FRAMING FRANCIS SCHAEFFER

FRAMING FRANCIS SCHAEFFER

APOLOGETICS AND PERSONAL INTEGRITY

Max H. Sotak, Ph.D.

Sotakoff
Publishing

FRAMING FRANCIS SCHAEFFER
Apologetics and Personal Integrity
Max H. Sotak

ISBN-10: 0-9896808-6-X
ISBN-13: 978-0-9896808-6-8

Published by: Sotakoff Publishing

Schaeffer, F.A. 1948. A Review of a Review. *The Bible Today*, 42(1): 7-9, Oct. Reprinted by permission of the PCA Historical Center, 478 Covenant Lane, St. Louis, MO 63141.

Front cover: Sketch of Francis Schaeffer by Ann Moore. Used by permission.

To John M. Frame
A Schaefferian apologist for the 21st Century

CONTENTS

PREFACE

The title of this book is not meant to announce a plot to make an innocent person look guilty. *Framing Francis Schaeffer* reflects a double-meaning combining the idea of a supporting or surrounding framework and the personal name of John Frame. The purpose of this book, then, is to *frame* the apologetic of Francis Schaeffer in light of John Frame's triperspectival theory of knowing, giving special attention to the existential perspective evident throughout Schaeffer's apologetic trilogy. By framing Francis Schaeffer, a clear picture of his apologetic approach comes into view, especially as he developed this in terms of personal integrity. Like a picture frame, this study has four sides or struts. First, the study discovers the ways in which Frame's triperspectivalism may be used in analyzing apologetic systems to reveal their strengths, weaknesses, and consistency. By giving attention to Frame's system as a meta-apologetic, it becomes evident that his approach is applicable to Schaeffer and to other apologists. Second, the study analyzes the ways in which Frame's triperspectivalism is reflected in Schaeffer's trilogy, highlighting the existential perspective. This "strut" establishes my central argument, which is that Frame's Christian epistemology reveals the underlying cogency and consistency of Schaeffer's apologetic credibly and does so most profoundly with respect to the existential perspective. Third, the study compares Schaeffer's existential perspective with that of Edward Carnell and secular existentialism, which both apologists confronted. Based on Carnell's critique of existentialism and his existential apologetic of personal rectitude or integrity, credible support is offered for Schaeffer's engagement with existential themes. Fourth, support is offered for the current relevance of Schaeffer's apologetic of personal integrity by showing how the postmodern situation he anticipated is best addressed using the apologetic tools he used so effectively and offers to us through his writings.

Framing Francis Schaeffer is really a story about two evangelical apologists who are known for their perspectival outlook and commitment to personal integrity in apologetics. While Schaeffer is the intuitive apologist and Frame the systematic apologist, both recognized that Christian knowledge is best understood in terms of multiple perspectives and the human need for integrity at the heart of religious belief. These insights—in my judgment—capture the essence of evangelical apologetics.

ACKNOWLEDGEMENTS

This book began as a dissertation that was originally submitted to North-West University of South Africa (Potchefstroom Campus) for the degree of Doctor of Philosophy (Ph.D.) in Dogmatic Theology (conferred 2012). The study was pursued under the direction of Drs. Daniel Lioy and Nico Vorster. My special thanks to Dr. Vorster of the Faculty of Theology (School of Human Sciences) for his patient review and critical perspective, especially on the finer theoretical details of the study. Sincere thanks are also due to Dr. John Frame who expressed interest in this study and offered positive comments on its central argument.

FRAMING FRANCIS SCHAEFFER

S ince his death in 1984, the influence of Francis Schaeffer has persisted through his published writings and the work of the L'Abri fellowships throughout the world. Popular and scholarly reflection on his work has been a mixture of appreciation and criticism. There is, however, unanimous agreement that the spiritual impact of Schaeffer's apologetic evangelism over the last fifty years represents one of the great accomplishments of evangelicalism in the 20th Century (Burson & Walls, 1998:17).

While much of the criticism of Schaeffer has focused on clarifying his apologetic method, the critics seem to have arrived at an impasse due to the lack of an adequate Christian epistemology to explain Schaeffer's work as consistent, albeit not systematic. He has been classified as a presuppositionalist (Morris, 1976:17, 36), a modified presuppositionalist (Frame, 2010a), an inconsistent presuppositionalist (Harper, 1976:138), a verificationalist (Lewis, 1986:77-78, 86; 1999), an evidentialist (Reymond, 1976:141-148), a pragmatist (Geisler, 1976:110-111), and an integrationist (Boa & Bowman, 2001:462-476). It is my contention that John Frame's triperspectival Christian epistemology provides the best tool for understanding Schaeffer's apologetic in general and the existential perspective of his apologetic in particular (Frame, 1976, 1982, 1987, 1994, 1995, 2000, 2006a, 2006b, 2008a, 2010a; Hughes, 2009). Frame (1999:7) offers a basic summary of his perspectival epistemology in his published lectures given at Trinity Evangelical Divinity School in 1988. Any item of knowledge can be viewed from three perspectives: (1) the correspondence of idea and object; (2) the "cognitive satisfaction" or confidence of the thinker; and (3) the agreement of thought with God's laws for thinking. These three views correspond to Frame's situational, existential, and normative perspectives. By "Framing" Francis Schaeffer, the enduring value of his apologetic system may be established and preserved for future applications.

Frame's Triperspectivalism

A significant factor in the application of John Frame's triperspectivalism to Francis Schaeffer's apologetic trilogy is the completion of Frame's major works. By 2010, not only had Frame completed his four-volume "Lordship" series, but in 2009 a massive *Festschrift* was published commemorating his seventieth birthday and over forty years of seminary teaching (Frame, 1987, 2002, 2008b, 2010c; Hughes, 2009). The full development of Frame's work in the three primary areas of his interest and teaching—theology, apologetics, and ethics—provides everything needed to apply his developed understanding to the work of other apologists who, like Schaeffer, lack Frame's depth and sophistication.

Indeed, the completion of Frame's central research agenda calls for useful applications of his work that demonstrate the power of his Christian epistemology to solve problems in Christian scholarship. Of his major works, *The Doctrine of the Knowledge of God* is the root from which perspectivalism is developed and applied in the later works (Frame, 1987:62-75, 89-90, 191-194, 200-204, 206-212, 235; 2002:1-115). Taking his cue from the first page of Calvin's (2008:4) *Institutes*, Frame (1987:89-90) states the first of two basic insights at the heart of his triperspectival epistemology: "I have argued that the knowledge of God's law, the world, and the self are interdependent and ultimately identical." Frame affirms with Calvin that knowledge of God and the self are interrelated but adds the world as the third perspective, making a triad. By studying the applications of God's law to the world and the self, all three are illuminated together, indicating that "the three kinds of knowledge . . . are identical but 'perspectivally' related". In agreement with Wittgenstein, Frame argues that "meaning and application are ultimately identical".

This epistemology is a major component in Frame's "Modified Presuppositionalism" and offers a useful tool for demonstrating the consistency of Schaeffer's practical apologetic (Frame, 2010a). In fact, Frame's method was significantly influenced by Schaeffer's apologetic, especially in some areas where Schaeffer differed from Cornelius Van Til (1955). (Van Til had been Schaeffer's professor at Westminster Seminary in the mid-1930's.) In addition, Frame's existential perspective may provide a fitting theoretical model through which to view the whole of Schaeffer's apologetic as he developed it in his apologetic trilogy: *The God Who is There, Escape from Reason*, and *He is There and He is Not Silent*. As will become evident throughout this study, Frame's perspectival epistemology suggests a systematic analysis of Schaeffer's non-systematic apologetic, highlighting the existential qualities of an approach that has earned the admiration of supporters and critics alike.

Presumptive evidence that Frame may provide the best tool for analyzing Schaeffer is provided in the exceptional work on apologetic methods by Boa and Bowman (2001:493-502). These authors provide what I consider to be the most reliable interpretation of Frame and Schaeffer available among all the general works on apologetic method surveyed to date. They demonstrate a detailed understanding of Frame's perspectival approach to apologetics as well as its relationship to other apologetic systems. The authors see Frame as "a presuppositionalist with a broadened understanding of that approach to include the others viewed as perspectivally related" (2001:502). Interestingly, Schaeffer and Frame are presented as representatives of essentially the same approach to apologetics, which echoes the main argument of this study.

The relevance of a perspectival analysis of Schaeffer is underscored by the fact that it has not been carried out by Frame himself or by anyone within Frame's circle of scholarship (Frame, 2010b; cf. Hughes, 2009). While a few scholars have recognized an existential emphasis in Schaeffer, they have not seen that perspective in relation to a triperspectival Christian epistemology. Many criticisms leveled against Schaeffer stem from an assumed inconsistency within his approach based on the attempt to classify him rigidly as a presuppositionalist, evidentialist, or verificationalist. Frame's analysis, however, represents an attempt to bring these classifications closer together on the basis of modifications to Van Til's (1955) presuppositionalism that Schaeffer (1948) himself inspired and articulated in simple form twenty years before the publication of his first book. In an interview with Steven Scrivener, Frame (2010a) explains the profound influence of Schaeffer's 1948 *Bible Today* article on his thinking and his decision to side with Schaeffer on certain critical points against Van Til (see Appendix). While Schaeffer did not anticipate in any detail what Frame would do with his early ideas, Schaeffer certainly embraced what Frame (1994:85-88) would later call "a presuppositionalism of the heart". The details of this analysis may provide the best account of Schaeffer's apologetic evangelism and its persuasive appeal as one of the great existential apologetic approaches of the 20th Century.

Schaeffer and Existentialism

Like Edward Carnell (2007a, 2007b. 2007c), who also developed an existential apologetic, Schaeffer confronted the secular existentialism of his time with a Christian existentialism that has rarely been recognized by his critics and supporters. Only a few have recognized this perspective as a dominant theme in Schaeffer, likely due to his strident criticisms of existentialism (Pinnock, 1977:32; Brown, 1984:82; Lewis, 1986:94). The irony of Schaeffer is that he fought secular existential fire with Christian existential fire, despite his seemingly complete repudiation of existentialism. With the application of Frame's triperspectivalism to Schaeffer's work, that strategy becomes obvious and more profound, supporting the cogency of an approach that is both properly rational and deeply existential. Frame (2010b:1) expressed enthusiasm for such a study in his response to my inquiry: "I don't know anyone who has studied this in Schaeffer, but I would be happy to see you develop the idea in greater depth. I think it's a very promising way to understand Schaeffer."

In fact, the cogency and relevance of Schaeffer's apologetic can be established by showing his relationship to both existentialism and post-modernism. With respect to existentialism, it is possible to show the similarity between Schaeffer's response to this philosophical movement and Carnell's more scholarly response. Given the respect for Carnell within the evangelical community as an expert on existential philosophy and theology—Kierkegaard's in particular—it is possible to show that Schaeffer was not advocating an unscholarly or idiosyncratic view of Kierkegaard's role in later existentialism and Neo-orthodoxy. Furthermore, Carnell shares with Schaeffer an existential perspective, which is explicit in Carnell and implicit in Schaeffer. With respect to postmodernism, it is possible to show that Schaeffer's own understanding of the flow of history and thought led him to correctly anticipate postmodern relativism and to address it through his existential apologetic in a manner that continues to be relevant today. While making these points would not amount to a complete vindication of Schaeffer as a philosopher and apologist, it would demonstrate—at the very least—a depth of insight and prescience to warrant respect for his apologetic and its continued relevance.

Comparing Schaeffer and Carnell is not a novel idea, although I know of no other scholar who has recognized the similarities between Schaeffer's existential perspective and Carnell's (2007b) formulation of an existential apologetic in *Christian Commitment*. As early as 1948, however, Schaeffer (1948:9) quotes Carnell, agreeing that "there is a point of contact with the unsaved man", even though there would be "absolutely no common ground whatever on any level" if the lost person were completely consistent with his unbelief. This crucial point of agreement with Carnell led Gordon Lewis (1976:300; 1986:102; 1999) to argue that Schaeffer is closer to Carnell than to Van Til. While this argument will be addressed and challenged, the similarities between Schaeffer and Carnell suggest that Carnell might also illuminate issues important to Schaeffer.

In fact, a closer inspection of Carnell's (2007a, 2007b, 2007c) work justifies this expectation. Carnell's (2007b) existential apologetic, while not developed exactly as Schaeffer develops his own, explicitly develops a number of Schaefferian themes within an existential context that might seem alien to Schaeffer but is not. What Schaeffer (1982a:144) refers to as "integrity" and "honesty" in the face of reality, Carnell (2007b: 16) refers to simply as "personal rectitude". Critical responses to Carnell's existential apologetic reflect its mixed reception among evangelicals during his lifetime (Spitz, 1957; Fowler, 1958; Shinn, 1958; Zetterholm, 1958; Holmes, 1959). But Carnell's (2007a:452) "third locus of truth—truth in the heart" is clearly in line with Frame's existential perspective and explains a great deal in Schaeffer that others have recognized as expressions of existential argumentation. In relation to Kierkegaard and secular existentialism, Carnell (2007a:449-507) develops a critique that echoes much in Schaeffer's own critique.

Schaeffer and Postmodernism

Schaeffer's understanding of absolutes and antithesis is the context for his anticipation of postmodernism and his response to the relativism of contemporary thought. For Schaeffer (1982a:8), antithesis is more than a logical distinction; it is a key "presupposition", a basis to distinguish truth and falsity: "We must not forget that historic Christianity stands on a basis of antithesis. Without it, historical Christianity is meaningless." The basic antithesis of Christianity is that God either exists or not, and one's stance on this point determines knowledge and morality.

Schaeffer's position on absolutes and antithesis implies an obvious response to postmodernism on his part. While his position is shared by many other evangelicals, one theologian in particular recognizes and elaborates Schaeffer's anticipation of the current postmodern situation (Erickson, 1998:63-80, 2001). Tinker and Tinker (2005:201), Groothuis (2000:50), and Pearcy (2004:110, 246) echo Erickson's treatment of Schaeffer in this connection, and Groothuis even dedicates his book to Schaeffer as one of two "intellectual mentors", Carl F. Henry being the other. Jones (2009) and Torres (2009) also mention Schaeffer's anticipation of postmodernism, and Edgar (1995b) engages the movement in relation to apologetics in much the same way that Schaeffer did.

An existential apologetic provides excellent resources for the Christian confronting a postmodern context today. Schaeffer's (1973:76; 1982a:189; 1985:80) stated goal to provide "honest answers to honest questions" reflects the existential impulse toward personal rectitude, which values the integrity of thought and life. While it might be thought that Schaeffer's heavy emphasis on the rationality of the Christian worldview is not compelling to postmodern thinkers, the integrity of thought and life certainly is relevant. Erickson (1998:63-64) recognizes that Schaeffer "was reacting to postmodernism, but before anyone, including the adherents themselves, knew what it was. . . . Thus, in many ways, Schaeffer was ahead of his time." It is at this point that the similarities between Schaeffer and Edward Carnell become important in understanding what Schaeffer was really trying to accomplish. Carnell's (2007b:16) existential approach embodies the "personal rectitude" or integrity that Schaeffer commended to his readers and listeners. Like Schaeffer, Carnell argues for the principle of antithesis and the drive for personal integrity as existentially compelling evidences for the truth of the Christian faith based on its livability. Carnell provides in depth what Schaeffer developed more simply and lived profoundly. While both apologists illustrate Frame's existential perspective in a way that is as important today as in their own time, Carnell provides Schaeffer with a kind of scholarly support that further validates Schaeffer's apologetic and critique of existentialism (cf. Carnell, 2007a:449-507).

Schaeffer's Apologetic Trilogy

Restricting the scope of this study to Francis Schaeffer's apologetic trilogy is based on two considerations. First, Schaeffer's *Complete Works* make up five sizeable volumes, but everything he wrote revolved around the content of the three books of the trilogy: *The God Who is There*, *Escape from Reason*, and *He is There and He is Not Silent*. The themes of Schaeffer's later work are all established in his first book, *The God Who is There*. The remaining two books in the trilogy merely elaborate further the foundational themes put forth in *The God Who is There*. This is why Schaeffer (1973:75, 1982a:x) indicated that all his other books "flowed out from that first book" and fit into the trilogy "as spokes of the wheel fit into the hub". Second, the trilogy reflects a congruity with Frame's "Lordship Series" at the level of its basic objective. Schaeffer (1982b:x) indicates that "the early books broke ground in calling for the Lordship of Christ in the arts—art, literature, cinema, philosophy, and so on". The remainder of his work elaborates the Lordship of Christ in these areas, but the trilogy provides all the foundational principles of Schaeffer's thinking in general and his apologetic in particular. My argument is that at the general level of method and strategy, Schaeffer's apologetic is consistent when viewed in light of

Frame's perspectivalism. This does not claim, of course, that all of the historical or philosophical details are above criticism. As the best scholars have contended, it is necessary to distinguish Schaeffer's general approach from arguable interpretations and errors in detail.

There are many inspiring passages in Schaeffer's other books that summarize his basic point of view with a clarity and practicality that explain why his work has been widely influential. An example of this, which gets to the very heart of Schaeffer's (1982b:38) existential perspective, is the following statement from *The Church at the End of the Twentieth Century*: "The final great concept of truth is that Christianity is true to what is there." Schaeffer goes on to explain what it means to say that "Christianity is true". Christians must be true to their creeds and to the Bible as God's word, but their knowledge must also be "practical", flowing from the whole person into the individual and corporate life of the church. I know of no other passage in all of Schaeffer's books that summarizes as well the whole of his work and the existential perspective at the heart of it. And yet, for all its value as a summary, it does not add anything that is not as clearly stated within the trilogy. Schaeffer employed repetition through-out his works very effectively to educate his readers in his basic principles and commitments. Outside the trilogy, the principles of his apologetic are repeated and applied, but no further clarification is supplied that is important to identifying his apologetic theory.

A host of books on the work of Francis Schaeffer have been published over the last fifty years, and a sizeable literature has accumulated in the form of journal articles (Brown, 1968; Franz, 1969; Holmes, 1969; Lakey, 1969; Geehan, 1972; Blomberg, 1975; Harper, 1976; Lewis, 1976; Morris, 1976; Reymond, 1976; Giacumakis & Tiffin, 1977; Pinnock, 1977; Rogers, 1977; Davis, 1978; Yancy, 1979a, 1979b, 1979c; Gill, 1981; Reugsegger, 1981, 1982, 1986a; Clark, 1982; Wells, 1983; Voss, 1984; Hill, 1985; Parkhurst, 1985; Dennis, 1986a; Packer, 1986; Stadler, 1989; Duriez, 1993, 2008; White, 1994; Edgar, 1995a; Burson & Walls, 1998; Geisler, 1999; Boa & Bowman, 2001; Pearcy, 2004; Follis, 2006; Hankins, 2008; Little, 2010). While some critics expressed doubt about his "staying power" and even charged him with "contributing to the scandal of the evangelical mind", Schaeffer has continued to attract interest up to the present time (Edwards, 1998:222, 223; cf. Noll, 1994). In his tribute, written shortly after Schaeffer's death, fellow classmate at Faith Seminary, Vernon Grounds (1984:62), wrote prophetically of Schaeffer's staying power, surmising that "Francis Schaeffer will be recognized as a key figure in twentieth-century evangelicalism" long after other popular authors have faded from the scene.

The Framework

The goal of this book is to show that the cogency of Francis Schaeffer's apologetic can be established on the basis of John Frame's triperspectival Christian epistemology, especially with respect to the existential perspective developed in Schaeffer's trilogy. To accomplish this task, it will be important to show that Frame's triperspectival method is a useful tool for evaluating apologetic systems in general and Schaeffer's in particular. By looking at Schaeffer's trilogy of books through the lens of Frame's existential perspective, it is possible to detect the existential heartbeat of the trilogy that admirers of Schaeffer have recognized as the true genius of his work. Because Schaeffer was often criticized for a lack of scholarly credentials, it will also be helpful to show how his existential perspective was anticipated by Edward Carnell and the existentialism both apologists opposed. Carnell was highly respected during his lifetime as a leading scholar of evangelicalism, and a comparison of his work with Schaeffer's shows that the great apologetic evangelist was in good company. Finally, the relevance of Schaeffer's contribution to apologetic evangelism will be confirmed by showing how his apologetic of personal integrity addressed the postmodern situation he anticipated.

It has been fifty years since the publication of *The God Who is There* in 1968, and Schaeffer's contributions to apologetics are still fresh and relevant. I attribute this to his deep insight into the human condition and his awareness that the modern mind is governed by a perspectival focus in knowing and personal integrity in believing. These insights have stood the test of time, and we can do no better than to place them at the center of our own apologetic evangelism.

FRAME'S TRIPERSPECTIVALISM

1 UNDERSTANDING TRIPERSPECTIVALISM

If the cogency of Francis Schaeffer's apologetic is to be assessed on the basis of John Frame's triperspectival epistemology, it is necessary to describe Frame's Christian theory of knowledge in detail. However, more than a detailed description is required. It must also be shown that triperspectivalism is useful as a tool for the analysis of apologetic systems, which is what I mean by a meta-apologetic. Put another way, Frame's epistemology must be more than a specific theory implying an apologetic; it must also entail a meta-apologetic capable of explaining a number of apologetic systems and Schaeffer's in particular. Since Schaeffer's work is controversial and not obviously systematic, the cogency of his apologetic is in question. If his apologetic is to be vindicated as internally consistent, a robust meta-apologetic that rises above the details of his popular apologetic may offer the best vantage point from which to approach the issue.

Explaining Frame's triperspectival epistemology also offers its own challenges. As a perspectival system, it is difficult to summarize using a linear presentation that progresses from first principles to the developed theory. In fact, the system itself reflects the "method of implication" described by Van Til (1969a:12) as "spiral reasoning": "We must go round and round a thing to see more of its dimensions and to know more about it, in general, unless we are larger than that which we are investigating." This approach, which explains Van Til's concept of "transcendental or circular argument", is also useful as a strategy for explaining Frame's system. Therefore, rather than using a linear approach, a spiral method will be used to bring out the structure of the system by turning the diamond, so to speak, to illuminate the apologetic facets of the system. These facets are really perspectives on the entire system, so they overlap and illuminate each other. Four apologetic facets may be identified as propositions: (1) The lordship attributes are based in Scripture and applied as epistemological perspectives; (2) Apologetics is a person-variable strategy reflecting scriptural antitheses, (3) Apologetic arguments are transcendental in goal and direct or indirect in form; (4) Interdependent epistemological perspectives justify an integrated meta-apologetic. A linear view of these facets could also be summarized according to Frame's definition of theology as application: Lordship attributes may be applied as epistemological perspectives that, in turn, apply to apologetics, which is the application of Scripture to unbelief.

Triperspectivalism has been described thus far in general terms as a Christian epistemology based on two insights inspired by Calvin and Van Til respectively: (1) The knowledge of God's word (law), the world, and the self are interdependent and yet ultimately identical perspectives, since they refer to the same content but from different points of view; (2) Ethical judgments always involve the application of a *norm* to a *situation* by a *person*. These insights affirm the same point in two ways: The knowledge of God's word is our *norm*, the world is our *situation* before God, the self is simply another term for a *person*, and all divine knowledge implies an obligation to believe and apply it to all of life. The knowledge of God, then, requires judgments in which persons apply God's word to the changing situations of life in the world. The context of this knowledge is God's lordship attributes of control, authority, and presence. Frame (1987:11-75) summarizes this epistemology in *The Doctrine of the Knowledge of God*. But is the developed theory faithful to the teaching of the Bible? Frame was aware that his early summary of perspectivalism called for a fuller biblical statement and defense. He provides this in his massive work, *The Doctrine of God* (Frame, 2002:1-115). In addressing the development of perspectivalism and its application to apologetics, it will be necessary to detail the biblical basis of an epistemology that promises to be one of the truly profound and powerful systems of our time.

Triperspectivalism is actually the product of a theological reconstruction of the doctrine of God's transcendence and immanence. Frame (2002:107-115; 1987:11-18) identifies several theological errors that have resulted from the influence of Greek philosophy on the Church's teaching concerning God's relationship to the world. By failing to grasp the covenantal context of God's transcendence and immanence in terms of the lordship attributes, modern theologians especially have either removed God from the world (e.g. deism and Barth's "wholly other" god), or they have identified him with the world (e.g. Process Theology and Tillich's "ground of Being" god). In Barth's case, while his theology is covenantal and Christocentric, his view of revelation is "so dynamic that it cannot be preserved beyond the moment of revelation" thereby reducing the abiding authority of God's written revelation (Frame, 2006c:59-60; cf. Deu 6:6-9). In Tillich's case, while his panentheism affirms divine transcendence, divine immanence is still defined unbiblically as a metaphysical identification with the world, rather than as a covenantal presence. In either case, God cannot speak an authoritative propositional word, leaving theologians to substitute their own thinking for the inspired revelation of God in Scripture. God's control, authority, and presence are modified or redefined, making God either "absent" from the world or "vested in the finite world" (2002:115). Either way, the human mind remains autonomous by default, since God either cannot speak in human language or speaks through a finite mind that mystically participates in the deity. Frame (2002:113) makes the point that such errors result from viewing transcendence as "hiddenness" rather than divine "control and authority" and from viewing immanence as "the autonomy of creatures" rather than "covenant presence". In the end, "pantheism and deism thus agree on the existence and importance of human autonomy" because both reject the biblical teaching that defines God's relationship to the world (2002:111).

While Frame's (1987:14; 2002:113) "square of religious opposition" provides a helpful account of both biblical and unbiblical approaches to divine transcendence and immanence and their implications, the goals of this study require an account of his covenantal reconstruction for the purposes of an apologetic application—not a critical evaluation of his views. I recognize that Frame's interpretations of panentheism and Barth are disputable. Frame is in essential agreement with Van Til's critique of Barth—a critique that has been recently analyzed and assessed in detail with mixed reviews (cf. McCormack & Anderson, 2011). But Frame's interpretation of these theological positions is not the basis of his understanding of the Lordship attributes; rather, his analysis follows from his biblical conclusions. Therefore, the remainder of this section will explain Frame's development of a covenant epistemology founded on Scripture.

The Covenantal Basis of Perspectivalism

The linchpin of Frame's (1987:40-49) epistemology is the covenant name of God. God is the covenant Lord, so the covenant name of God, Yahweh, is the key to perspectivalism. Frame's approach is to provide a thorough analysis of God's revelation of himself as Lord throughout Scripture, concluding that God's immanence and transcendence should be understood—not from two perspectives—but three: control, authority, and presence. These are God's lordship attributes, and they capture the central message of the Bible, which is that "God is Lord" (Frame, 2002:25). While the full detail of Frame's analysis will not be presented here, the structure and rationale of his epistemology will be presented according to the controlling ideas and their biblical basis (cf. Frame, 2008a; Anderson, 2009:432-436).

God's encounter with Moses at the burning bush provides a paradigm case for an understanding of the lordship attributes. In Exodus 3, God reveals himself as Yahweh, or Lord, the Redeemer of his covenant people Israel. Yahweh is the name by which the Lord is "to be remembered from generation to generation" (EXO 3:15). This name is a personal and proper name, clearly designating God as a person. Frame (2002:25) views the term *person* as an extrabiblical word that—like *Trinity*—cannot be avoided: "Only in biblical religion is there an absolute principle that is personal. Other religions have personal gods, but those are not absolute." As an absolute person, the Lord is revealed as holy, which grounds his right to our reverence and obedience: "Who among the gods is like you, O Lord? Who is like you—majestic in holiness, awesome in glory, working wonders?" (EXO 15:11.) God's holiness in the biblical context is not simply his transcendence; it is also his imminent presence to redeem his "servants or vassals" and to go with them (2002:29). Therefore, divine transcendence and immanence describe God's relationship to his people, not simply an abstract relationship to the world. This gives rise to the covenant concept, which defines the relationship between the Lord and his servants.

Frame's (2002:31) biblical understanding of the covenant is taken from Meredith Kline (1972), who identified the elements of a "suzerainty treaty" in Exodus 20:1-17 (cf. Walton, 2006:287-311). After redeeming Israel from Egypt, God demands their obedience, reflecting a relationship of both grace and law. God's treaty document has five characteristics: (1) the announcement of the King's name; (2) the historical prologue stating the past benefits vassals have received from the King; (3) the "stipulations" that vassals are expected to obey in love and gratitude for past benefits; (4) the covenant "sanctions" of blessing for obedience and cursing for disobedience; (5) the "continuity" provisions for the perpetuation of the treaty among God's people across future generations.

Israel's treaty document has implications for God's relationship to his people throughout redemptive history (Frame, 2002:32-35, 37): (1) The treaty document is an authoritative written document, "holy writing" that becomes the paradigm for the "holy Scriptures" of both testaments (ROM 1:2); (2) God's people may not add to or take away from the holy writings of the Lord (DEU 4:2, 12:32); (3) Grace precedes law, identifying love as the proper motivation to obey Yahweh under the old covenant and Jesus under the new (JOH 14:15, 21, 33; GAL 5:6); (4) Sonship is covenantal, being defined as adoption through union with Christ, the Savior and Lord of the covenant (ROM 8:15); (5) God's Kingship extends beyond Israel to all nations and all of creation (PSA 47:7-9; MAT 28:18-20; PHP 2:9-10); (6) What pertains to Yahweh under the old covenant pertains to Jesus under the new, since the Septuagint consistently uses *kyrios* (Lord) as equivalent to *Yahweh*, and Jesus is referred to as both Lord and God in the New Testament (ROM 10:9; PHP 2:11; cf. ISA 45:23; TIT 2:10, 13).

So how does the suzerainty treaty explicitly reflect the lordship attributes of control, authority, and presence? After announcing his name in the covenant prologue, Yahweh affirms his *control* by appealing to his powerful deliverance of his people in the past. In the present, he imposes the terms of the covenant on his vassals, implying his control over all aspects of the relationship. After the prologue, Yahweh asserts his *authority* to command a loving obedience from his subjects, imposing sanctions of blessing and cursing, which require his abiding *presence* to apply these sanctions from generation to generation (Frame, 2002:42).

Frame's (2002:35) central point is that the name *Lord* (Yahweh) designates a covenant head: "His essential relationship to us is that of a great king who has delivered us from death and calls us to serve him by obeying his written word." By defining God's transcendence and immanence in the relational terms of a covenant Lord, the two attributes become complementary instead of dialectical, as in much of modern theology. To facilitate this understanding, Frame employs three lordship attributes that specify God's transcendence and immanence with respect to those he calls his servants, sons, and friends (JOH 1:12; 15:14-15).

God's Transcendence: Control and Authority

Frame defines divine transcendence in terms of control and authority. As mentioned above, all the lordship attributes are derived from the divine name. To observe this, it is necessary to return to Exodus 3:13-15:

> Moses said to God, "Suppose I go to the Israelites and say to them, 'The God of your fathers has sent me to you,' and they ask me, 'What is his name?' Then what shall I tell them?" God said to Moses, "I AM WHO I AM. This is what you are to say to the Israelites: 'I AM has sent me to you.'" God also said to Moses, "Say to the Israelites, 'The Lord, the God of your fathers—the God of Abraham, the God of Isaac and the God of Jacob—has sent me to you.' This is my name forever, the name by which I am to be remembered from generation to generation."

In these verses, the proper name of God, Yahweh in verse 15, is equated with the name I AM. Frame (2002:37-39) discusses the controversy surrounding the mysterious names by which God reveals himself, challenging several theologians who contend that God used such names to avoid answering Moses' question or to proclaim his incomprehensibility (Thielicke), hiddenness (Barth), or metaphysical Being (Aquinas). Frame logically reasons that God must have intended to reveal himself in a way that would motivate the Israelites to listen to Moses and to believe that the Lord was able and willing to deliver them. In keeping with more recent scholarship on Exodus 3:14, Frame (2002:39) concludes that "God is saying, in effect, 'I will be present (to deliver you)'. This interpretation sometimes takes the verb in the sense of 'be present'." Frame agrees with Carl Henry (cited in Frame, 2002:40) that this interpretation has much to commend it, since "similar 'to be' language is found in Revelation 1:4, 8; 4:8; 11:17 in contexts dealing with God's presence and coming". Because the two mysterious names are equated in this context, the verb explains the proper name and the proper name the verb. Yahweh, therefore, is the redemptive name of God. Numerous passages in the Old Testament reinforce this interpretation, presenting God as coming to the rescue of his people for his name's sake (PSA 23:3, 143:11; JER 14:7). In combination with other Old Testament passages explaining the name of Yahweh (PSA 135:13; ISA 26:4-8; HOS 12:4-9, 13:4; MAL 3:6), the "I am" sayings of Jesus in the Gospel of John (6:48; 8:12, 58; 9:5; 10:7, 14; 11:25; 14:6; 15:1, 5; 18:5-8) provide sufficient evidence in favor of Frame's interpretation (2002:41-42). The "I am" statements of Jesus, in particular, show that "Christ is not just God in some general sense, but actually the covenant Lord, Yahweh" (2002:42). The biblical evidence summarized here is merely a sampling of the massive testimony Frame presents in support of his thesis.

The concept of redemption alone, however, does not exhaust the meaning of the divine name. As Frame (2002:45) says, "Exodus 3:14 emphasizes divine sovereignty in God's being, decisions, and actions." The "I am he" passages also stress God's sovereignty in redemption (DEU 32:39; ISA 41:4; 43:11-13). God's sovereignty in salvation and judgment raises the question of the relationship between control and authority. Is God simply an absolute power for whom might makes right? The Bible teaches that God has both the power to direct all of nature and history and the right to do so as the Creator and Sovereign over all things. Therefore, he has the right to tell his creatures what to do. As Frame (2002:81) puts it, "Since God created and governs all things, he is the original interpreter of creation, the one who understands . . . its ultimate meaning and purpose." Unlike the false gods, the Lord is also able to foretell future events because he is in control of nature and history (ISA 40:1-31; 41:21-29; 43:8-13). He is the owner of all things, which also implies control and authority (DEU 10:14; EXO 19:5; 1CH 29:11; JOB 41:11; PSA 24:1-2, 82:8, 89:11; ROM 11:35).

As the original interpreter of creation, God's interpretation must stand without question (Frame, 2002:82). The finite creature simply has no ultimate reference point from which to question God or to argue with his standards (ISA 45:9-11; MAT 20:1-16). In Frame's (2002:83) words, "God's kind of might actually embraces right. . . . So with God, might and right coalesce." There is a sense in which only the presuppositionalist can fully appreciate this point. There is simply no standpoint above God from which finite creatures can evaluate the relationship between his power and authority. God must simply be taken at his word because of his comprehensive knowledge and sovereignty. Thus, might and right, control and authority, are "mutually perspectival" within God. This is clearly not the case with finite humans who must derive both might and right from God, the ultimate reference point. God is the potter; his creatures are the clay. This is consistent with the suzerainty treaty form in which God declares his name, describes his redemption, and delivers his requirements—control and authority in tandem. Frame (2002:86) uses Abraham as an example of unreserved trust in God's control and authority, having believed God's promise even against empirical evidence (ROM 4:16-22). Epistemologically speaking, this is what it means to have no other gods before the Lord (EXO 20:3; DEU 6:14; MAT 22:37).

According to Frame (2002:83), control and authority are also "mutually perspectival" with respect to the divine name. In Leviticus, "I am the Lord" appears as the exclamation point at the end of God's commands (2002:84; LEV 18:6, 21, 30; 19:3-4, 10, 12, 14, 16, 30-32, 34, 37). The same pattern is reflected in the New Testament in Jesus' words, "Why do you call me 'Lord, Lord,' and do not do what I say?" (2002:85; LUK 6:46.) In this verse, Jesus' lordship implies his authority: "So again Jesus stands in the place of Yahweh as the great king, the head of his covenant people." So whether exercising *control* over the wind and sea (MAR 4:35-41) or exercising the *authority* to forgive sins (MAR 2:7), Jesus exercises the sovereignty of Yahweh (2002:86). Clearly, the lordship attributes of control and authority are woven so tightly into the fabric of Scripture that once they are brought to light, the evidence for them becomes obvious and overwhelming.

A final issue of importance related to the lordship attribute of authority is its comprehensive scope. Because God is absolute, his authority governs every area of life. As indicated above, God's written word is the "covenant constitution of the people of God" (Frame, 2002:91; 2010c). Frame (2002:89) notes that the New Testament, even more explicitly than the Old, asserts God's authority over all of life (ROM 9:23; 1CO 10:31; COL 3:17, 24; 2CO 10:5). Furthermore, "absolute authority entails infallibility" (2002:92). Therefore, the word of God is above criticism. This does not mean that interpreters do not judge Scripture or its meaning; rather, they "may never judge it to have failed or to have been mistaken". Like Schaeffer, Frame affirms the infallibility and inerrancy of Scripture as an implication of God's covenantal authority. Without "holy Scriptures", God simply cannot exercise his authority over his people (cf. Perez, 2009; Frame, 2010c:335-346).

Does inspiration require inerrancy? Frame's (2006c:60-65) argument for inerrancy is based on his understanding of Near Eastern covenant treaty documents: "In these treaties and emphatically in biblical covenants, the great king is the author of the document." (2006c:61.) The treaty document functions as "God's witness against Israel by which God will hold Israel accountable" (cf. DEU 31:26). The writings of the prophets were "added to the covenant documents" and were "preserved for future generations" as a further witness against Israel and as a basis to test the predictions of prophets (JOS 24:25-26; DEU 18:22). By the time of Jesus' ministry, the collected writings of the Old Testament were referred to as "the oracles of God" (ROM 3:2), "the holy Scriptures" (2TI 3:15), and the "royal law" (JAM 2:8; 2006c:62; cf. 2010c:105-117).

Following Warfield, Frame (2006c:62) affirms that "Scripture is the words of the Holy Spirit given through human writers (as Acts 1:16)." Because "the Holy Spirit spoke long ago through the mouth of David", it is reasonable to conclude that "what 'Scripture says,' to the New Testament writers, is what 'God says'". Jesus reinforces this understanding by assuring the Jews that the Scriptures were fulfilled in him and could not be broken (JOH 5:45; 10:33-36). Paul supports this view by describing the Scriptures as "breathed out" by God (2TI 3:15-17), and Peter describes the prophetic word as the production of the Holy Spirit (2PE 1:19-21). Men spoke "as they were carried along by the Holy Spirit". Frame (2006c:64) extrapolates the inspiration of the New Testament from the Old on the basis of the following principle: "the religion of the New Testament is essentially the same as that of the Old, centered on the Word of God". The words of Jesus are "the words of eternal life" (JOH 6:68), and Paul told hearers that his own words were the Lord's command (1CO 14:37). At bottom, "the New Testament is just as word-centered as the Old Testament" and is given to be passed on as a "tradition" for future generations (1CO 15:2-3; 2TH 2:15, 3:6; 1TI 6:20; 2TI 2:2; 2PE 2:21; JDE 3). Finally, "Paul quotes Luke as an authoritative word from God", and Peter classes the writings of Paul as "Scriptures" (1TI 5:18; 2PE 3:16): "Paul's letters are Scripture, like the books of Moses." (Frame, 2006c:65; cf. 2010c:118-132.)

This view of inspiration implies inerrancy as a corollary. Frame essentially holds Millard Erickson's view (although he never cites him), which is that the Bible is inerrant with respect to its truth claims, or in Erickson's (1983:234) terms, in all that it "affirms". Frame's approach seems more illuminating, however, in that it reflects his view of theology as application. While affirming the traditional qualifications of inerrancy made by Erickson (1983:233-240), Frame (2010c:174) says these are not "qualifications". Rather, they are different "applications" of the scriptural teaching on the truth of God's word. Like Erickson, Frame affirms that inerrancy is compatible with imprecise grammar, narratives, numbers, quotations, descriptions, and pre-scientific statements. As Erickson (1983:234) puts it, "Inerrancy pertains to what is affirmed or asserted rather than to what is merely reported." Therefore, the Bible should be held only to the claims it makes for itself—no more and no less. Discussions of the "phenomena of Scripture" typically bias the question of inerrancy by their reliance on an inductive method, which reasons from the appearance of errors in Scripture to their actual existence (Frame, 2010c:178). The problem is that an inductive method assumes that one can draw conclusions about Bible difficulties without the normative authority of Scripture to ground and guide induction. This is no better than the deductive method eschewed by the opponents of inerrancy. Frame believes that Scripture's claims for itself support inerrancy. Inerrancy is not simply a deduction from a few verses of Scripture; it is the expression of "Scripture's claim to be the Word of God" (2010c:179). Frame's case for inerrancy is an application of his perspectival epistemology based on lordship attributes.

God's Immanence: Presence

Like the previous lordship attributes, the attribute of presence is also derived from the meaning of the divine name. It should be recalled that Frame (2002:39) concluded that the divine name in Exodus 3:14 means, "I will be present (to deliver you)." Obviously, God cannot deliver his people if he is not there to do it. This is why Frame (2002:94) would say that "the presence of God is a consequence of his control and authority". This presence must not be viewed as physical, however, since God is invisible. Rather, God's presence is covenantal: "He is present with his creatures to bless and judge them in accordance with the terms of his covenant." Thus, this attribute is defined as "a presence of power and authority", not a metaphysical identification with the world, as in much of modern theology (Frame, 1994:44).

One of the notable coincidences of this study is that Frame's (2002:95) definition of Yahweh as "the God who 'is there,' present to deliver his people from Egypt" is also captured in the title of the key book in Francis Schaeffer's trilogy, *The God Who is There*. The lordship attribute of presence, which corresponds to Frame's existential perspective, is literally the title of Schaeffer's main book! This is clear evidence of the existential perspective at the heart of Schaeffer's work and accounts for the original intuition that Schaeffer is best understood through the lens of Frame's perspectivalism.

Frame illuminates this lordship attribute in some fascinating ways. Returning to Exodus 3:11-12, Frame (2002:95) makes the interesting observation that when Moses asks God the question, "Who am I", God answers by saying, "I will be with you." As Frame puts it, "Who is Moses? He is the man with whom God is. God has covenanted to stand with Moses in his confrontation with Pharaoh." Frame (2002:98) calls this "the Immanuel principle" (ISA 7:14; MAT 1:23). God dwells with his people to deliver them from their enemies and from their sins. This principle is evident in God's many dwelling places from the Garden of Eden to the tabernacle to the Temple to Jesus himself, who tabernacled among us in human flesh (JOH 1:14; 2:21). This attribute too must be understood according to the suzerainty treaty form. God is present with us and within us as our deliverer, lawgiver, and ruler (EXO 3:6-8). The Church—God's people—is now the Temple in which he dwells (1CO 3:16; 1PE 2:4-5). This is the intimate presence of the redemptive fellowship of the covenant, not the metaphysical participation of a pantheistic theology.

Frame (2002:98) makes the point that this covenant presence spans all time and space. Jesus said, "before Abraham was born, I AM!" (JOH 8:58). Jesus spans the ages and is "present to all times". He is, therefore, the Lord of time. God's covenant presence, however, is not simply his being there: "Although God's people may wait long for him, he is always there, always ready to bless his people and judge his enemies." (2002:99.) God must go with his people to bless their efforts and to thwart their enemies; otherwise they cannot be successful (cf. JOH 15:5). Frame (2002:100) notes Moses' very significant response to God along these lines: "If your presence does not go with us, do not send us up from here." (EXO 33:15.) Other "Yahweh passages" associate blessing and judgment in connection with the Lord's name. When the Lord passes before Moses, he proclaims his name and his dual presence (EXO 34:6-7). It is also notable that God proclaims his covenant name twice: "The Lord, The Lord"—Yahweh, Yahweh.

The covenantal presence of the Lord is also universal with respect to the nations. The creation itself "is a covenant" in which God separates the light from the darkness, the land from the waters, and brings forth living things (GEN 1). Adam is created in covenant with God—and with him the entire human race (GEN 1:26; ROM 5:12-21). From their very creation, Adam and Eve received God's covenantal blessings and commands (GEN 1:27-30). The Lord walks and talks with them "in the garden in the cool of the day", reflecting the intimacy of covenant fellowship (GEN 3:8). Frame (2002:102) observes that "the Noahic covenant is made not only with Noah's family, the human race, but also with 'every living creature on earth'" (GEN 9:10). In both Testaments, the presence of Yahweh is inescapable (PSA 139:7-10; EPH 4:7-10).

The evidence provided by Frame does not exhaust the biblical witness to the lordship attribute of presence. Indeed, this substantial testimony merely sensitizes the reader to the theme of the Lord's covenant presence throughout the Bible. The New Testament teachings concerning the coming of the Holy Spirit on the Day of Pentecost and the second coming of Christ are also interesting "presence" doctrines (ACT 2:1-28; 1TH 4:13-17). In the case of both doctrines, the Lord's presence with his people or their presence with him is central. But the goal here is not an exhaustive account of the biblical evidence but the establishment of the lordship attributes as the proper context for understanding God's relationship to the world. It remains, therefore, to clarify the development of perspectivalism by showing how the lordship attributes function as normative, situational, and existential perspectives.

Lordship Attributes as Perspectives

The transition from lordship attributes to epistemological perspectives is based on the application of Scripture to the philosophical question of how God's personal creatures know what they know (Frame, 1987:62-75). The lordship attributes explain God's relationship to the world, but how does a finite knower created in God's image relate to those attributes? For Frame (1987:xv, 63), epistemology is "the theology of knowledge", an analysis of "the norms that govern thought". Specifically, it "analyzes the norms for belief", focusing on what and how one "ought" to believe and the acceptable justifications for such beliefs. Defining epistemology as a branch of ethics disallows autonomy, requiring instead dependence on the knowledge of God as he has revealed himself. This is where the lordship attributes come in. Torres (2009:115) refers to them as the "three theological axioms" from which multiperspectivalism is derived (cf. Anderson, 2009:436-442).

As a Christian epistemology, perspectivalism cannot settle for a simple restatement of the biblical teaching on God's transcendence and immanence. It must apply this scriptural testimony to the realities of human knowing. God is the "ultimate criterion" of truth, and his word is the "standard", but epistemology deals with how human beings "apprehend" divine revelation through reason, sense experience, and subjectivity (Frame, 1999:6). Even the subjectivity of human consciousness must be taken into account, since feelings and intuitions clearly play a role in human knowing—and they should play a role if God is the author of human subjectivity. One might summarize Frame's position by saying that reason, sense experience, and subjectivity are the components of the human decoder designed for God's encoded revelation. All important here is the fact that the components—reason, sense experience, and subjectivity—are finite receptive faculties, not ultimate criteria of knowledge. We know God *through* these faculties, not *in* them as ultimate criteria. And yet, all are necessary and function as "mutually dependent" in knowing God—"they work together in producing human knowledge". In essence, each faculty provides a perspective on human knowledge, but each perspective is necessary to the others as well (1999:7; cf. 1987:89-90, 191-194).

Correlated with this triad of reason, sense experience, and subjectivity is another triad that explains "any act of knowledge" (Frame, 1999:7): (1) the object of knowledge, (2) the subject of knowledge, and (3) the standard by which knowledge claims are justified. Put simply, this triad refers to what is known, who knows it, and how it is known to be true. Like the knowing faculties, these three elements are mutually dependent and "each may be defined in terms of the other two". So, for example, the object of knowledge refers to the "facts to be known". And yet, the norm and subject are objects of knowledge, and "the object and norm are also elements of subjective experience".

The Existential Perspective

To fully understand Frame (2010c:344), one must recognize that episte-mological perspectives are "ways of looking at Scripture that necessitate and imply one another". As human perspectives, no one perspective—not even the normative—is simply equivalent to Scripture. As epistemological perspectives, they refer to the human apprehension of God's revelation with Scripture taking priority over all other forms of normative revelation (Frame, 1987:137-139). The beauty of this approach is that it unifies what other philosophers separate and compartmentalize. Most secular episte-mologies tend to be monoperspectival, making reason, sense experience, or subjectivity the sole faculty of knowing and exalting the chosen faculty to a normative status (1987:123). One might generalize secular epistemologies by saying that they grant normative status to rational, empirical, or subjective criteria, bypassing knowledge of God's revelation as normative. This is an accurate description of the strategy of intellectual autonomy.

This analysis leads to an understanding of "any piece of human knowledge" as a three-fold relationship: A "warranted cognitive satisfac-tion" within a subject concerning the correspondence of an idea and its object—all in accordance with "God's laws for thought" (Frame, 1999:7). This three-fold relationship corresponds respectively to Frame's existential, situational, and normative perspectives. This human relationship to the world also corresponds to the divine relationship: (1) God is personally *present* in blessing and judging all *persons*; (2) God is the Creator and therefore exercises *control* over all *situations*; (3) God is the ultimate *authority* over all knowing. Another way to put this is to say that God is present to persons, the source of all situations, and the ultimate criterion of knowledge. For purposes of this study, the existential perspective is most important: "His presence is the source of our existential perspective, for it means that we can find God's reality in the deepest recesses of ourselves as his image." (2002:7-8.) This is just Frame's way of saying with Calvin that to know the self one must know God, and to know God one must know the self.

2 THE APPLICATION TO APOLOGETICS

The application of triperspectivalism to apologetics requires a unified understanding of Frame's presuppositional approach. While key features of his apologetic have been discussed, the general cast of Frame's presuppositionalism must be clear if the perspectival component of that apologetic is to stand out in bold relief. Therefore, it will be helpful at this point to pull together the strands of Frame's approach as these have been presented thus far. Frame (2000:219-223) provides a summary of his apologetic method in the form of eight conclusions drawn from the biblical teaching. Scrivener (2009:541) cites this summary as the most concise presentation of Frame's apologetic in all of his writings. As an introduction to the application of perspectivalism to apologetics, it will unify the presuppositional context, giving a definite shape to the essential components of Frame's apologetic.

It was noted that Frame's (2000:219-223) eight apologetic conclusions are drawn from biblical teaching, not from a neutral philosophical method. As conclusions, some will simply restate points already made above, and others will draw conclusions from what has been presented: (1) Apologetics is for both believers (as training) and unbelievers (as evangelism), its goal being "to evoke or strengthen faith, not merely to bring intellectual persuasion" (2000:219); (2) First Peter 3:15-16 stresses the importance of the character of the apologist, not his or her intellectual ability, thus commending godliness, gentleness, and respect as proper attitudes for defending a comprehensive "way of life" as opposed to a mere "intellectual system" (2000:220); (3) A biblical apologetic will present God as "the sovereign Lord of heaven and earth", meaning that God controls all things and is "the source of all meaning and rationality"; (4) Because God is the source of meaning and rationality, apologetic argument should be transcendental, meaning that the God of the Bible is both the conclusion of the argument as well as the One who makes all argument possible; (5) A transcendental conclusion can be reached by many argument types, including many traditional arguments, as long as the conclusion is biblical truth and the logic of the argument does not claim neutrality; (6) The apologist should not reinforce the pretended "autonomy and neutrality" of the unbeliever, arguing as if a secular method may be used as a neutral tool to judge biblical truth (2000:221); (7) Apologetics is "person-variable" (Mavrodes), which means that it deals with "the inquirer's specific form of unbelief" by using arguments and dialogue that serve the needs of the person and a transcendental conclusion (2000:222, 223); (8) It is helpful in apologetics to expose unbelief by showing "how unbelief itself is a systematic source of error", leading to both rationalism and irrationality in the unbeliever's position (2000:223). Given this general context, the application of perspectivalism to apologetics is more easily understood (cf. Davis, 2009:511).

Apologetics as a Person-Variable Strategy

It is common in academic circles to focus on apologetic methods. Certainly there is nothing wrong with analyzing apologetic methods in order to sort them out (Sotak, 2016). For Frame, however, apologetics is explained primarily in terms of defensive and offensive *strategies*. While Frame (1987:347) discusses this issue in a chapter entitled, "Method in Apologetics", he also makes it clear that there is no one set of questions or topics "that must be treated in a fixed order". The influence of Mavrodes (1970) on Frame's thinking is obvious, and Frame (1987:348) acknowledges that he quotes Mavrodes often throughout *The Doctrine of the Knowledge of God*. Specifically, Frame (1987:347, 348-349) relies on Mavrodes for his insight that apologetics is "person-variable" and for his explanation of a three-fold strategy that closely corresponds to the existential, situational, and normative perspectives.

In general, this means that the apologist will use the three perspectives in offering "broadly circular arguments" based on Scripture, extrabiblical resources, and the apologists own gifts, ability, and "godly character" (Frame, 1987:348). It is important to distinguish Frame's notion of broad circularity from the narrow circularity reflected in the fallacy of begging the question, or assuming what needs to be proved. According to Frame (1987:130), circularity within a system of belief is justifiable at one point only: "in an argument for the *ultimate* criterion of the system". Frame shows that such circularity characterizes all belief systems. The rationalist must presuppose the authority of reason, since one must use reason to justify reason. The same goes for the empiricist and the subjectivist: At the level of the ultimate criteria of knowing, circularity is unavoidable for all thinkers—Christian or not. So what distinguishes "broad" from "narrow" circularity? The difference is in the amount of biblical and extrabiblical data brought into the argument (1987:131). Such data might include biblical facts as well as the facts of archeology, history, philosophy, and forms of argument and types of evidence validated by Scripture.

While the distinction between broad and narrow circularity may seem like a mere device to justify a dogmatic starting point, it really is not. The distinction explains all theoretical thought, regardless of the ultimate religious commitment. It also reveals the ultimate goal of Christian apologetics: "a broadly circular argument for Christianity will display the internal coherence of the Christian position—the fact that it 'holds together' on its own terms" (Frame, 1987:132). Presuppositional apologetics seeks to answer a simple question: Does the center hold? Comparing the coherence of belief systems as wholes is not an exact science because it also involves subjective and spiritual factors. But such a comparison is not only possible; it is the only way apologetics can be done given biblical teaching and the realities of theoretical thought.

The Christian proof is really about proclaiming the "rationale" for the truth (Frame, 1987:131). Therefore, the "normative perspective" reflects a specific type of "Christian rationalism", the situational perspective a kind of Christian empiricism, and the existential perspective a kind of Christian subjectivism or existentialism (1987:133, 145-148). Christian rationalism does not affirm a deductive system, since the "apparent contradictions" of Scripture require commitment to an "analogical system" and "analogical reasoning" (Frame, 1976:306-310; 1987:18-40). Certain doctrines in Scripture, such as the necessity and freedom of God's will, are "paradoxically related" (1976:310). Since God's revelation presents him from a human perspective, apparent contradictions "arise from our ignorance concerning the precise senses of key terms". Of course, there are no contradictions in the mind of God. Human reasoning, however, is analogical, presupposing the authority of God and his revelation despite the fact that divine revelation leads to some paradoxical formulations. Human thought is a finite replica of God's original thought and therefore reflects an analogical system—a system *like* God's own understanding, based on his revelation, neither univocal nor equivocal. But within its own principles, the Christian system explains both reason and its limits in relation to the revelation of God. Likewise, with respect to evidence and subjectivity, the revelation of God must have normative authority. In short, human beings must think God's thoughts after him, not with him or for him (PSA 36:9; 2CO 10:5). Frame (1987:40) aptly calls this "servant thinking" (cf. Meek, 2009:614-616).

The three-fold strategy suggested by Mavrodes (1970:82ff.) is based on "the ways we seek to help people share in other sorts of experiences" (Frame, 1987:348). First, the apologist attempts "to place the other person in circumstances that are similar to our own". Second, the person must be told "what to look for" (quoted by Frame, 1987:349). Third, the apologist must seek to integrate the experience with other experiences, using "a conceptual framework that exhibits the meaning of the particular experience" (quoted by Frame, 1987:349). Frame summarizes this strategy in perspectival terms by saying that the unbeliever needs to be placed in new circumstances (existential) and then given the facts (situational) and a system (normative) that integrates the total experience, allowing its "meanings" to be apprehended. This is the "methodological triad" that defines the defensive and offensive strategies of Frame's apologetic.

Apologetics as Defense

Defensive apologetics takes its cue from the unbeliever who takes the "initiative": "The unbeliever raises an objection, the believer responds." (Frame, 1987:349.) Biblically, Paul addresses this in terms of the defense and confirmation of the gospel (PHP 1:7, 16; Frame, 1994:2). Unlike many apologists who begin with a consideration of common objections to Christian faith raised by unbelievers, Frame offers a perspectival analysis of defensive apologetics before dealing with common objections (1987:348-358, 1994:2, 149-190). Frame (1987:349) logically begins with the normative perspective, since it concerns "the 'conceptual framework' or 'system' in terms of which the meanings of facts are apprehended". Since the teaching of Scripture is the norm for all apologetic activity, it is inevitable that Scripture will have to be defended against objections to its authority. This requires considerable knowledge on the part of the apologist, including knowledge of the Bible, extrabiblical information, and preferably the original languages.

The use of the Bible as the Christian's ultimate authority must be defended on the grounds that all knowing is "broadly circular" (1987:350). An open admission of this in every apologetic encounter is not necessary, but nor should this be hidden or downplayed. For Frame, the normative defense boils down to "a demand for a change in presuppositions". Therefore, the defense of the Christian's complex presupposition is implicit in every encounter if not explicit. It all depends on the intellectual sophistication of the hearer and the situation at hand. "The important thing", writes Frame, "is not to *talk* about our presuppositions but to *obey* them in our thought, speech and life". Many non-Christians accept Christian presuppositions on a number of issues, so it may not be necessary to openly discuss them, especially as part of a "canned" or scripted approach to apologetics, which Frame criticizes as unskillful (1987:347). It all depends on the situation and the person.

Frame (1987:365-368) takes for granted, along with Van Til, that there are no neutral criteria of truth shared by the Christian and the non-Christian, although there may be points of contact or agreement. Given the fact that the unbeliever—by definition—does not believe the Christian message, the apologist demands a change in presuppositions through the gentle method of calling the non-Christian to accept Christian criteria "for the sake of argument" (1987:351). While this may seem like commending the Christian system to the non-Christian as a hypothesis to be evaluated on alien presuppositions, it is not (cf. Lewis, 1971:349-368). Rather, the unbeliever is being asked to look at the facts from a Christian point of view. The word "hypothesis" is defined in three senses, all of which reflect Frame's view with proper qualifications: "1. A tentative explanation that accounts for a set of facts and can be tested by further investigation; a theory. 2. Something taken to be true for the purpose of argument or investigation; an assumption. 3. The antecedent of a conditional statement." (AHCD:670.)

Within presuppositionalism, hypothetical reasoning is valid. Assuming the Christian position for the sake of argument means that the Christian "hypothesis" will be tested by its own internal criteria, not allegedly neutral external criteria (Frame, 1995:291-294). Obviously, the Christian assumption will be held hypothetically by an unbeliever until it is accepted as categorically true. Thus, the Christian position is "tentative" only with respect to the unbeliever who has yet to recognize it as absolutely true. But the fact that such an exercise reflects a form of hypothetical reasoning neither demands nor implies autonomy or neutral criteria. Christian proclamation is a demand for agreement with God, not an invitation to allegedly neutral hypothesis testing. On this point, Frame (1995:293) sees "a difference in clarity and completeness" between Van Til and Carnell, not a difference "in substance, as Van Til thinks".

The goal of the normative defense is to invite the non-Christian to apply a *reductio ad absurdum* argument to the Christian system in exchange for the same opportunity on the part of the Christian with respect to the unbeliever's worldview (Frame, 1987:351). This approach will not enable the Christian to answer every objection the unbeliever raises, since the Christian system does not answer all questions for either party. The Bible defines areas of ignorance with respect to things God has left unrevealed (DEU 29:29). In addition, there are vast areas of factual information the apologist may be lacking as a result of intellectual or educational deficiencies. And yet, both believers and unbelievers share this problem, and Christians should be honest and up-front about the fact that God alone is omniscient. Such humility represents a challenge to the many false certainties of the non-Christian.

The situational defense employs extrabiblical evidence interpreted biblically (Frame, 1987:352-354; 1994:57-60). While the non-Christian has sufficient evidence for the Christian system in nature, Scripture, and the self, the apologist "has the obligation to underscore that evidence, to show the unbeliever 'what to look for' (Mavrodes), as well as how to look for it and how to look at it" (1987:352). Frame (1987:353) acknowledges that presuppositionalists have not given adequate attention to the use of evidences in apologetics, and he acknowledges the "positive value" of many of the popular offerings by evangelical evidentialists. The problem with most evidentialists, however, is that they fail to recognize that evidential arguments are only intelligible within a Christian framework: "They are intelligible only within the 'broad circle' of Christian argument. Outside that circle, the arguments can be evaded easily." In perspectival terms, evidential arguments require the normative perspective; they cannot be approached from the situational perspective of factuality alone, since the Bible also supplies a philosophy of fact. By recognizing the normative context of evidences, the apologist presents those evidences within the context of the Christian worldview.

Philosophically sophisticated unbelievers will recognize the Christian presuppositions implicit in an evidential defense of the faith, and their objections will require the apologist to turn the tables with respect to the non-Christian's philosophy of fact and probability (offensive apologetics). The non-Christian can always argue against Christian evidences like the resurrection on the basis of their inherent improbability, as David Hume did, but the very notion of probability itself is not intelligible apart from Christian presuppositions. For this reason, the evidential apologist must also be a philosophical apologist, since—eventually—the issues of epistemology will come up. So while it is true that the presuppositionalist school has done little with the specific use of evidences in apologetics, it has addressed in detail the philosophy of Christian evidences (Van Til, 1951; Notaro, 1980).

Frame's (1987:355-358; 1994:57-80) concept of proof is properly discussed in relation to the existential perspective. This perspective takes into account proof as the apologetic means and persuasion as the evangelistic end or goal of the Christian defense (ACT 18:4, 28; 19:8). Thus, apologetics and evangelism are "perspectivally related", which is another way of saying that "godly reasoning based on Scripture" is perspectivally related to "the conversion of sinners" (1987:355).

The complexity of apologetics is based primarily on the complexity of the self, which is central to the existential perspective. The problem, of course, is that both proof and persuasion are "person-variable", which means that there is no set of proofs and no method of persuasion that appeals to all persons. In addition, the role of the sovereign work of the Holy Spirit in the persuasion of sinners further complicates the existential defense, since no method of proof or persuasion—however necessary—provides a sufficient condition for salvation. With respect to "the mystery of persuasion", the self of the hearer is not the only factor. Adding yet more complication to the picture, the self of the apologetic evangelist must be considered along with the self of the hearer and the divine Self of the Spirit. The godly character and love of the apologist is also a necessary factor in apologetic evangelism, adding to the mystery of "that 'cognitive rest' that marks the moment of persuasion" (Frame, 1987:355). Without the "gentleness and respect" commended in 1 Peter 3:15, the Christian system (normative) and its evidence (situational) lack a fully personal (existential) defense.

Given the person-relativity of both proof and persuasion, what constitutes proof? To answer this question, Frame returns to the concept of broad circularity, which is based on the biblical teaching that all things testify of God to the unbeliever. Proofs, therefore, formalize the revelation of God in nature, Scripture, and the self into apologetic-evangelistic appeals to the unbeliever. Given the comprehensive scope of the evidence for the Christian faith from these sources, the non-Christian is without excuse before God and really should require no argument at all (ROM 1:18-21). All valid (biblically based) proofs, therefore, "ought to persuade" (Frame, 1994:63). Consistent with the dynamics of the existential perspective, it is clear that apologetic proofs should consider the facts and experience of the unbeliever, and a "godly pragmatism" dictates that "broader arguments just seem to work best". Therefore, apologetic proofs must adapt broader arguments to the situation of the inquirer, employing true premises and valid logic. Such arguments must also be consistent with biblical teaching and epistemology and be sensitive to the inquirer's education, interests, questions, and needs (1994:63-64).

Based on this description of the existential perspective, it is clear that it is not Frame's goal to specify a set of proofs or a scripted method for applying them to all situations. The person-variability of proof and persuasion simply forbids that. However, all evidence validated by Scripture and a biblical epistemology is potentially useful to apologetic evangelism. Frame (1994:89-190) offers specific arguments and evidences that are useful to defensive apologetics, but his goal is to provide samples and exemplars, not a complete catalogue of apologetic arguments. Recognizing that many other apologists have made worthy contributions that simply require adaptation to presuppositional principles, Frame gives more meta-apologetic advice than he does arguments and resources. As an ecumenical apologist, he sees no reason to have the last word on apologetic resources.

Apologetics as Offense

Offensive apologetics takes its cue from the believer who responds with "an attack . . . against unbelieving thought and action" (Frame, 1987:358; cf. 1994:192). Offensive apologetics could be viewed as "the *primary* function of apologetics", since "God has nothing to defend, nothing to 'apologize' for" (1987:358). Christ's present reign over history involves putting down his enemies, and apologetics is part of that goal (COL 2:15; 2CO 10:4-5). Just as the non-believer is asked to stand on the position of the believer for the sake of argument (defensive apologetics), so the believer takes a stand on the unbeliever's position (offensive apologetics) "so that the believer can present a *reductio*, a demonstration that the unbeliever's premises lead to total unintelligibility" (1987:359). Accepting a non-Christian stance for the sake of argument does not mean adopting unbelief hypothetically. Rather, the Christian explains clearly how the non-Christian's position looks from a Christian point of view (1987:360). In both defensive and offensive strategies, each party is asking for agreement with the other's presuppositions to see which position provides a basis for intelligibility. Like the defensive strategy, the offensive strategy is also triperspectival.

A normative offense typically centers on the relationship of faith and reason. Non-Christians usually charge believers with arguing by faith rather than on the basis of reason conceived as an allegedly objective criterion. The Christian knows, however, that the unbeliever also has faith and "argues in a circle" (Frame, 1987:360). But the unbeliever has no basis to believe in the reliability of reason, given an ultimately impersonal worldview, so he ends up practicing a blind faith while alleging neutral objectivity. It is remarkable the extent to which even Christian apologists fail to understand this point in presuppositional apologetics. Frame exposes John Warwick Montgomery to criticism on this point for admitting that facts require "a *gestalt* or system of thought" in order to become intelligible, and yet he fails to recognize that this affirmation agrees with Frame and Van Til and conflicts with his own radical empiricism (1987:354). Even Christian apologists emulate unbelievers in pretending neutrality and refusing to acknowledge that the situational perspective (in Montgomery's case) requires the normative authority of God's revelation in nature, Scripture, and the self for its intelligibility; "monoperspectivalism" rules in much of evangelical apologetics (Frame, 1982:8).

For Frame, theoretical thought is shut up to only two alternatives: It is either scriptural or dialectical. If one does not reason on the basis of Scripture, one will inevitably become mired in both rational and irrational claims simultaneously. As Frame (1987:361) puts it, "the non-Christian has no right to have faith in reason". So, for example, the claim to authoritative neutral criteria for one's thought is rationalistic, and yet attempting to ground such criteria in the autonomous self or an impersonal worldview is irrational. Postmodernism has done much to expose the irrationalism of autonomous thought, and yet it also reflects the rationalist-irrationalist dialectic in its dogmatic commitment to relativism as an absolute. Because the world is what God says it is, "the facts never fit into his godless system", and the unbeliever is forever frustrated in his thought as long as he refuses to agree with God. Over time, he becomes mired in the "fantasy world" of his own thought life, which is irrational. At a deeper level, the frustration of unbelieving thought derives from a finite knower assuming omniscience. A finite reference point simply provides no basis from which to know the whole of reality (cf. Sotak, 2017:450-451; Frame, 1987:362). Only a personal being who is omnipotent and omniscient is in the proper position to interpret all of reality. In short, only a being with lordship attributes is sufficient to ground reliable knowledge. In the end, the unbeliever is completely stifled in his attempt to distinguish between the capabilities and limits of reason, infusing the whole of his thought with irrationality.

In reasoning like an omniscient being and assuming the competence of unaided reason, the non-Christian really borrows Christian presuppositions. Because all know God, all know that God is the author of reason and its abilities; the unbeliever, however, refuses to acknowledge these things (ROM 1:18-21), choosing instead a "parasitic" strategy that lives off the borrowed capital of the Christian faith in order to deny that faith (Frame, 1987:362). As Frame (1987:363) says, "rationalism feeds on the Christian premise that the world is governed by a fully rational plan, that nothing can be known unless someone knows everything". But the unbeliever also feeds off the Christian premise that human knowledge is limited, "that much of the world is mysterious to us, being beyond the capacity of our reason". The unbeliever, therefore, oscillates back and forth between rationalism and irrationality as it suits his purpose, trading on the fact that reason is both capable and limited. In framing his arguments against the Christian faith, he affirms reason's reliability; when pressed with questions he cannot answer, the unbeliever takes refuge in reason's limits. The problem, of course, is that the autonomous mind, not God's revelation, acts as the normative authority over where one draws the line. The arbitrariness of this intellectual oscillation between rationalism and irrationality is what opens the unbeliever to the Christian's normative attack. The more consistently rational the unbeliever becomes, the more strongly he defends his own autonomous system of thought. The more consistently irrational he becomes, the more he defends the irrationality of all thought, even to the point of swamping himself and the Christian in a sea of unintelligible facts. The goal of this strategy, of course, is to leave autonomy intact. For after all, if everyone is overboard with respect to truth, each person must find his or her own way to remain afloat. The opportunities for apologetic engagement around these issues are obvious, and presuppositionalism has profoundly analyzed them.

A situational offense requires attacking unbelief with respect to matters of fact, whereas the normative offense focuses on presuppositions. Factual "unclarities" and inaccuracies naturally abound in discussions of Christianity, and many of these result from the errors of Christians themselves (Frame 1987:363-364). Unclarities often typically result from the parasitic strategy described above. Borrowed Christian capital is distorted through its reinterpretation and adaptation to non-Christian philosophic systems, thus contradicting scriptural teaching while being "made to *sound* very biblical" (1987:364). Frame's discussion of transcendence and immanence, it should be recalled, illustrates this point. Unclarities must be exposed for what they are, especially in light of their role in intellectual and spiritual deception. All deception trades on unclarity and the resemblance between errors and the truth (cf. GEN 3:1-7).

Factual and logical errors must also be exposed. The problem with such errors is that unbelievers have special reasons for making them. If, as the Bible teaches, the unbeliever refuses "to love the truth and so be saved" (2TH 2:10), then factual and logical integrity will be impossible to maintain with respect to the Christian system. Again, Christians are also subject to breaches of fact and logic due to their own ignorance and willful tendencies. But the non-Christian bears the burden of remaking the world to fit his own belief system. The problem, of course, is that God has created the world, and the attempt to live in another world is doomed to frustration. To the extent that this project of unbelief is carried out, errors of fact and *non sequiturs* will increase accordingly.

The existential offense requires specific knowledge of one's audience: "Each inquirer is different, though all have essentially the same problem and need." (Frame, 1987:365.) This goal requires dialogue and sympathetic listening to determine "where the inquirer is in his thought and life". One must listen for what Os Guinness calls the unbeliever's "dilemma" and "diversion"—a situation equivalent to Frame's rationalist-irrationalist dialectic (quoted by Frame, 1987:365). This is really the point of inconsistency at the heart of the inquirer's position, "not only in his theorizing but particularly between his theorizing and his life". The problem with the unbeliever is that "he is an irrationalist who nevertheless needs to live in a rational world". All human beings strive for meaning, and yet the dilemma of the non-Christian is that the meaning he seeks (rationality) is continually being undermined by his irrationality. The Christian, however, relies on God to define both the meaning of life as well as the realm of what is unknown or mysterious, so what the believer cannot rationalize is nevertheless rational in God's mind. This preserves Christian rationality in the face of what the Christian cannot explain within an analogical system.

Sensitivity to individuals requires sensitivity to their cultural influences—what Frame (1987:366) calls "points of contact". Frame lists several apologists—Francis Schaeffer being the very first—who provide useful information on modern culture and its drift toward "secularization, pluralization, and privatization of religion". A Christian apologist simply cannot speak effectively to modern inquirers without some "responsible (scripturally based) opinions" on these matters. These issues become "points of contact", not *the* point of contact, which represents an "ambiguous" concept in apologetics. Frame recognizes that in the practical outworking of apologetics, the strategic question centers on points of contact or communication that facilitate the effective proclamation and defense of the gospel. While rejecting a neutral criterion of truth shared by believer and unbeliever, Frame does accept "some facts or norms that both the believer and unbeliever know". There are, therefore, "many points of contact", including the unbeliever's suppressed knowledge as well as "some psychological faculty (perhaps the heart itself) that can be reached by a gospel presentation or apologetic argument, if God wills" (1987:366-367; cf. 1994:82-85). This is what Frame means by "points of contact". While the apologist should not "identify" with unbelievers, she "must seek to look at the world through their eyes as much as possible so that our message is not obscured by cultural or traditional factors that are irrelevant to the gospel" (1987:367; cf. Jones, 2009; 1Co 9:22).

Frame (1987:367) appeals to Paul's example on this point, showing how the apostle appealed to "the prophets, the customs, and the ideas of the unbeliever" in Acts 17:16-34. Paul appealed to the clear and inescapable knowledge of God in line with his argument in Romans 1, rebuking the Athenians for having resisted this revelation (cf. ROM 1:21). Paul also notes the Athenians' recognition of "their own ignorance (v. 23) and God's immanence (v. 28)" but corrects their pagan, Stoic, and Epicurean misconceptions in light of the biblical teaching that God is "immaterial, personal, and sovereign". While not directly quoting the Old Testament, Paul is clearly alluding to several biblical passages (1987:368; EXO 20:3ff.; DEU 32:8; 1KI 8:27; PSA 50:9-12). Frame's point here is that Paul acknowledges both the truths of his audience as well as their errors. Apologists should not assume that the point of contact is merely the point of conflict. Rather, common truths should be acknowledged in the course of correcting errors. Also significant is the fact that Paul refers to biblical teaching without directly quoting chapter and verse. This demonstrates that offensive apologetics must be scripturally based but does not require the explicit use of Scriptural references to validate arguments, even though such references are appropriate and powerful at times.

Frame's (1987:368) point about the truth of "certain elements of unbelieving thought" is vitally important to establishing the argument of this study. Presuppositionalism is often interpreted to mean that there are no common truths, no common ground, between believers and unbelievers because their respective belief systems differ fundamentally. This would mean that any apparent agreement between the believer and unbeliever is merely formal. Frame's (1995:305) precise position is that "there is no common ground in principle, but there is common ground in debate". The reason for this is that the non-Christian is not fully consistent with his unbelieving principles and therefore embraces some Christian truths while resisting others. Frame (1995:197, 188) criticizes the "extreme antithetical formulations" of Van Til as "overstated", acknowledging that there may be common truths, even though such truths are affirmed within a context of unbelief. Thus, the correct view affirms both depravity and common grace as pervasive: "There is no commonality without difference." (1995:207; cf. Edgar, 2009:419-424.)

The antithesis between the believer and unbeliever, then, may be understood triperspectivally as an opposition "in principle" regarding their respective systems of belief (normative), their interpretation of facts (situational), and their ethical motivation with respect to the love of God (existential). This understanding of antithesis is not merely intellectual, "as if it were merely about one group of propositions contradicting one another" (Frame, 1995: 211). In fact, the doctrine of antithesis is about the orientation of the human heart with respect to all of life. Frame (1995:212) affirms that "the chief antithesis is between belief and unbelief as such rather than between varieties of belief or various formulations of the truth". This point is critical in understanding Frame's specific version of presuppositionalism (and Schaeffer's, as will be evident in the next section). The antithesis cannot be identified with a rigid set of "conceptual oppositions" that distinguish believers and unbelievers. Presenting antithesis this way, as Van Til sometimes did, fails to do justice to the complexity of "the precise relationship between heart condition and verbal confession". While doctrine and words are related to the condition of the heart (MAT 12:34), the two heart conditions do not lead to identical confessions of belief and unbelief. Just as there are denominational differences among Christian believers, so there are schools of thought among unbelievers as well. Just as there is no commonality without difference between believers and unbelievers, so this situation prevails to a lesser extent within each group. Frame's commitment to commonality with differences explains his notion of a "presuppositionalism of the heart" in apologetics. Various forms of believing argument reflect the regenerate condition of the heart, despite differing formulations, denominational differences, and strategies. Various forms of unbelieving argument may be described likewise. Antithesis is ultimately "a doctrine about the human heart".

Apologetics and Antithesis

Despite the complex relationship between the condition of the heart and the confession of belief, it is possible to arrive at general descriptions of belief and unbelief that hold firmly in the face of the complexities of philosophy and theology. Frame (1994:31-55; 191-202; cf. 2002:185-237) presents a number of foundational beliefs that distinguish Christian and non-Christian thought. By presenting Christianity as a philosophy, the antithesis between the believing and unbelieving heart becomes evident. Regardless of areas of commonality and complex differences, the overflow of the heart speaks clearly of its orientation to God. These conceptual oppositions are all-important to apologetics, representing a short list of the fundamentals of belief and unbelief organized in terms of metaphysics, epistemology, and ethics. What Frame shows is that—ultimately—one has only two choices, Christian belief being the only alternative to "conventional wisdom" (1994:34). In the case of each Christian philosophical principle or fundamental, Frame explains the corresponding principle of all unbelief.

One can derive seven paired principles reflecting the antithesis from Frame's (1994:34-55) discussion of the apologist's message. While he does not organize his material around paired principles, this is a helpful way to reorganize his discussion to bring out the antithesis of belief and unbelief in terms of cognitive opposites. Of the seven antitheses listed below, four are metaphysical, one is epistemological, and the last two are ethical: (1) God as ultimate Personality versus impersonal reality as ultimate; (2) A two-level concept of reality versus a one-level concept of reality; (3) The sovereignty of God versus the determinism of impersonal forces or laws; (4) The triune God as the eternal One and Many versus the dialectic of absolute oneness and absolute pluralism; (5) God as the supreme standard of truth and error versus human autonomy with respect to the final standard of knowledge; (6) God as the supreme standard of good and evil versus human autonomy with respect to the final standard of ethics; (7) The gospel as the solution to the problem of human sin versus works-righteousness or effort as the solution to the problem of human finitude. While Frame does not state it, the seven antitheses are perspectivally related and could be reduced to three simple antitheses: (1) Ultimate personality versus an impersonal ultimate; (2) God's sovereignty versus human autonomy; (3) Righteousness in Christ versus works righteousness (cf. 1994:55).

Antithesis One: God as ultimate Personality versus impersonal reality as ultimate. A Christian metaphysics begins with God as the absolute personality (Frame, 1994:34; cf. 2002:387-401). As the Creator and ground of all reality, God is "self-existent and self-sufficient". The biblical testimony presents God as an eternal Spirit who is infinite, timeless, omniscient, omnipotent, unchangeable, just, truthful, and good (DEU 32:40; PSA 90:2, 93:2, 102:26-27; ISA 41:4, 44:7-8; JOH 1:1, 4:24, 16:13-14; ACT 10:19, 17:25; ROM 8:14, 16-17, 15:30; 1CO 2:10; GAL 4:4; EPH 1:11; 1TI

6:16; HEB 1:10-12; 1PE 3:15; REV 10:6). Frame (1994:35) raises the central question of modernity in relation to this testimony: "Granted that the universe contains both persons and impersonal structures (like matter, motion, chance, time, space, and physical laws), which is fundamental?" The answer to this question depends on one's spiritual orientation to God. The Christian believer affirms that the impersonal is grounded in the ultimate personality of God; the unbeliever affirms that the impersonal is ultimate, all personal qualities being merely products or epiphenomena of impersonal laws. The philosophical liabilities of an impersonal metaphysics are obvious: "What we call reason and value are the unintended, accidental consequences of chance events." This being the case, there is no reason to trust reason, and virtue, love, and beauty have no ultimate meaning, "for they are reducible to blind, uncaring process" (1994:36). Clearly, if the personal is ultimate, the world reflects a rational plan and purpose that is apprehensible to some extent by personal creatures whose "thoughts, plans, trust, love, and achievements have eternal consequences after all" (1994:37).

Among non-Christian worldviews, there are a number of options that approach the idea of a personal absolute but they fall short. Some forms of pantheism (Hinduism and Buddhism) are theistic, but it is clear that the deities of these religions are not absolute, the absolute being ultimately impersonal. Likewise, "in Greek polytheism . . . the gods are personal but not absolute" (1994:38). Frame notes that in Greek polytheism, fate serves as "a kind of impersonal absolute". Therefore, while a personal nonabsolutism may *resemble* the biblical position, in fact, the two positions are worldviews apart (cf. Sotak, 2017:457-458). Other theistic belief systems such as deism, Judaism, and Islam also fall short of absolute personality due to their unitarian conceptions of God, but more will be said about those options below. With respect to the antithetical principles of a personal and impersonal ultimate, it should be evident that the latter must be held by a blind faith. An impersonal absolute is blind and therefore provides no basis for a belief in the reliability of reason or the intelligibility of the world. While few non-Christians reason consistently on the basis of their impersonal absolute, most professing faith in the rationality of the universe and life as meaningful, it is clear that they have no right to such commitments based on their ultimate metaphysical presupposition.

Antithesis Two: A two-level concept of reality versus a one-level concept of reality. As the ultimate Personality, God has entered into fellowship with his creatures, a relationship Frame (1994:42) calls "the Creator-creature distinction". Though God's personality is original and underived, human personality is derivative and "dependent on impersonal matter (the 'dust' [GEN 2:7]) and forces to keep us alive" (Frame, 1994:41). This antithesis grows out of a consideration of God's transcendence and immanence, which was detailed above in terms of the Lordship attributes. Frame's point with respect to this antithesis is to affirm the Creator's place as the sole authority and standard according to his revelation. Unbelief denies the Creator-creature distinction, reasoning that either the world or the human mind is "the ultimate standard of truth and rightness" (1994:42). These dynamics were presented above as motivated by "a desire to escape responsibility to God's word" (1994:43; cf. ROM 1:21ff.). A one-level view of reality makes the world its own ground, leading to the worship of the creature, not the Creator: "it either raises man to God's level or lowers God to man's".

Antithesis Three: The sovereignty of God versus the determinism of impersonal forces or laws. Like the previous antithesis, this one is also based on the Lordship attributes. Ephesians 1:11 teaches that "God directs all things" according to his divine will (Frame, 1994:44; cf. 2002:115-159). God not only foreknows free decisions; he also creates the world so that the decisions he foreknows come to pass. "Creation sets the whole universe in motion", so it is not overstating to say that God's foreknowledge "causes" the free decisions he foreknows (1994:45). On this point, the evangelical Arminian would come only half way with Frame, affirming that God creates a world in which foreknown decisions come to pass but denying foreknowledge as the cause. On Frame's view, the Arminian must either embrace a causeless action, which is absurd, or a "mysterious" cause. On the Arminian view, an appeal to mystery on this complex issue is reasonable given Frame's view of paradox and mystery. The unbeliever, of course, faces the same problem. Apart from a sovereign God, impersonal laws or another god must govern the world. In any case, "the unbeliever's pretense of autonomy" is destroyed. An impersonal ultimate cannot interpret the world for a personal being, and a finite god is also at the mercy of fate or chance. Only a sovereign God is sufficient to control and interpret all things.

Antithesis Four: The triune God as the eternal One and Many versus the dialectic of absolute oneness and absolute pluralism. In accord with the Nicene Creed, Frame (1994:46) affirms that "the Christian God is three in one" or "one God, three persons" (GEN 1:2; DEU 6:4ff.; Ps. 110:1ff.; ISA 44:6, 63:9-10; JOH 1:1, 20:17; ACT 2; ROM 8, 9:5; COL 2:9; 1TH 1:5; HEB 1:10ff.).

While Christians do not profess to know "precisely" how three are one and one is three, "all three have all the divine attributes". The doctrine of the Trinity is unique among the world's religions, despite some "threefold distinctions" in some religions (Hinduism) and philosophies (Hegel). The Trinity has a unique role in presuppositional apologetics that it has in no other system. For Frame, Schaeffer, and Van Til, the Trinity is necessary to a fully personal conception of God and an intelligible creation.

Unitarian conceptions of God tend "to lose definition and the marks of personality" (Frame, 1994:47). A God of "pure oneness" becomes an inconceivable "blank oneness"—"wholly other"—unless he is defined as a "perfect unity" of qualities separated in creation. However, defining God in relation to the creation implies a "chain of being" metaphysics, which reflects a dialectical relationship "between the unknowable God and the knowable world" (1994:48). The unitarians of the early church (Gnostics, Arians, Neoplatonists) viewed God as relative to the world rather than as sovereign over it, and the doctrine of creation was distorted into a doctrine of emanation. Thus, the roots of the modern dialectical conceptions of God's transcendence and immanence are found in the early Christian era. Judaism, Islam, and deism also reflect these problematics. The Trinity, of course, is the only alternative to this dialectical approach. The Creator-creature distinction represents two levels of being, not one level with degrees of being. The blank oneness of the one-level approach is challenged by the absolute personality of the Sovereign Lord. The unknowable and "wholly other" One becomes the knowable One and Many revealed in Scripture: "Since God is both three and one, he can be described in personal terms without being made relative to the world." A self-sufficient being can *be* love as a trinity of persons (1Jn 4:8); he does not need to create a world to define himself as loving. Therefore, none of God's attributes depend on the world.

The One and Many God is also the answer to the one and many of creation. Unbelieving thought oscillates between monism and pluralism because it lacks "the resources to define a position between the two extremes, and because it seeks an absolute at one extreme or the other" (Frame, 1994:49). The problem, of course, is that monism (Parmenides) destroys any intelligible plurality, and pluralism (Heraclitus) destroys "any universal oneness". The Christian, however, seeks neither absolute unity nor plurality, since "these exist neither in the world nor in the world's Creator" (1994:49-50). Since an "utter uniqueness" or an "utter disunity" is humanly unknowable, God must furnish "the ultimate criteria for human thought", revealing his plan for and interpretation of the created world. The unbeliever, however, posits his own interpretation of the world, seeking to negotiate the utter unity and disunity of the world in the futility of a finite and fallen mind.

Antithesis Five: God as the supreme standard of truth and error versus human autonomy with respect to the final standard of knowledge. Since much of Frame's epistemology has already been discussed at length, the goal here is merely to express the antithesis at the heart of his view. Given the Creator-creature distinction, it is logical to think God's thoughts after him, taking into account the implications of a "Trinitarian epistemology" (Frame, 1994:50). Because God is omnipotent, omniscient, and controls all things according to his plan, human knowledge must begin in "the fear of the Lord" (PRO 1:7; HEB 4:12-13; 1JO 3:20). Again, the Lordship attributes—and God's authority in particular—imply this principle. Human autonomy, however, leads to the distortion of knowledge (ROM 1:12-25; 1CO 1:18-2:5; 2CO 4:4). The conflicting truth claims of rationalism, empiricism, subjectivism, and skepticism are products of the "free thought" that rejects God's right to tell his free creatures what to believe (1994:51; cf. 1987:109-122; 2002:211-213). As Frame points out, liberal theologians have been only too willing to follow free thinkers, "and the Christian heresies continue to manipulate the biblical message as they see fit". Given the uniqueness of a trinitarian epistemology, "Christianity is *the* alternative to conventional wisdom." (1994:52.)

Antithesis Six: God as the supreme standard of good and evil versus human autonomy with respect to the final standard of ethics. The ethical implications of the Creator-creature distinction also require little more than a statement of the antithesis. If God has supreme authority, then he is also the "supreme standard of what is good and evil, right and wrong. And he has expressed his standard in his words to us" (Frame, 1994:52). Unbelievers disobey God's laws and reject responsibility for what, according to Scripture, they know in their hearts (ROM 1:26-32). As in epistemology, so in ethics various systems have been constructed that separate and distort the perspectives of the Christian system, placing them under the authority of the autonomous mind (cf. Frame, 2008b:72-125). Teleological ethics reflects the situational perspective in basing values on sense experience, "but it cannot bridge the gap between the 'is' of experience and the 'ought' of value" (Frame, 1994:53). Deontological ethics reflects the normative perspective in claiming "a source of duty beyond experience, but that source is ultimately mysterious". Whatever the source, Kant's deontology affirms emphatically that one's duty must be autonomously chosen and cannot be imposed from without. Subjectivist ethics reflects the existential perspective in basing value on feelings, "but why should one person's feelings command anyone else's attention or behavior?" Again, Christianity represents *the* alternative to conventional wisdom, although autonomous systems resemble the Christian system with respect to goals, norms, and motivations.

Antithesis Seven: The gospel as the solution to the problem of human sin versus works righteousness or effort as the solution to the problem of human finitude. Frame (1994:53) presents the Christian principle of this antithesis as "good news" and not in terms of ethics, but logically he could have done so. What is the central problem of human life, and what ought to be done about it? The problem, according to the Christian worldview, is primarily ethical (sinfulness), not metaphysical, so the solution is believing the gospel unto the forgiveness of sins, not working at controlling the environment or the self or becoming God. Obviously, this antithesis might have been discussed first, since it addresses the central issue of all the antitheses, which is the spiritual condition of the human heart. All non-Christian philosophies and religions deny the Christian gospel, either by "the hollow advice to try harder, or the false and morally destructive claim that God will forgive without demanding anything" (1994:54).

Christian Faith or Conventional Wisdom?

By reconstructing Frame's discussion of the apologist's message as a series of antitheses, what is stated often throughout the discussion becomes clear: Christianity is *the* alternative to all conventional wisdom, which comprises all non-Christian philosophies and religions. While conventional wisdom requires different apologetic strategies depending on whether it is expressed as a form of atheism or idolatry, the antitheses described above define the cognitive oppositions at issue in all apologetic evangelism (cf. Frame, 1994:191-202). Even more important to the goals of this study, however, is the fact that Frame's presuppositional apologetic reduces the apologetic appeal to a choice between only two mutually exclusive alternatives: Christianity and conventional wisdom. Given the common principles of all conventional wisdom and the uniqueness of Christianity, human knowledge inevitably and necessarily boils down to a binary decision.

This doctrine of the antithesis is unique to presuppositionalism, and from an existential perspective looks very different from other apologetic systems where Christianity is presented as the most plausible, probable, or practical alternative among others. Frame's (2008a:8) existential perspective asks the question, "What belief is most satisfying to the human heart?" Obviously, a choice between two mutually exclusive alternatives is more satisfying than a choice among a large number of possibilities varying in merit and probability. Experience shows that pluralism tends to weaken conviction with respect to all the options. In other apologetic systems, Christianity is the best choice among many possibilities. In Frame's presuppositionalism, Christianity is the only reasonable choice, and the antithesis of belief and unbelief explains why. As will be evident in the next section, Francis Schaeffer agrees with this analysis.

3 THE TRANSCENDENTAL GOAL OF APOLOGETICS

The doctrine of antithesis implies a transcendental mode of argumentation. If all theoretical thought is fundamentally religious in orientation, reflecting belief or unbelief, and if Christian presuppositions are necessary to knowing anything at all, then presuppositional or transcendental reasoning is the Christian mode of reasoning. However, Frame (1994:69; 1995:320) disagrees with Van Til's commitment to transcendental argument as the only acceptable argument type, arguing that other forms of argument may be transcendental in goal (conclusion), direction, or purpose even if they are inductive or deductive in form: "I believe that much of Van Til's presuppositionalism should be understood as an appeal to the heart rather than as a straightforward apologetic method." (1995:320.) Methodologically, a transcendental goal allows for a "richness and variety" in presuppositional apologetics never envisioned by Van Til (Frame, 1995:322). First Peter 3:15 requires that the Christian apologist "set apart Christ as Lord", which means the Lordship attributes regulate apologetic argument and strategy (Frame, 1994:3-9). But with respect to the form apologetic arguments take, all forms—direct and indirect, negative and positive—are possible under the Lordship of Christ.

Transcendental Argument

The presuppositional or transcendental argument developed on the basis of Immanuel Kant's response to David Hume's skepticism (Frame, 1994:69-70; cf. 2006b:716-717). Hume's pure empiricism reduces all knowledge except mathematics and logic to sense experience. The implication of Hume's view is that metaphysical propositions cannot be proved on the basis of sense experience alone, relegating propositions about God, freedom, the self, causality, and moral values to the category of practical beliefs—not knowledge. While accepting Hume's belief that knowledge is restricted to experience, Kant adopted a transcendental method: "That method does not try to prove that genuine knowledge is possible; rather, it presupposes that it is." (1994:70.) It then asks "what the necessary conditions of human knowledge are". Van Til studied this idealistic method at Princeton University in the 1920's and developed a "distinctively Christian" version of this method for apologetics. Unlike Kant and Hegel, however, Van Til recognized that only the Christian God could provide the necessary preconditions of knowledge, since God alone is the source of all meaning, rationality, and possibility. Kant's transcendental method rooted in the finite self of the knower is simply not a sufficient ground for knowledge, since it ultimately reduces all knowledge to subjectivism. But the Christian starting point provides both a basis for knowledge and "the only legitimate proof of God's existence": "Without God there is no meaning (truth, rationality, etc.); therefore, God exists." For the presuppositionalist, all legitimate theistic proof reduces to "the possibility of predication": "God exists ... because without him it would not be possible to reason, to think, or even to attach a predicate to a subject." (1994:70-71.) Given Van Til's exhaustive development of presuppositionalism and his longevity as a seminary professor, this approach became "Westminster's Apologetic" (Knudsen, 1986).

Frame (1994:71) was also schooled in this approach at Westminster Seminary and agreed that "theistic argument should have a transcendental goal" to prove the Christian system as a whole. But he also raised some legitimate questions with respect to Van Til's formulation of the transcendental argument. Most notably, Frame questions "whether the transcendental argument can function without the help of subsidiary arguments of a more traditional kind". For example, it is not immediately evident that there is no meaning without God, since in proving this premise one must define the "meaning-structure" of reality. Is it design, efficient cause, values, or all of these? If it is one or all of these definitions, then meaning entails a designer, a first cause, or a valuer, which is precisely what the traditional theistic proofs set out to prove. As long as the traditional arguments are not framed to prove that God is "merely" a designer, first cause, or valuer, they may be used in a complex argument with a transcendental goal or direction. Moreover, the transcendental goal actually requires these arguments (cf. Frame, 1995:241-297; 311-322; Edgar, 2009:424-428).

Frame (1994:71-72) makes the same point by claiming that the traditional arguments often work because "they presuppose a Christian worldview". The Christian system alone explains design, causality, and value, but non-Christians who resist the traditional arguments do so by taking refuge in worldviews that redefine these concepts in order to circumvent and invalidate the arguments. For example, by redefining these concepts, Kant and Hume can reject the conclusion of the traditional proofs by reducing their central concepts to the subjective functions of individual psychology. Non-Christians who accept the validity of these arguments do so because they have not repressed the revelation of design, causality, and value reflected in the arguments. Different responses to traditional arguments by unbelievers determine the extent to which presuppositional differences must be addressed. The more "sophisticated and philosophical" the discussion becomes, "the more explicitly transcendental" the argument becomes (1994:72). Frame recognizes that good communication requires sensitivity to the "person-variability" of apologetics and avoiding more sophistication in argument than each hearer requires. He even affirms that, with "unsophisticated inquirers, one or more of the traditional arguments may be sufficient". This is a remarkable qualification of presuppositional apologetics that accounts for the rich possibilities of Frame's approach.

Defending Christian theism holistically, then, is not possible using "a single argument, unless that argument is highly complex" (Frame, 1994:72). In fact, Frame believes that Van Til himself was not "sufficiently holistic" in his own formulation of the Christian proof (1994:73). Many arguments are needed in a system of apologetics "that establishes the entire organism of Christian truth". Therefore, individual arguments should not be criticized simply because they do not bear the entire burden of proof in apologetics. This insight is important to understanding why Frame deplores the party spirit among many Christian apologists. Given the complexity of a comprehensive argument for Christian theism, apologetic approaches should be assessed for their contributions to the transcendental goal of apologetics and the extent to which they avoid compromising Christian doctrines. This is why Frame's work contains far more commendation than criticism for apologists of other schools. On the basis of his system, most apologists are making useful contributions, despite occasional concessions to autonomy and neutral standards (Frame, 2000:229).

Every individual apologetic argument, therefore, fails to prove the entire Christian system for two reasons: (1) No argument has universal rational appeal; (2) No argument is beyond "additional questioning" (Frame, 1994:73). Therefore, no argument—Van Til's included—"is sufficient by itself to prove the existence of the biblical God to everyone's satisfaction". For this reason, we may speak of a "transcendental goal" for apologetics, but "not a distinctively 'transcendental argument' which rules out all other kinds of argument". The God of the Bible is the source of meaning, possibility, and predication, but there is no single argument or argument form that proves all that. Nor must the apologist explicitly state the transcendental goal of apologetics in every encounter. It is often enough simply to avoid saying anything to suggest to the inquirer that reasoning and predication are possible without God. In dealing with intellectuals who proudly advocate autonomy, neutrality, and objectivity, it will be necessary "to stress the transcendental direction" on those occasions (1994:74).

Valid Forms of Argument

Based on the conclusions of the previous section, it is clear that "positive" as well as "negative" forms of argument are valid in Frame's version of presuppositional apologetics (Frame, 1994:75). For Van Til, a transcendental argument is only a negative or "indirect" argument, "a *reductio ad absurdum*". The *reductio* assumes a proposition "for the sake of argument" and then proceeds to refute it by deducing "a logical contradiction or some proposition that is obviously false". Provided that the false proposition does not result from a fallacy or an additional premise, the opposite proposition would be established. Frame (1994:76) states Van Til's argument in this form: "God doesn't exist; therefore, causality...is meaningless." Therefore, "God does exist."

Frame (1994:76) acknowledges the "rhetorical" value of this indirect form of argument but asks what really distinguishes it from a direct or positive form of the argument. At bottom, "it doesn't make much difference whether you say 'Causality, therefore God' or 'Without God, no causality, therefore God'". Because any indirect (negative) argument can be converted into a direct (positive) argument "by some creative rephrasing", "the indirect argument becomes nothing more than a prolegomenon to the direct". For this reason, Van Til's restriction of the transcendental argument to the indirect-negative form only is not cogent: "Positive arguments can be just as transcendental in their thrust as negative ones, and negative arguments are just as likely as positive ones to express a spirit of autonomy." (1994:76-77.) While the negative form "tends to take overconfident unbelievers by surprise", no form of argument is a silver bullet against autonomy and unbelief (1994:76). Frame (2009:962-968) and Scrivener (2009:540-546) have defended this formulation against objections from both Collett (2009:470-487) and Bahnsen (1998:501-502).

Frame also calls into question Van Til's account of the Christian theistic proof as absolutely certain. Frame (1994:77) recognizes that certainty is a "problematic concept". While the Bible clearly affirms that the Christian should be certain of the gospel of Christ and salvation (LUK 1:4;

1JO 5:13), it does not affirm that such certainty is merely the function of an argument (1994:77-78). In fact, the believer presupposes God's word as certain because it is "the very criterion of certainty" (1994:78). In addition to this presupposition as "a logical fact", the believer is also assured by the Holy Spirit, who testifies to the gospel and the believer's relationship to Christ (1CO 2:4-5; 1TH 1:5; ROM 8:16). Based on these resources, the believer has "the right . . . to come to full assurance on at least the major points of the gospel message". Perspectivally speaking, the Scripture and the Spirit account for the normative and existential perspectives on certainty. Situationally speaking, it is also necessary to speak of "the certainty of the evidence", which is "evidence warranting certainty of belief". Just as the clarity of general revelation is sufficient to leave all without excuse (ROM 1:19-20), so the miracles of Jesus and his post-resurrection appearances provide "signs" and "convincing proofs" for the Christian worldview (JOH 20:31; ACT 1:3). Thus, certainty applies to both persons and evidences (cf. Frame, 2006a:141-145). But does it apply to arguments as well?

While Van Til attributed absolute certainty to the transcendental argument, Frame's position is more nuanced. For Frame (1994:79), certainty may be applied to arguments only to the extent that the apologist's arguments convey biblical content and evidence: "Insofar as his argument communicates truly the evidence that God has revealed in nature and Scripture, it may be said to convey the certainty of that evidence." The opposite, however, is also true. Insofar as an argument fails in presenting the evidence accurately, "it lacks authority and therefore may not boast absolute certainty" (1994:80). Van Til mistakenly assumed that certain evidence required an absolutely certain argument, but Frame does not. Frame's position leaves "room for error to enter in" resulting in "a possible loss of certainty" due to inadequacies in argument. This opens the door to probable arguments that fall short of absolute certainty, not due to uncertain evidence in nature and Scripture, but due to arguments that fail to convey certain evidence cogently. So while the evidence is absolutely certain, the argument "conveys the evidence more or less adequately" (1994:82). Put another way: "Insofar as the argument conveys the evidence truly, it also conveys the absolute certainty inherent in the evidence."

But how, then, does the apologist judge the adequacy of his own argument? How does he know that his argument conveys the evidence truly and therefore certainly? Frame (1994:83) answers this question in a single pregnant sentence: "And where there is suspicion of at least some legitimacy to uncertain reasoning, we may speak of some degree of probability." In short, the apologist's own level of confidence in the cogency of his argument reflects the extent to which the argument conveys the certainty of the evidence. This may be illustrated by comparing arguments for well-established Christian doctrines with more controversial doctrines. The Christian's argument for the Trinity will likely be more certain than his argument for a specific position on the second coming of Christ. In the end, the revelation of God (normative perspective) and the evidence for God (situational perspective) safeguard Christian certainty without guaranteeing the individual Christian's every argument or belief (existential perspective). This is consistent with Frame's triperspectival apologetic, since persons are subject to sin, ignorance, and error, whereas the revelation of God is not. In effect, the revelation of God becomes the mast to which the believer is tied with the cords of certain faith rooted in the gospel and salvation.

This allows the Christian to have certainty with respect to the Christian faith itself, even though some Christian beliefs may be less certain or doubtful. In the end, a lack of certainty is not attributed to inadequacies in divine revelation but to defects in the created decoder of that revelation. Thus, Frame's presuppositionalism allows for both absolute certainty and probability, neither contradicting nor infecting the other in the believer's experience. On the contrary, the believer's normative and situational certainty supports and stabilizes faith in the face of those beliefs held as less certain. I know of no other apologetic position that makes this psychological dynamic possible. In other apologetic systems, a subjective certainty usually exists in tension with an objective probability with respect to both evidence and argument, thus infecting subjective certainty with objective uncertainty (cf. Ramm, 1972:73). Frame's (1994:86) position provides a way to "rehabilitate" probability in Reformed apologetics without threatening the certainty of faith.

Bahnsen's (1998:81-82) criticism of Frame on this point overlooks—in my view—the perspectival distinctions that explain Frame's position. Bahnsen argues that distinguishing between certain evidence and probable argument vitiates the certainty of the evidence, since it cannot receive more than a probable embodiment in an argument. Frame does not argue, however, that all arguments are probable embodiments of certain evidence. Only some arguments fit that description. Frame's position captures the existential reality of Christian faith as comprising both certain beliefs and probable beliefs striving toward complete certainty through better arguments. Bahnsen's alternative would seem to require that all Christian beliefs on all points of doctrine should be held with absolute certainty lest all become infected with uncertainty. The progress of dogma in history, however, reflects the Church's goal to improve its understanding of scriptural evidence and argument in order to certify more Christian doctrines (Orr, 2000:3-32). The alternative would be a dogmatic view in which all Christian doctrines are held with equal certainty on the basis of certain evidence that acknowledges no deficiencies or errors in argument.

A Presuppositionalism of the Heart

The practical import of Frame's (1994:85) presuppositional approach is to show that "there is less distance between Van Til's apologetics and the traditional apologetics than most partisans on either side (including Van Til) have been willing to grant". In fact, Frame thinks that possibly all traditional arguments may be useful in a complex argument with "a transcendental purpose" (1994:86). While the central arguments for the Christian faith are not probable, some are because they leave "room for error in their formulation". But no argument—direct or indirect—necessarily presupposes autonomy purely by virtue of its form. As long as an argument proceeds from the belief that nothing is intelligible apart from God, it may be transcendentally valid, even though it does not represent a complete argument for the Christian faith. One problem evident among academic apologists is the tendency to criticize other apologists for not representing a complete or adequate argument for the Christian faith. Frame recognizes the difficulty of requiring any one apologist to offer a complete argument for the faith that is both sufficiently comprehensive and fully cogent. Perhaps a better approach would be to assess individual apologetic contributions in terms of a transcendental attitude: Does the apologist argue with a transcendental purpose, avoid communicating or reinforcing autonomy, and display the Christian piety appropriate to commending the gospel of Christ? If so, the apologist and apologetic are approved by God (cf. Davis, 2009:508-509).

This is in line with Frame's (1994:87) conviction that presuppositionalism may be more "an attitude of the heart, a spiritual condition, than an easily describable, empirical phenomenon". He recognizes and rejects the tendency in Van Til to confuse issues of piety and method. Is the apologist's presuppositional loyalty really compromised by proving a conclusion directly rather than by disproving its opposite? While this might be the case, "we must be careful before we, in effect, impute evil motives to apologists who simply prefer to do things in a different order". In the final analysis, presuppositionalism is not distinguished by a mere form of argument or a specific view of certainty and probability. It might be better distinguished by four spiritual commitments in apologetics: (1) A commitment to a Christian-theistic epistemology; (2) A commitment to presenting "the full teaching of Scripture" wisely and without compromise; (3) A commitment to presenting "God as fully sovereign" and the authoritative source of all meaning and intelligibility; (4) A commitment to understanding the unbeliever's knowledge of God and rebellion against that knowledge (1994:88).

Self-Attesting Evidence

This study contends that only Frame's version of presuppositionalism makes sense of the apologetic task and the biblical witness. The classic version of presuppositionalism represented by Van Til is counter-intuitive, and Frame (1994:87) explains why in a brief but important footnote: "The words 'nature itself reveals God' suggest a direct argument more naturally than they suggest an indirect one." This single observation summarizes the apologetic import of Psalm 19:1 and Romans 1:20, perhaps the most important verses in the Bible related to apologetics. Christian apologists studying the Bible simply do not see the *reductio* argument as the central component of a biblical apologetic. Certainly it is used in apologetic contexts (e.g. ACT 17:24-29; 1CO 15:12-19, 29-32). But other passages appeal directly to the revelation of God as fully evident to unbelievers such that they are atheistic "fools" and "without excuse" (PSA 14:1, 19:1-6; ROM 1:18-20). Scripturally speaking, "what may be known about God is plain" to unbelievers from nature and the self alone.

The revelation of God within and without the unbeliever testifies to God without a *reductio* argument—indeed without any argument at all! "To my knowledge, Scripture does not trace the mechanism by which this knowledge from nature and the human self reaches us." (Frame, 1982:6; cf. 2000:215-216.) Frame's point here is one few apologists recognize, and it cannot be overemphasized: The evidence of God's revelation that holds all "without excuse" may be embodied in an argument but does not require one—biblically it is self-attesting! The heavens themselves "declare the glory of God", showing that the evidence itself is both certain and sufficient to leave unbelievers "without excuse" before God (PSA 19:1; ROM 1:20). Frame (2011a) refers to this knowledge as intuition, which "is primary, though of course argument is usually a way to put intuitive insights into language". It is clear, then, that the Bible warrants a variety of argument forms for apologetic engagement, but no one form takes priority and no argument is required to prove God's existence or moral accountability to him. On this point, Frame agrees with Reformed epistemologists (Frame, 2000:307; 1987:382-400; Anderson, 2009:443-446; Plantinga, 1979; Hoitenga, 1991). An overemphasis on argumentative form may even detract from the apologetic task, since the negative form of the transcendental argument is understandable only to those with the intellectual sophistication to fully grasp the argument. Furthermore, assuming that an absolutely certain argument or proof is required to convey certain evidence may actually justify the unbeliever's rejection of the Christian system. In rejecting an incomplete or inadequate Christian proof, the unbeliever may be left to assume that there is no other compelling evidence behind or in addition to the proof that remains to be considered. According to Scripture, however, the evidence without the argument remains absolutely certain because God's world constitutes a fully revelational environment. Thus, Frame's distinction between evidence and argument explains why a presuppositionalism of the heart best explains a highly personalized approach to apologetic evangelism.

4 TRIPERSPECTIVALISM AS A META-APOLOGETIC

O n the basis of the foregoing discussion, it is now possible to fully grasp Frame's triperspectivalism as a meta-apologetic. In fact, Frame (1982:1) stated his apologetic approach in the form of a "meta-apologetic discussion" even before publishing his foundational work on Christian epistemology in the Lordship Series. Frame read his paper, "Epistemological Perspectives and Evangelical Apologetics", as an address to the Evangelical Theological Society, but the paper was not fully appreciated at the time and brought no significant response, even though it represents a "prequel" to *The Doctrine of the Knowledge of God* (Frame, 2011b:1). Frame expressed his agreement with me that this piece in particular is critically important among his writings as a meta-apologetic statement of triperspectivalism. As a basis to understand not only his apologetic system as a whole but also his approach to evidences and verificational tests, this essay is—in my judgment—Frame's single most important offering. It may be viewed as either the cornerstone (prequel) of Frame's work on apologetics or the capstone. For purposes of this study, it serves as the capstone, demonstrating the profound scope and explanatory power of this apologetic system.

Epistemological Perspectives and Apologetics

Like the great meta-philosophical essay by W.T. Jones (1986:24), Frame (1982:1) rises above the "different parties" and "partisan commitments" of apologetics to look at what Jones calls the "cognitive and evaluative sets" (worldviews) by which apologetic disagreements may be understood and possibly resolved. While Jones (1986:29) analyzes philosophical disagreements in terms of three "dimensions", Frame, of course, employs three perspectives that actually align "roughly" with Jones's dimensions (Frame, 2011b). The point here is not to explain Frame in terms of Jones's analysis, since Frame's analysis was published first, but rather to indicate that a quite similar and compelling meta-analysis has also been done by a leading philosophical historian. This suggests that Frame's belief in a triperspectival meta-apologetic puts him on the cutting edge of apologetics in much the same way that Jones reflects the cutting edge of philosophical analysis.

Frame's (1982:1) analysis begins by distinguishing "three general types of epistemology", three "tendencies". Frame enumerates these tendencies as rationalism, empiricism, and subjectivism. Rationalism (*a priorism*) represents the tendency to presuppose principles that govern the interpretation of sense experience, empiricism the tendency to base knowledge on "the data of sense experience", and subjectivism the tendency to verify personal knowledge "by criteria internal to the subject" (1982:2). Unlike the other two tendencies, subjectivism does not affirm objective truth. These perspectives are referred to as "tendencies" because "no philosopher has succeeded in being a consistent rationalist, empiricist or subjectivist", despite a few notable attempts by Parmenides (rationalism), John Stuart Mill (empiricism), and Protagoras and the sophists (subjectivism). Frame notes that the great philosophers (Plato, Aristotle, Aquinas, Kant) tend to address these tendencies in some combination but at the expense of consistency. The traditional tendencies simply cannot be harmonized without significant problems arising from the basic principles of each tendency.

For example, sense experience and subjectivism are "always problematic" because they are subject to various interpretations, and the principles by which their respective data is interpreted are questionable (Frame, 1982:2). How can principles for interpreting sense experience or subjective experience be derived from those experiences? Both call for interpretive principles from some other source to address this "problematic data". The rationalist claims to supply these prior principles to illuminate experience, arguing that to deny such principles in denying objective truth is self-defeating. Without objective truth, both sense and subjective experience forfeit any claim to objective truth. While the subjectivist may happily forfeit such a claim, he cannot do so without contradiction, since truth—even for the knowing subject alone—is either a claim of personal objectivity or no truth at all. At bottom, the rationalist argues that no claim to experiential truth—sense or subjective—can avoid a rational judgment that goes beyond such experience, since "feelings often mislead" and the future may not resemble the past, rendering judgments based on past experience as problematic as feelings are (1982:3).

Does the rationalist, then, win by default? In fact, "claims to a priori truth are also problematic" (Frame, 1982:3). What can be known *a priori* is as arguable as what is known on the basis of experience (*a posteriori*). If philosophers contradict one another on what they claim to know prior to experience, then why should the empiricist and subjectivist take their word for it? "There must be checking procedures available to all, not just to the individual making the claim." However, no such "public" checking procedures are available. Claims to truth on the basis of reason, sense, or the self are clearly personal, not public. The empiricist will argue that sense experience alone is common and therefore public, and the subjectivist will argue that both sense experience and the claim to *a priori* principles are subjective (1982:4). The empiricist asks what good are the laws of logic without sense experiences to which they may be applied and on which they depend. The subjectivist asks what makes rational principles more than subjective judgments, since the knower must adopt them by a subjective act—a decision based on persuasion.

As it turns out, Christian apologetics reflects the very same epistemological tendencies (Frame, 1982:5). There are rationalists (Clark), empiricists (Montgomery), and combinationalists (Geisler, Carnell, Van Til). Geisler represents a combination of rationalism and empiricism along Thomistic lines, and Van Til and Carnell represent a combination of all three tendencies, Carnell also developing a Christian subjectivism. Frame notes that Carnell's (2007c) book, *The Kingdom of Love and the Pride of Life*, suggests that "there may be a kind of subjectivism [existentialism] which is compatible with other epistemological principles"—a suggestion taken very seriously in this study.

The three epistemological tendencies "correlate roughly" with Scripture, nature, and the self, requiring some biblical adjustments (Frame, 1982:5). The *a priori* principle is correlated with God's word (law), which provides the "criterion" of truth and error with respect to "the interpretation of sense experience and subjective states" (1982:6). Since God's word is also available within nature and the human self (possibly conscience), both are inseparable from the law: "The logical distinction between them is that nature is the environment in which we are called to live obediently to the law." This also implies that "nature could yield moral knowledge", thus relieving Hume's problem of deriving *ought* from *is* (cf. ROM 1:18-20; 2:15). Human conscience may be the "mechanism" of such natural knowledge, but whatever the means, Scripture affirms that "God gets his message through."

Given that "the word of God governs all our activity in the world" and that the entire world reveals God, we must study both God's law-word and the world to arrive at the "concrete meaning" of the word of God: "we must study the world in order to properly exegete God's word" (Frame, 1982:6, 7). As Frame puts it, "The word directs us to the world; and in the world we find more of the meaning of the word." (1982:7.) Human nature is the most "philosophically difficult" member of the triad, and yet, everything else is known through the human self. Frame notes the paradox of the self: "The self seems to be everywhere and nowhere. We know it, but only as we know other things." This is, of course, Calvin's point at the beginning of the *Institutes*. The self reflects its "ultimate environment" in God, in his revelation, and in its own ethical response to God (ROM 12:1ff., EPH 5:8-10; PHP 1:10; HEB 5:11-14). Thus, "knowing God always involves attention to ourselves".

The point here is that "law, object and subject are distinguishable, but not discovered separately" (Frame, 1982:7). These three "aspects" or "perspectives" are inseparable in every act of knowing, each perspective being reflected in the others. This is why the traditional epistemologies inevitably fail to do justice to knowledge: They either separate the perspectives, forcing a choice between rationalism, empiricism, and subjectivism, or they give one priority over the others thereby reducing the act of knowing to one type of mental process (1982:8). A perspectival epistemology recognizes that the senses and the self are fallible and require an infallible ground, thus validating the rationalist's concern. But human reason alone is also fallible and merely formal, thus validating the empiricist's and subjectivist's concern. The answer to human fallibility is God's infallible word: "Only God's word furnishes an ultimate ground, and God's word is available to us in all three perspectives." Only the Christian system provides an epistemology of "checks and balances" in which God coordinates "the law, the world and the self". Without infallible revelation to ground knowledge, the three perspectives will not cohere, thus forcing a choice between them on the basis of which one is believed to be most reliable (1982:9). With God's revelation, rational, empirical, and subjective tests may all be applied to knowledge claims—literally a Christian method of "triangulation" (Edgar, 2009:404).

For Frame, while God's law-word provides an infallible ground for knowledge, it does not thereby guarantee infallible knowledge. Each perspective is fallible, reflecting as it does human thinking. But each perspective also "brings us into contact with God's [infallible] truth" (Frame, 1982:9). So while human thought "is fallible at every point, it is not *so* fallible that any of us has an excuse for failing to know God (Romans 1:20) or for failing to live obediently before him". This might be viewed as a difficulty in Frame's thinking, but he is simply affirming a Christian epistemological dualism. For Frame, the knowing mind is not identified with the object of knowledge (Young, 1954:67). The problem, of course, is that epistemological dualism may be argued to agnosticism, since "getting the idea and the object together" is problematic (1954:68). So how does one know that an idea truly represents its object? The Christian answers this question by affirming that the idea and the object correspond, even if the knower cannot explain precisely how this works. Young (1954:71) is in line with Frame in saying that "the exact manner in which the mind is able to grasp the object 'out there' will probably always remain beyond the realm of human understanding". Nevertheless, the normative perspective resolves this problem by the scriptural affirmation that God is truly known, even if he is not known completely or infallibly. Thus, the problem of epistemological dualism in Frame illustrates why a triperspectival epistemology is necessary to guarantee human knowledge.

Poythress (2001:45) further illuminates this issue by distinguishing between "absolute truth" and "relative knowledge". While any propositional truth may be absolute, "human beings are limited. Our knowledge of the truth is partial". In other words, "We know truth, but not all of the truth." (cf. 1Co 13:9-12.) Human knowledge also reflects limitation in its perspectival focus—a limitation God does not have. Therefore, human knowledge is relative with respect to its *content*, since we know only in part what God knows exhaustively (2001:46). Furthermore, individual situations, proclivities, and presuppositions also "influence which particular truths we come to know". As Poythress puts it, "Any particular bit of truth is always related to other bits. The exact relations we see and use depends on us." Human knowledge is also relative with respect to *use*. Like Frame, Poythress recognizes that "meaning is use", so knowing how to apply truth correctly is a measure of true understanding: "Knowledge is thus always knowledge *in relation to* other truths and situations of possible use." Human knowledge is also relative to *time*, being subject to growth, limitations of memory, and changes in belief. The relativity of human knowledge is important to a meta-apologetic, since the Christian apologist defends God's absolute truth acknowledging the relativity of that truth for finite knowers. This is not relativism but a Christian doctrine of epistemological relativity (cf. Ladd, 1959:73-74; Niebuhr, 2001:235ff.). Apologetics requires an absolute standard of truth as a ground for human knowledge, as an ultimate reference point, but it does not require the epistemological monism of Aristotle, Berkeley, and naive realists (Young, 1954:65-67). Human knowers relate to absolute truth; they do not possess it. In other words, "we advance toward it step by step" (Frame, 2008a:3).

Christian Evidences and Verificational Tests

At this point, it is relatively easy to draw out the apologetic implications of Frame's meta-analysis. Evangelicals have developed three types of apologetic systems corresponding to each of the epistemological tendencies. The rationalist, empiricist, and subjectivist tendencies result in normative, situational, and existential apologetic types. Not only are all three types warranted on the basis of a biblical epistemology, but each is "found in Scripture explicitly" (Frame, 1982:9). A normative apologetic is reflected "in the explicit appeals by prophets, Jesus and the apostles to the law of God in Scripture" and implicitly in scriptural responses to "doubting questions" (1982:9, 10; JOB 38-42; EZE 18:25; MAT 20:1-15; ROM 3:3ff., 6:1ff., 7:7). Because no one may claim ignorance of God's law, "we *have no right* to doubt God's truth". This normative apologetic perspective is also present when interpreting sense and subjective experience, since these are also to be interpreted by Scripture: "Such data do not lead merely to probable or optional conclusions; they lead to certainty, because indeed they are law-laden." (cf. ACT 17:30.)

A situational apologetic is "the most obvious of the three" in the Bible, reflected in the "mighty acts of God in nature and redemptive history, pre-eminently the resurrection of Christ" (Frame, 1982:10). Like the normative apologetic, the situational is a perspective on the other two, since biblical proclamation—the gospel especially—appeals to historical facts. An existential apologetic is also evident in biblical instances of belief in response to proclamations of truth. Frame specifically mentions the disciples on the road to Emmaus: "when Jesus taught, their hearts burned within them" (LUK 24:32). Biblical psalms, sermons, and letters appeal to "the whole range of human subjectivity" (1982:11). It is also possible to say—as with the other two types—that all biblical apologetics is existential: "For Scripture *always* addresses the full range of human subjectivity; it always seeks comprehensive inner change, 'heart change'."

What is fascinating about Frame's (1982:11) analysis is that he locates the mistake of traditional methods, not in the methods themselves as somehow unbiblical, but in their lack of perspectival integration: "Thus, all three methods are biblically legitimate, as long as neither seeks to claim ultimate priority or to exclude another as a complementary perspective." The major contribution of presuppositionalism, then, is not in offering a new system of apologetics, but in its contention that "knowledge is impossible without law and that the ultimate law is Scripture". Frame has no argument against the evidentialist's concern for "publically observable events of nature and history" or the Reformed epistemologist's concern for properly functioning knowing faculties. In fact, all approaches must be "present implicitly" regardless of the specific approach used in an apologetic encounter. Thus, Frame's notion of the identity of perspectives is the key to apologetic eclecticism and creativity. The Bible's own "wonderfully rich" use of methods should have led apologists away from "stereotyped patterns" in apologetics to a multi-perspectival approach that is truly "integrationist" at its core (1982:11, 12; Boa & Bowman, 2001:462). In my view, Frame's (1982:12) approach to apologetics has the creative potential "to show the world that indeed every fact of experience, every principle of reason, every burden of the human heart, has God's name upon it".

This meta-analysis of apologetics illuminates Frame's dialogue with other Christian apologists with respect to the use of evidences and verificational tests. In responding to classical apologist, William Craig (2000:26-55), Frame (2000:74) points out that "the role of the Word of God" is "entirely missing" from Craig's approach. While the attempt to balance the testimony of the Holy Spirit, reason and evidences is evident, an important apologetic question must be answered: "What is it, after all, that the Spirit testifies to? In the Scripture, the Spirit testifies to the truth of the Word." Based on Frame's meta-analysis, Craig has not recognized that the normative perspective is also a perspective on the situational evidences and the existential witness of the Holy Spirit. By separating reason from the principles of the word of God, reason becomes neutral, and the witness of the Holy Spirit becomes "an ineffable mystical experience" (2000:75-76). While Craig's apologetic is focused on establishing biblical truth and assessing biblical evidences, "he assigns no distinct role to Scripture in his epistemology" (2000:76). Thus Craig's apologetic is situational (objective) and existential (subjective) but not properly normative—a two-legged stool. Notwithstanding, Frame (2000:81) says that Craig's books on the evidences for Christ's resurrection "are among the best accounts of these evidences".

In responding to evidential apologist, Gary Habermas (2000:92-121), Frame (2000:132) sees the same problem in Habermas concerning the witness of the Holy Spirit that was noted in Craig. At bottom, Frame sees no great difference between the methods of Craig and Habermas. Whether the apologist begins with theistic proofs or evidences, "without the biblical God there is no reason to suppose that there is a rational, causal order leading to a first cause" or to meaningful evidences—both presuppose God's existence (2000:133). With the Christian presupposition, either a theistic or evidential argument may be transcendental in form or direction, starting "from any fact in the universe". Habermas also fails to do justice to the role of the word of God in the interpretation of historical evidences. While neither Habermas nor Frame believe in brute factuality, Habermas (2000:95) attempts to illuminate evidences on the basis of "the canons of historical research" understood in terms of a general ethic of historical research. Frame (2000:134) argues, however, that the canons of historical research also must be informed by Scripture and what it tells us about good and bad biases, miracles, divine providence, and its own uniqueness as an inspired document. Because the Bible is inspired, it is "not subject to the types of criticism appropriate to other historical witnesses". Faith, then, is not grounded "in scholarly consensus" but in an argument that includes the normative perspective of God's word (2000:135). Frame also commends Habermas for having "done a masterful job of summarizing our Lord's claims and the evidences of his death and resurrection". But apart from the presupposition of Christian theism—"without which no other reasoning (either about miracles or non-miracles) makes sense"—a traditional evidentialism is inadequate to deal with the skepticism of Hume, postmodernism, the Jesus Seminar, or many skeptical people today (2000:137).

The Reformed epistemology apologetics of Kelly Clark (2000:266-284) would seem to be in closer alignment with Frame's own Reformed epistemology because of their common thesis "that it can be rational to believe in God (and in other things) without argument" (Frame, 2000:307). This is a point on which Frame agrees "entirely" with just one qualification: "Warranted belief does not need to be based on argument, but it does need to be based on fact, on reality." (This qualification will be important in establishing Schaeffer's congruence with Frame.) The problem with Clark's (Plantinga's) position is not the claim to an "unargued theism" but to the fact that it is a reduced theism—reduced in terms of certainty. Clark defines the epistemic status of Christian belief in terms of "rational believability", a claim Frame (2000:308) thinks is "about the weakest claim that could be made for Christian theism". Equally problematic is Clark's view that Christian belief is defeasible given sufficient evidence to the contrary. Frame (2000:308-309) rejects this view due to the lack of a properly normative perspective: "We are not merely *permitted* to believe in God until we are persuaded otherwise; rather, we are *obligated* to believe in him." Since Scripture is the Christian's "ultimate criterion of truth and falsity", it cannot be held with a tentative or defeasible faith. The Christian is not merely rational in holding Christian faith—rationality itself depends upon Christian faith. Perspectively speaking, the lack of a properly normative perspective in Clark's view is reflected also in a reduced faith (existential perspective) and a commitment to neutral evidences (situational perspective) that may ultimately speak against faith and potentially defeat it. The classical apologist and evidentialist reflect these perspectival dynamics as well, since arguing for "demonstration" (Craig) and "best explanation" (Habermas) also falls short of the biblical standard of Christian certainty (2000:307, 308). Nevertheless, Frame praises Clark for "accepting God as an epistemic starting point" and for defending faith as an essential component of knowledge and rejecting faithless epistemic foundations (2000:310, 311).

The cumulative case apologetic of Paul Feinberg (2000:148-172) addresses the issue of verificational tests in relation to a presuppositional approach. Frame (2000:194) commends Feinberg's definition of a "demonstrably sound argument" as one that is valid, sound, and coercive for "anyone who wants to retain rationality". This definition reflects both a transcendental goal and an epistemic obligation to believe a demonstrably sound argument. The problem, however, is that Feinberg fails to press this obligation in his apologetic approach, since this particular epistemic norm is derived from Scripture, and Feinberg wants to escape the supposed circularity of such an appeal. Instead, he proposes a series of verificational tests for use in apologetics, but scripture is not one of them. Frame's point is that, without the epistemic normativity of the scriptural test, the sound arguments of the cumulative case cannot be pressed as epistemic obligations. What good are arguments that reinforce each other if key scriptural premises among these arguments may be rejected off hand by the nontheist? For example, Feinberg (2000:148) rejects the ontological argument as unsound because the premise of God's necessary existence is unacceptable to the nontheist, but Frame (2000:194) recognizes this as a scriptural premise that vindicates the argument as sound. Therefore, the lack of a normative scriptural test compromises the persuasive force of the other tests: consistency, correspondence, comprehensiveness, simplicity, livability, fruitfulness, and conservation (Feinberg, 2000:153-156).

Frame (2000:196) even goes so far as to identify presuppositionalism with the cumulative case approach: "Presuppositionalism may be understood as a cumulative case approach that recognizes the problem of epistemic normativity." Unfortunately, Feinberg and the other apologists ignore this problem because of its connection to circularity. But "scripturality is the major test", without which the other tests become neutral and problematic (2000:197). As Frame (2000:198) says, "Christian theism and nontheism are *systems*; and, contra Feinberg, these systems include their own distinctive tests for truth." Thus, the Christian system supplies the "rationale" for verificational tests, conveying the obligation to believe and the corresponding certainty of a normative epistemology (1987:131).

In summarizing Frame's response to apologists of other schools, the goal is not to provide a comprehensive analysis but an illustration of how a triperspectival apologetic integrates the contributions of other approaches, enabling a presuppositional use of evidences and verificational tests. The four approaches engaged above all reflect a significant problem in their failure to "honor the Word of God as the ultimate authority" (Davis, 2009:511). As Davis points out, "The issue here is the normative perspective." Most apologists opt for neutrality at this point in an attempt to avoid circularity, but in so doing, they overlook the inevitable circularity of all theoretical thought. All belief systems are justifiably circular only with respect to their ultimate criterion. Frame (1987:130-131) addresses this issue by broadening the circle with more biblical, extrabiblical, and experiential data, thus overcoming vicious or narrow circularity. The result is that the meaning and rationale of the Christian conclusion is set forth more persuasively, which is "all that an argument can do" (1987:131). Without a properly normative approach, the whole apologetic argument becomes reduced and compromised. The interpretation of evidences reduces to a mere probable case, thus reducing the certainty of the conclusion, and the interpreter becomes the *de facto* arbiter of truth, thus compromising God's lordship attributes.

A Christian Existentialism in Apologetics

Giving special attention to the existential perspective in this study requires the clarification of Frame's meta-apologetic in existential terms. The value of an existential apologetic has been affirmed in a recent offering on the subject by Williams (2011). And certainly Schaeffer was ahead of his time in developing his own existential perspective in apologetics. For Frame (2010c:11), the existential perspective focuses "on our own inwardness, our personal experience, in which God has chosen to be near us". In the preceding discussion, this perspective has been developed according to several issues that are expected to resurface in Schaeffer: The certainty of faith as "cognitive rest" or confidence, the antithesis of belief and unbelief in terms of personal choice, faith as an expression of personal rectitude or integrity, and the interdependence of perspectives.

These issues may be captured in an existential (and homiletical) triad that reflects the interdependence of the three perspectives: presupposition, proof, persuasion. Clearly, each perspective in this triad is relative to the others, and all are person-variable. The self chooses presuppositions and acknowledges proof as persuasive. Furthermore, the Holy Spirit's (existential) presence is required to change a person's heart, which leads—in turn—to a change of presuppositions and a believing response to persuasive proof. Thus, the existential goal of apologetic evangelism is "nothing less than conversion, a fundamental change of heart, in those to whom we witness" (Frame, 1987:355). In relation to the normative perspective, the existential perspective is concerned with what *should* convince an individual inquirer. But in relation to the situational perspective, the existential perspective must also be concerned with the kind of proof that *will* convince a specific unbeliever, assuming—of course—the regenerating presence of the Holy Spirit. Practically, this means that apologetic evangelism requires arguments and reasons that embody the evidence of God's revelation—what should convince—but it also wisely selects from among these arguments what might appeal to the individual inquirer.

In addition to the personal presence of the Holy Spirit, the personal presence of the apologist is also important to the existential perspective. The apologist is part of the inquirer's situation in addition to being a personal embodiment of the evidence for the Christian faith (cf. 1PE 3:16; Davis, 2009:500-505). Therefore, the person to person encounter of apologetic evangelism is crucial to the existential perspective in apologetics, not only in presenting gospel information (normative perspective) and relevant proofs (situational perspective), but also in urging a decision to believe out of a sincere love for the inquirer and a godly example (existential perspective).

The issue of personal integrity is also deeply existential, since individuals inevitably seek some degree of consistency between their basic presuppositions—believing or unbelieving—and their thought processes (epistemology) and moral choices (ethics). Because the perspectives are interdependent, this issue also influences the kind of proof an individual finds challenging or persuasive. To the extent that an individual suppresses God's revelation on some point, proofs related to that point will represent an immediate challenge to unbelief and a call for decision. So, for example, a Humean skeptic will not find a teleological argument immediately persuasive, having repressed God's revelation of purposeful design in the world and himself. He may, however, affirm the principle of this argument in the ethical realm by treating individuals as valuable and worthy of respect and by viewing his own life as meaningful. The apologist, therefore, will use the appeal of personal rectitude to attempt to draw the skeptic into greater personal consistency and integrity. While non-Christians are both rational and irrational, they tend to think of their personal belief systems as consistent on some level, their rational principles somehow justifying the irrationalities and mysteries they embrace.

Any apologetic method, therefore, that is strategically focused on this rationalist-irrationalist dialectic and its corollary, personal integrity, is an existential apologetic at the core. Calling individuals to greater intellectual and moral consistency reflects a direct challenge to personal unbelief. Placing before individuals a choice between two alternatives—only one of which is certain—is obviously existential, since the antithesis in Frame's epistemology is a doctrine concerning the human heart in relation to God. Regardless of how complex the arguments become, if the goal is to put the Christian antithesis before the unbeliever for a decision between only two basic choices, that apologetic method is rightly characterized as existential. That such an approach may also be transcendental, evidential, and verificational goes without saying within Frame's perspectival system. But an apologetic that calls for greater personal integrity before the triune God of the Bible represents a truly Christian existentialism. It remains, then, to discover these elements in the trilogy of Francis Schaeffer.

A Tool for Apologetic Analysis

By arriving at a summary of Frame's perspectival system as a meta-apologetic, it was intended that the reader would gain a comprehensive and integrated understanding of the details of this many-faceted system. On one level, the system is quite simple: The three lordship attributes correlate with three epistemological perspectives that explain the historic discussions of the theory of knowledge and apologetics. The result is an epistemology that triangulates human knowledge and an apologetic that is biblically normative, situational, and existential in orientation. The goal of Christian defense, then, is the conversion of inquirers through a multiplicity of arguments with a transcendental direction reflecting biblical norms—an application of theology best termed apologetic evangelism. The only alternative to the Christian faith is conventional wisdom, which proves its futility despite many permutations and combinations in the realm of ideas. Lacking the ability to triangulate knowledge, conventional wisdom falls prey to the weakness of all mono-perspectival or di-perspectival systems:

The lack of a sufficient norm to ground the sources of knowledge within the philosophic system. Unfortunately, Christian apologists also fall prey to the same weakness, assuming an allegedly neutral method for fear that circularity with respect to their ultimate criterion poisons the apologetic well with fallacious reasoning.

In hindsight, it is clear that the issue of circularity represents the offense of presuppositionalism. Concerning this issue, there is one crucial question: Is Frame (1987:130) correct that all theoretical systems are circular with respect to their ultimate criterion? Given the nature of theoretical thought as he understands it, I see no reason to disagree with Frame (cf. Sotak, 2017:448-449). One or more criteria must be assumed as authoritative in order to predicate anything at all. If Frame is correct, it would seem that his meta-apologetic is essentially sound and useful as a tool for the analysis of apologetic systems.

An additional benefit of Frame's system is that it is presented in a manner that makes it easy to apply to other apologetic systems. The clarity of Frame's writing has been noted by Edgar (2009:430): "His style is lucid, personal, and almost conversational." Edgar also notes Frame's ability "to translate large, complex issues into everyday theology". These qualities have also been attributed to Schaeffer, but Frame brings a higher level of scholarship to these qualities. Also, like Schaeffer, Frame applies his approach to almost every issue he engages, so there is sufficient repetition throughout his work to insure an accurate understanding by comparing his applications. All that remains, then, is to show that Frame's triperspectival Christian epistemology provides the best tool for understanding Schaeffer's apologetic in general and his existential perspective in particular.

SCHAEFFER'S APOLOGETIC TRILOGY

5 THE GOD WHO IS THERE

Analyzing Schaeffer's apologetic in light of Frame's triperspectivalism requires a detailed and accurate understanding of Schaeffer's method. Given his popular style, this would seem to be relatively easy, but a popular style is also less precise and therefore requires more careful interpretation. The creativity of Schaeffer's system, his desire to avoid overly technical discussions, and his very personal definitions of some key terms challenge his readers. While I have observed a remarkable consistency at the heart of Schaeffer's thinking, seeing it requires a careful reading of the trilogy and close attention to the controlling ideas embedded in his popular language. If the ways in which triperspectivalism is reflected in Schaeffer's trilogy are to be discovered—especially the existential perspective—one must read the three books in light of each other. The goal of this section, then, is not to criticize or evaluate his method. Rather, the goal is to explain and analyze Schaeffer's views in light of Frame's model. This goal will be achieved in two steps: (1) by explaining Schaeffer's apologetic within the trilogy, considering each book individually; (2) by analyzing his method using Frame's meta-theory to reveal an underlying perspectival consistency.

At the beginning of *He is There and He is Not Silent*, Schaeffer (1982a:275) explains the relationship between the three books of the trilogy. *The God Who is There* was "written first" and provides the foundational issues and terminology for the other two books. *Escape from Reason* presents Christianity as a balanced biblical system touching all of life with truth—a system worked out philosophically in terms of nature and grace. In more detail than the first book, the second traces the "polluted roots" of modern culture to the late Middle Ages. *He is There and He is Not Silent* deals with the "fundamental" question of epistemology, arguing for "God's being there and not being silent" as a philosophical necessity. The "link" with *The God Who is There* is evident in the title of this third book (1982a:276). The three books together form "a unified base" and "a conscious unity" reflecting the unity of biblical teaching. In fact, each book covers the same themes from a different point of view, namely, the logical, historical, and philosophical respectively. In Frame's terms, the books are perspectivally related.

The Concept of Truth

Schaeffer (1982a:5) begins *The God Who is There* with a discussion of the nature of truth. The present generation gap is the result of "a change in the concept of truth". There is a new method that is "almost monolithic" and challenges the previous approach to truth. This method is characterized by "the lack of absolutes and antithesis, leading to pragmatic relativism" (1982a:11). Schaeffer begins with epistemology because he sees the concept of truth as the most pressing problem Christians face in our time. This change in the concept of truth took place by about 1890 in Europe and 1935 in America (1982a:6). These dates mark the points at which pragmatic relativism filtered down into the popular culture. Prior to these dates, both Christians and non-Christians shared essentially the same "presuppositions" with respect to "epistemology and methodology". Both presupposed the possibility of absolutes in truth and morals, which made it possible to "reason together on the classical basis of antithesis". This meant that if anything was true or right, then the opposite was false. A basic axiom of Schaeffer is that "absolutes imply antithesis" (1982a:10). Whether or not anyone has a sufficient basis for absolutes, a common commitment to them makes it possible to communicate Christian content and to be understood.

Schaeffer (1982a:7) says that a presuppositional apologetic would have "stopped the decay" in epistemology, enabling Christian thinkers to help upcoming generations avoid the shift. Even today, many Christians are still behind the times because they are not taught to think in presuppositional terms about truth, thereby failing to lead in "defense and communication". This failure allows secular philosophy and modern theology to flood the Church. For Schaeffer, "defense and communication" really capture his entire approach to apologetics as pre-evangelism, and the concept of truth is the epistemological center. Prior to the shift, classical apologetics could take advantage of a common presuppositional context; after the shift, however, it could not bear the load of the modern view of truth since classical apologetics does not take presuppositions into account at the outset.

The concept of truth as antithesis is not grounded in Aristotle's logic but in the truth of Christianity. Specifically, "it is rooted in reality" (Schaeffer, 1982a:184). The human mind was created for antithetical thought and "fits" the reality of God's existence and created order. In what may be the central passage of the trilogy, Schaeffer (1982a:8), grounds this concept in God's existence: "We must not forget that historic Christianity stands on a basis of antithesis. Without it, historic Christianity is meaningless. The basic antithesis is that God objectively exists in contrast (in antithesis) to his not existing. Which of these two are the reality, changes everything in the area of knowledge and morals and in the whole of life."

The shift away from antithesis to pragmatic relativism was progressive, filtering down through the disciplines from philosophy to art, music, and general culture, and finally to theology (Schaeffer, 1982a:27-41). This relativistic mindset also filters through society beginning with the intellectuals and progressing to workers and the middle class last of all. Once modern people crossed "the line of despair", moving away from antithesis to relativism, it was no longer possible to take for granted that Christian concepts would be understood within the culture as they had before (1982a:8). So spirituality, for example, becomes distorted into its opposite (1982a:9). Non-Christian thought has thus become humanistic and rationalistic (cf. Knudsen, 1971:289-290).

For Schaeffer (1982a:9), the definitions of humanism and rationalism are critical to his entire system of thought and apologetics. Employing a "wider" definition than that often employed by secular humanists themselves, Schaeffer defines these terms as perspectival synonyms. Humanism is the attempt to build a system of thought from the individual as "the integration point" for all knowledge, meaning, and value. Rationalism is synonymous with the definition of humanism but must be distinguished from the word *rational*, which refers to what is "not contrary to reason". So the Christian position is rational while being the opposite of rationalism. In fact, non-Christian thought has always been based on the principle of autonomy. But the line of despair represents a "titanic" shift within "the unity of rationalism" (1982a:10). This is an important qualification, since Schaeffer is often accused of ignoring non-Christian antithesis philosophy as humanistic and rationalistic, especially Greek philosophy. In fact, his definitions cover all non-Christian thought while attempting to characterize the unity of non-Christian thought in the present time in terms of relativism. The real difference is that above the line of despair, "people were rationalistic optimists", commending a "unified optimistic humanism". Below the line, the search for "a unified rationalistic circle" of thought is given up. Thus, when the philosophers departed from antithesis thinking, the concept of truth was shifted and "modern man was born".

According to Schaeffer (1982a:13, 14), Hegel was the first modern philosopher to "open the door" to the line of despair by introducing "the concept of dialectical thinking", replacing the concept of antithesis with the idea of a synthesis that resolves a thesis and its antithesis. The "straight line" of thought before Hegel becomes a "triangle" afterwards (1982a:14).

Retaining the optimistic rationalism of previous philosophers, Hegel opened the door to the line of despair but did not go below the line himself. Schaeffer does not teach, contra Reugsegger (1986b:116-117), that Hegel was a relativist. Rather, Kierkegaard was the first to go below the line of despair. The second book of the trilogy, *Escape from Reason*, details the development of earlier philosophy leading to Kierkegaard through Kant and Hegel, while *The God Who is There* merely summarizes this development and its significance (cf. 1982a:207-270).

Kierkegaard is identified as the father of modern existentialism, the secular and the religious (Schaeffer, 1982a:14-17, 21, 199; cf. 237-244; Reugsegger, 1986b:118-120; Nash, 1986:61-62, 225). Kierkegaard's key insight, according to Schaeffer (1982a:15), is the "leap of faith", which means that a synthesis of all knowledge is not possible through reason. Kierkegaard's writings and his interpretation of Abraham's act of faith in offering his son Isaac as a sacrifice "gradually led" to the separation of faith and rationality, since this act was allegedly performed without a rational basis (1982a:16). In fact, counters Schaeffer, Abraham actually had "much propositional revelation" upon which to base his action, including God's "fulfilled promises" (1982a:15). Abraham's act was not, therefore, a non-rational leap. Schaeffer is careful to qualify his interpretation by saying that Kierkegaard would not likely agree with the secular or religious existentialism that developed from his thinking. The historical "result" is not necessarily in keeping with the original intent of the philosopher (1982a:16). This principle is an important axiom in Schaeffer that explains much of his interpretation of the history of philosophy. What a philosopher intends to achieve and what actually results may be two different things—a principle that justifies both Schaeffer and critics like Reugsegger who interpret so-called contradictions in Hegel and Kierkegaard as logical contraries and not true contradictions. Interestingly, Schaeffer defines antithesis as a "direct opposition of contrast between two things", a definition broad enough to cover both contraries and contradictories (1982a:199). The bottom line is that, from Kierkegaard on, important aspirations like love and purpose become purely existential experiences (Sartre) that cannot be communicated. As a non-rational experience, the leap of faith is viewed as "angst" (Heidegger) or a "final" (Karl Jaspers) or "first-order" (Aldous Huxley) experience, while the rational-logical area has "only particulars" without purpose or meaning (1982a:19, 17, 22, 16). The new uniformity in unbelieving thought, then, radically denies the possibility of a unified rational circle encompassing all thought. Philosophy has thus become "antiphilosophy" and humanity has become "a machine". Anti-philosophy makes no claim to being systematic in the way that classical philosophy was: "In it language leads to neither values nor facts, but only to language." (1982a:21.)

It is unfortunate that critics of Schaeffer have failed to read him responsibly with respect to Kierkegaard (cf. Dennis, 1986b:114-117, 230-231). Schaeffer (1982a:15) specifically asks "what proposition"—what principle— Kierkegaard added to the "flow of thought" that made a historic difference. The proposition is that one cannot "arrive at a synthesis by reason". This principle "gradually led" to the total separation of faith and reason (1982a:16; cf. Boa & Bowman, 2001:474). Whether Schaeffer was correct in believing that Kierkegaard made such a total separation in his own thinking is really incidental to his point. What contemporary Kierkegaard scholar would disagree with the principle Schaeffer observes in Kierkegaard? The Danish philosopher did not believe one could synthesize knowledge according to reason, and this was the basis for his argument against Hegel. The fact that Kierkegaard himself may not have advocated a *total* separation of faith and reason only means that Schaeffer's view of Kierkegaard's personal philosophy is out of sync with more recent scholarship on the question (cf. Evans, 2009:156-159; 1998:13-14, 21; 2006). It does not invalidate the principle he observes in Kierkegaard or his contention that it gradually led to pragmatic relativism in the 20th Century. Dennis (1986b:231-234) responds to several other examples of irresponsible criticism of Schaeffer in a lengthy footnote to his essay.

The alternative to this pragmatic relativism is the unity of believing thought grounded in God's creation of "a real, external world" (Schaeffer, 1982a:24). While anti-philosophies seek a non-rational experience of something of ultimate significance, the Christian worldview guarantees the possibility of "touching" the real world in the unity of the total personality. The "objective reality" of the world and the "mannishness" (uniqueness) of human beings are inescapable because the true God is the Creator of both the world and the human self: "God shuts us up to reality." (1982a:178.) Thus the existence of God and the doctrine of creation provide the metaphysical foundation for Schaeffer's concept of truth, and these are presupposed as necessities of predication. In short, a Christian view of being determines a Christian view of knowing.

For Schaeffer (1982a:43), then, the contemporary mindset and culture is understood in terms of the "unifying concept" of pragmatic relativism, which refers to "a divided field of knowledge". Because of this unifying concept, the Christian apologist must employ antithesis in order to challenge those who embrace the new thinking adapted from Hegel's dialectical method. If the antithesis is maintained, the apologist can take advantage of the death of romanticism and its optimistic answers—answers that now appear hollow to modern people living below the line of despair (1982a:45). The Christian offers realistic answers, affirming that there is no hope without truth and no truth without an "adequate base". Contrary to optimistic humanism and nihilism, neither of which can provide an adequate diagnosis or treatment for the world's ills, Christianity provides both a diagnosis and a solid basis for an answer. Christians should be glad, then, that the romantic answers are discredited, since modern people now agree with Christians—metaphysically, at least—"that man is dead, dead in the sense of being meaningless" (1982a:46). This provides an opportunity for an apologetic based on an antithesis concept of truth to address the contemporary despair. But if antithesis is forsaken, Christians become "nothing", having "nothing to say" (1982a:47). Nothing is left, then, but an "outward institutional form". Only by restoring "the mentality and practice of antithesis . . . in doctrine and life" will Christians avoid aiding and abetting the surrounding relativism. In apologetics, this will require "pre-evangelism" to establish a proper concept of truth as a first step: "Before a man is ready to become a Christian, he must have a proper understanding of truth, whether he has fully analyzed his concept of truth or not." (1982a:149, 155.) Adopting a proper concept of truth is a necessary condition for accepting true content.

Non-Rational Leaps of Faith

For Schaeffer (1982a:63), there are only three ways modern people respond to the modern despair concerning a unified field of knowledge: "(1) simple nihilism; (2) the acceptance of the absolute dichotomy; (3) a semantic mysticism based on connotation words". The first of these options, simple nihilism (the first level of despair), is unlivable because it contradicts human nature, which requires an optimistic alternative. Because human beings are made in the divine image, they cannot live without hope (faith) and meaning (1982a:61). It is noteworthy that Schaeffer's analysis of the modern situation is not based on a neutral concept of human nature but on the biblical presupposition of creation in God's image within an environment of rational divine revelation. This basic biblical presupposition is captured in the titles of all three books of the trilogy combined: God is "there" and is "not silent", which means that to avoid God, one must "escape from reason". The second and third alternatives above explain categorically the two optimistic leaps of faith acceptable to modern unbelief. Thus, the dichotomy at the heart of these two leaps is an answer to the despair of nihilism, but they come at the high cost of "any unified concept of knowing" and a unified self (1982a:58). Human beings are rational by nature, and this is undeniably evident in experience, since even communication within the self requires antithesis thinking. Therefore, in rejecting antithesis (which itself requires antithetical reasoning), the individual becomes self-alienated to the extent this is carried out consistently. Clearly, for Schaeffer, the principle of antithesis is not a neutral epistemological first principle; rather, it is an existential principle based on the created nature of the self and its revelational environment. Thus, predication requires antithesis, which—in turn—is based on a Christian presupposition. This explains why "Christianity is not just a better dialectic" (1982a:164).

Ironically, the methodology of antithesis is rejected by affirming the antithesis of rationality and meaning. Schaeffer (1982a:57, 58) refers to this in terms of "two totally watertight compartments": "The downstairs has no relationship to meaning; the upstairs no relationship to reason." By dividing the field of knowledge, the rationalistic man divides himself by an antithetical act of reason that denies reason. This is why, for Schaeffer, the modern irrationalist is still a rationalist. Schaeffer simply affirms here the rationalist-irrationalist dialectic of Van Til and Frame in terms of contemporary examples and simple analogies. But the same point is made: The unbeliever must use reason to escape from reason, thus infusing his thought with a dialectical tension that is not purely logical. Being divided from himself as a thinking being, he is also psychologically and morally divided.

The sponsors of this dichotomy of reason and meaning, depending on their level of optimism, will resort to one of two strategies representing the second and third levels of despair. On the second level, the dichotomy exists in tension with moral attitudes that imply a rationally meaningful basis. Schaeffer (1982a:58-59) cites Sartre and Camus as examples of the modern dichotomy who contradicted their own relativism by adopting non-relative moral attitudes. At this second level, tension is evident in the lack of consistency between one's moral motions and a meaningful basis for morality. Neo-orthodoxy, which represents a religious form of existentialism, seems to offer an improvement by moving to a third level of despair, making use of religious words that connote personality and meaning. The problem, however, is that the use of such words gives only "an illusion of communication" (1982a:59). This "semantic mysticism" trades on synonymous definitions with different connotations and is employed by theologians and philosophers alike. So a Christian symbol or word "stirs the mind" of those exposed to a Christian culture, but lacking a concrete definition, the "illusion of communication and content" allows hearers to be moved psychologically while leaving content in obscurity (1982a:59). This explains a defining principle of modern theology: "To the new theology, the usefulness of a symbol is in direct proportion to its obscurity." (1982a:60.) For Schaeffer, the "new theology" refers primarily to the Neo-orthodoxy of Barth, Bultmann, and Tillich, "men who have particularly applied the dialectical methodology of Hegel and Kierkegaard's 'leap' to the Christian faith" (1982a:201).

In other words, the new theology trades on the resemblance between contemporary and traditional usages, commending the new usage on the basis of a non-rational faith. Schaeffer (1982a:60) points to Tillich's phrase, "God behind God", as a clear example that amounts to a deceptive bait-and-switch routine in which an orthodox theism is replaced by a pantheistic conception of God. Not all Neo-orthodox theologians go as far as Tillich, but even Barth's system, which is more biblical and orthodox than Tillich's, "is not open to verification, it must simply be believed" (1982a:55). While Barth affirms a historical resurrection, as salvation history this event is not subject to historical investigation and remains, therefore, an upper-story leap of faith (1982:86-88). Schaeffer's point is not to argue that the new theology lacks any Christian content; rather, he contends that its method provides no way to defend Christian content on a rational or verificational basis, relying instead on a mere resemblance between the old Christian terminology and the new. A "living orthodoxy", however, concerns the whole person—rationality included (1982a:61). But the new theology, according to Schaeffer (1982a:85, 84), offers the extremes of a "vague pantheism" of the upper story ascribing transcendental status to both God and man (Tillich) or affirming a non-transcendental naturalism of the lower story using religious words "with *upper-story* overtones" (God is Dead theology). Practically, both amount to a denial of the unity of truth and the knower under God—both biblical presuppositions. This crucial concept of unified truth is clearly overlooked in Pinnock's (1986:183-193) criticism of Schaeffer's allegedly unfair view of Kierkegaard and Barth, the two conservative examples of upper-story theology. Rejecting presuppositionalism, this critic evaluates Schaeffer in terms of his own "nonpresuppositional apologetic" inspired by Hackett (1984), charging him with rationalism, voluntarism, and offering his own existential upper-story theology (1986:189, 193; cf. Pinnock, 1977:32).

Some find fault with Schaeffer's (1982a:64) concept of the modern dichotomy, which he presents as a dichotomy between "contentless faith" with "no rationality" in the upper story and "rationality" with "no meaning" in the lower story: "Rationality and faith are out of contact with each other." On the surface, this seems to be a simple overgeneralization. Do not existential theologies and philosophies reflect some rational structure to upper story beliefs, and is not some of this content, at least, in agreement with Scripture? And what of the following assertion: "All the new theology and mysticism is nothing more than a faith contrary to rationality, deprived of content and incapable of contentful communication." As if these generalizations were not sharp enough, Schaeffer offers an even stronger one: "All that the new theology has above this line [of anthropology] is the 'philosophic other,' a metaphysical infinite, which is unknown and unknowable." As Schaeffer (1982a:257) says, "This brings us in Western thought into proximity with the East."

Like his teacher, Van Til, Schaeffer (1982a:64) often stated the logical conclusion of an opponent's method rather than giving an account of specific beliefs on a continuum. The rationalist-irrationalist dialectic exposes beliefs for which there is no adequate basis, and this is what Schaeffer is doing. The new theology "knows nothing of man being created in the image of God, nor of God revealing Himself truly in the Scriptures". Because of the lack of these biblical presuppositions as normative revelation, the new theology reduces to "faith in faith", not faith directed to a real object. The Christian faith must be "open to discussion and verification" on its own terms or it can have "no certain object" (1982a:65). While the existential theologian may personally believe that God is there; the point is that he can provide no rational account or verification for such a belief (cf. 1982a:351-352). Thus, the new theology lacks the rationale of the biblical worldview and therefore lacks its content as well. Put simply, being dialectical and unverifiable, the new theology is not truly biblical—it is relativistic! What it can account for, then, is far less than what individual theologians may affirm.

The scandal of Schaeffer's presuppositionalism is really the same as Van Til's: The inability to give an account of one's theological or philosophical content invalidates the content itself. Unless religious experience can be discussed in scientific or rational terms, it is ultimately without content in the biblical sense. For evangelical theologians taking a critically appreciative or "dialectical" approach to modern theologians, Schaeffer's view will appear parochial and harsh (cf. Ramm, 2000:109). However, learning from modern theologians does not require "rapprochement" or building on their foundations (Brown, 1986:22).

In summary, because the modern theologian's concept of faith is different than the Bible's, so is the content. One may disagree with Schaeffer (and Van Til) on this point, as many do, but he should not be charged with overgeneralization on his own terms. If the content of Christian faith is not "open to discussion and verification", it does not represent "the God who is there" and the Christ who died and rose again "in space and in time" (Schaeffer, 1982a:65). Having "no certain object", the "introverted" faith of modern theology rejects the infallible *kerygma* by misrepresenting it. The result—in Neo-orthodoxy at least—is a relativistic variety of content that testifies to Schaeffer's point. Truth content is not measured on a continuum where the theologian draws the line between rationality and faith; rather, it is measured by biblical norms. The conservatism of Barth and the liberalism of Bultmann and Tillich demonstrate the lack of biblical presuppositions functioning as norms within a theological movement that rejects discussion about verification. The most liberal expressions of Neo-orthodoxy merely reflect the end game of a new modernism that lacks a scriptural basis for its affirmations: "There is no certainty that a god is there" (1982a:75; cf. Brown, 1986:20-21).

This is in antithesis to the biblical teaching that God is certainly there and is known by all. Therefore, in one sense, it makes no difference where the new theologian is located on the continuum of conservatism and liberalism; his confession is a leap of faith based on an objective uncertainty and his own judgment, which—in essence—is pragmatic relativism. For Schaeffer, as for Van Til, method and content are inseparable. Applying Jones's (1986:30-35) meta-philosophy, one could argue that Schaeffer reflects a "continuity" orientation that is challenged by his critics' "discreteness" orientation. Veith (1986:47) would likely agree: "Schaeffer offers not so much a philosophy as what many contemporary theorists would describe as a meta-philosophy . . . a way to look at philosophy as a whole."

Christian Being and Knowing

The burden of Schaeffer's (1982a:93) apologetic is to show that the Christian system provides answers for the "basic needs" of modern people.

Contrary to the new theology, which has "no adequate basis" for rational and livable answers, the Christian system provides good and sufficient answers to basic human needs, the first of which is the need to explain "the reality of individual personality". The Christian system affirms that personality is fundamental, God being personal "on the high order of Trinity". Unlike worldviews that ground the personal in an impersonal ultimate, Christianity affirms an eternal, triune Person sharing "real love and real communication" before the creation of the world (1982a:94). As the image of God, mankind was created to reflect God's personality. Just as water cannot rise higher than its source, so there is no way to explain the complexity of human personality in terms of "the impersonal (plus time, plus chance)". Thus, the Christian faith adequately explains the origin and meaning of human personality in rational terms.

For Schaeffer (1982a:94), there are only two "clearcut" alternatives: "Either there is a personal beginning to everything, or one has what the impersonal throws up by chance out of the time sequence." The use of connotation words, such as Tillich's "Ground of Being", only veils the absurdity of deriving the personal from the impersonal through a semantic mysticism that does not fit the facts of experience. Thus, personality appears "out of the hat" and the water rises "above its source" (1982a:95). The end result is that personality is either a "mirage" or is affirmed through a leap of faith. Acting as if God exists (Julian Huxley) is also not a reasonable answer but a lie. Based on an impersonal ground, human aspirations, such as hope, purpose, love, moral motions, beauty, communication, and compassion—all are beyond fulfillment and meaningless.

Since God is personal and has created personal images who speak, it is logical to expect that God also speaks: "Why should God not communicate *propositionally* to the man, the verbalizing being, whom He made in such a way that we communicate propositionally to each other?" (Schaeffer, 1982a:99-100.) Schaeffer asks a rhetorical question that affirms a basic Christian presupposition supporting "the possibility of verifiable facts" (1982a:100). Because God speaks, religious, historical, and scientific truths may be verified on the basis of God's revelation in nature and Scripture—a revelation set in history and in the universe and addressed to historical creatures living in that world. Given this situation, Schaeffer logically asks, "What sense then would it make for God to give His revelation in a book that was wrong concerning the universe?" The answer is obvious: "No sense at all!" The point here is that the Bible reflects a unity of truth across all areas of knowledge—upstairs and downstairs—by virtue of its "linguistic and propositional form". While Christians may differ over how to interpret nature and Scripture, they may nevertheless affirm the consistency of nature and Scripture as "certain" witnesses to a holistic truth that is not exhaustive.

With all of Schaeffer's emphasis on antithesis and absolutes, it is easy to overlook a very important qualification in his theory of knowing. Schaeffer actually acknowledges a principle of limited relativity in the biblical epistemology. His notion of a balance of form and freedom in the biblical revelation is really a balance of absolute truth and bounded relativity. While Schaeffer would not have called this principle of freedom *relativity*, this term may be applied to what he describes. So while the Bible functions as the authority in the sciences and humanities, it does so by setting "some absolute limits", some "guiding boundaries" in three areas: "right and wrong in dogmatic systems, objectivity and subjectivity in history, and justification and sanctification" (Duriez, 2008:168). In an important appendix to *The Church Before a Watching World*, Schaeffer (1982b:169-175) sets absolute limits beyond which theologians must not go in formulating doctrines: "the Christian doctrinal and intellectual position lays down a circle rather than a point", within which there is "freedom to express doctrines in various ways" (1982b:166). The edge of the doctrinal circle functions "as an absolute limit past which we 'fall off the edge of the cliff' and are no longer Christians at this particular point in our thinking". This is simply a popular version of Van Til's (1972:v-vi) notion of limiting concepts in theology expanded to include issues of Christian practice that Van Til did not discuss. Van Til put forward this notion in order to reject the idea of a deductive theology (scholastic orthodoxy) at one extreme and the post-Kantian idea of truth as "nothing but a limiting concept" (Neo-orthodoxy) on the other.

Schaeffer's simple appendix is a critical methodological essay within his complete works. In his own rejection of a deductive theology, he allows for theological variations within the absolute boundaries provided in Scripture. In one example of an orthodox young person who goes to the university, Schaeffer (1982b:166, 167) counsels the student to distinguish between "a repetitive orthodoxy" as a "projection" of a particular position and the position itself. By studying the Scriptures and "the swings of the pendulum in church history", it is possible to discover both the boundary limits and the freedom to "reformulate, phrase, and rephrase" creeds and doctrinal standards (1982a:167). Note that the freedom here is not simply in the phrasing and rephrasing of creeds, but also in their formulation.

Thus, both the certainty and propositional form of biblical truth are secured while acknowledging significant freedom in the formulation of truth. This is not simple absolutism; it is relativity without relativism—a middle path between scholastic orthodoxy and Neo-orthodoxy.

The problem with the new theology is that it compromises both the certainty and propositional form of God's revelation—a disclosure made necessary by human finitude, which is not a sufficient "reference point" for certain knowledge (Schaeffer, 1982a:100). Neo-orthodoxy seeks to "secure" the Christian message by denying the possibility of its verification, which actually has the opposite effect (1982a:101). Nothing can be secured by a mere declaration of such "immunity from proof", and this shows the "fatal flaw" and irrationality of modern theology: "That is, all the new theology can do is preach and ask the people to believe or not to believe, without the exercise of reason."

The Christian position, however, affirms what the infinite, impersonal gods of the East and the finite, personal gods of the West cannot, namely, that an infinite personal God has created the world in "various orders", making distinctions between himself, his human images, and other creatures (Schaeffer, 1982a:100, 101). Thus, "man can know God truly, though he cannot know God exhaustively" (1982a:102). The biblical view does not leave the Christian with the dilemma of complete knowledge or complete ignorance of God. Interestingly, Schaeffer recognized that driving a "wedge" between the personal and the infinite was the mistake of modern philosophy and theology—a mistake trinitarian theism would never make owing to its doctrine of human creation in the divine image (1982a:103). Human personality is limited because it is created, not because it is personal. A finite personality may not know God exhaustively, but God and the world may be known truly because God authorizes the communication (1982a:104). The horizontal love shared among the persons of the Trinity defines the meaning of love shared in human relationships: "The validity and meaning of love rest upon the reality that love exists between the Father and Son in the Trinity." (1982a:106.) Thus, God is not defined by a set of finite qualities separated in the world; rather, God's characteristics are original—and human qualities are finite expressions of their divine originals, which are revealed in Scripture. This is simply Van Til's (1967:12-15; 1969b:16-17) doctrine of analogical reasoning in popular form. For Schaeffer (1982a:107), the Trinity gives a "basis for verifiable facts and knowing", which includes the God-words in our theology and apologetics.

The Trinity, then, is a key biblical presupposition in Schaeffer's Christian epistemology.

Human knowing is now complicated by the abnormality of the universe and humankind (Schaeffer, 1982a:120). The Bible affirms "a historic space-time Fall" of the human race into sin, which means that human beings are now separated from their "only sufficient reference point" by a "true moral guilt" requiring justification through faith in Christ's substitutionary work on the cross (1982a:114; cf. 109-118). The world is also fallen and abnormal—a truth that makes sense only in light of the biblical account in Genesis. The problem, then, is that the human knower is confronted with the existence and form of the world and himself but lacks the resources to interpret either one (1982:119-120). Schaeffer describes the problem of how these two things cohere and make sense in terms of the analogy of a torn book. A torn book with only "one inch of printed matter on each page" requires its complement of "torn-off parts" in order to be rationally understood (1982a:119). If these are found in the attic, the mystery of the book would be solved, and the "completed story" could be read by the whole person, his reason being "the first to tell him that the portions which were discovered were the proper solution to the problem of the ripped book". Through this analogy, Schaeffer is saying that the ripped pages correspond to the abnormal world and the abnormal person, and the torn-off parts found in the attic correspond to the Scriptures. The question of verification enters in deciding whether God's communication "completes and explains" what was obvious but unexplained before the discovery (1982a:120). In other words, verification answers the question of whether or not the Bible explains the existence and form of the world and human uniqueness (cf. 1982a:184-185).

Beginning from himself as autonomous and the world as merely given, the fallen individual cannot give an adequate answer on the basis of the world or himself alone. Without the Scriptures to interpret the world and himself, the fallen knower "would never have had the answer" (Schaeffer, 1982a:120). But given propositional revelation as a guide, "the pieces match up in a coherent whole over the whole unified field of knowledge".

Thus, verification is confirming the unique sufficiency of the Christian answer with respect to two criteria. Suggesting that scientific, philosophical, and religious proof follow the same rules, Schaeffer commends two truth tests: "A. The theory must be noncontradictory and must give an answer to the phenomenon in question. B. We must be able to live consistently with our theory." These tests may be applied positively to the

Christian answer regarding mankind as unique and to non-Christian answers as well. As these tests are described, they actually represent the two traditional truth tests of coherence and correspondence (cf. Adler, 1990:98). A coherent theory must be internally consistent (non-contradictory) and adequately explanatory; a correspondent theory must conform to empirical observation as well as a broad observation of human nature and behavior. Schaeffer's particular twist on these tests is to include explanatory adequacy as a qualification of the coherence test and experiential fit as a qualification of the correspondence test. A non-contradictory answer is not true simply as a postulate; it must also be sufficient to explain what is being tested. Similarly, a theory must correspond to what personal creatures observe and experience and therefore must fit experientially as well as empirically. These qualifications reflect the existential needs of rational creatures applying these truth tests as whole persons.

The use of such verificational tests has led some interpreters to conclude that Schaeffer stepped out of presuppositionalism and into verificationalism by virtue of these tests (Lewis, 1986:86; Follis, 2006:99). However, in an illuminating study, Leigh (1990) argues that Schaeffer took his understanding of verification directly from Van Til. Going back to the early syllabi in the Van Til archives at Westminster Seminary, which Schaeffer would have read as a student in the mid-1930's, Leigh proves that Van Til did not reject a verificational method but qualified its proper use. Van Til (quoted by Leigh, 1990:28) wrote the following in his 1935 *Christian Theistic Evidences* syllabus: "Is the method of hypothesis and verification then inherently anti-theistic? Not so if only a hypothesis and verification be based upon the presupposition of God." Leigh (1990:29) points out that "Van Til's methodological nomenclature did not change" in the years that followed his early syllabi. Therefore, the traditional method fails—not because it is verificational—but because it fails to take Christian presuppositions into account. Schaeffer's own statements concerning the necessity of revelation and the futility of autonomous reason are sufficient to prove that he was following Van Til's original verificational method, not the verificational method of natural theology or evidentialism. Schaeffer's (1982a:101) own explicit statement is clear: "The historic Christian answer concerning verifiable facts and knowing depends on who God is, on who is there." In this context, Schaeffer is referring to "the personal-infinite God", the "God who is there according to the Scriptures", not the god of general theism. Thus, Leigh (1990:96) concludes that, for Schaeffer, "the ultimate source of verification is God, and the God who reveals himself propositionally in the Bible". Therefore, it is no surprise that in applying verificational tests to Christian and non-Christian answers in *He is There and He is Not Silent*, Schaeffer resorts to a presuppositional or transcendental argument in framing his proof. Schaeffer's view of evidences also reflects this same dependence on biblical truth (Leigh, 1990:104-109).

So what does Schaeffer (1982a:121) conclude from the application of his verificational tests to the Christian worldview and its non-Christian rivals? The Christian answer does "conform to and explain" human nature and self-knowledge. Human beings and their "present abnormality" are best explained only by a personal source. The theory that "the impersonal plus time plus chance" produced human personality is against all experience and leads to the conclusion that "personality is an illusion". While this theory could be non-contradictory (test A), it is not livable (test B), since human beings cannot live as machines determined by impersonal forces of nature. Evidences from art, artifacts, and burial rites also testify against this theory. The irrational leap is itself a "desperate attempt to have answers at the expense of reason" and thereby testifies to the inadequacy of the impersonal option and the need for the Christian answer (1982a:122). Any hope for another answer in the future is also unlivable, since life in the present requires "a working hypothesis from which to start". The scientific theory of relativity also offers no hope of a sufficient answer, since the theory is based on physical laws that are constant—not relative: "Therefore it does not mean that 'anything goes,' as it does when relativity is applied to human values." The third book in the trilogy, *He is There and He is Not Silent*, provides an expanded account of the basic argument presented in this context (Schaeffer, 1982a:275-352).

Of critical importance here is the manner in which Schaeffer applies these tests. Following Van Til, Schaeffer (1982a:122) evaluates Christian and non-Christian answers holistically, adopting these for the sake of argument (hypothetically) to see which answer offers a non-contradictory answer that "explains the phenomena" and supports all of life and scholarship. Each answer reflects a total *rationale* that is either sufficient or not. The truth tests, in other words, are applied to an entire system of belief, not to individual tenets evaluated in piecemeal fashion. This is essential to the presuppositional cast of Schaeffer's apologetic and explains the transcendental method of his expanded argument in the third book of the trilogy. Also of critical importance is the fact that rationality is not the highest value in this apologetic approach. Rather, "rationality provides a form for the whole" (1982a:124). Figures of speech and other forms of "enrichment" must "fit into a framework of defined speech" in order to know what the enrichments mean. Thus, the Christian system must be rational if it is to provide a rationale for "testing the spirits". Reason begins a knowing process that ultimately involves the whole person: "Much can be added to the rational, but if we give up the rational everything is lost." (1982a:125.) Only then can communication with the infinite-personal God be restored.

What may not be obvious in Schaeffer's discussion of Christian being and knowing but is solidly evident is the fact that the Christian rationale stands behind both his verificational tests and the way he applies these to modern answers. Apologists presupposing the requirement of neutral tests and rejecting any notion of circularity will automatically cry foul by this point in Schaeffer's discussion. But it should be remembered that Schaeffer never affirmed the possibility of neutral hypothesis testing anywhere in his apologetic discussion. Indeed, his definitions of rationalism and humanism explicitly deny the possibility of knowledge beginning from one's own autonomous reason. The Christian answer, therefore, informs the discussion of epistemology and apologetic method—inevitably and inescapably. The Christian answer, like any non-Christian answer, is a *total* rationale, which means that it must serve as a normative guide in knowing and verification. Though not as explicit as Van Til and Frame, Schaeffer affirms the broad circularity of being and knowing, and the discerning reader can hear it humming quietly in the background of his entire apologetic trilogy.

Apologetics as Pre-Evangelism

Schaeffer (1982a:151) defines his apologetic method in terms of two purposes: "The first is defense. The second is to communicate Christianity in a way that any given generation can understand." Defense is understood as providing sufficient answers to objections through dialogue, understanding the specific "attack" of one's generation and communicating the gospel in understandable terms. Thus, relevant defense is the negative side of apologetic evangelism, and gospel communication is the "positive side" (1982a:153). Throughout the endeavor, the apologist must remain in contact with the real questions being asked by the current and next generation. The work of the Holy Spirit, prayer, and love for hearers as fellow divine image-bearers are also necessary along with the scriptural "space-time proofs" that provide "good and sufficient evidence" that Christ is the Messiah of the Old Testament and the Son of God (1982a:153, 154). It is notable that "space-time evidence" is scriptural evidence that is "open to verification by eyewitnesses" (1982a:154; cf. LUK 1:1-4; ACT 1:1-3; 1CO 15:1-

8). What is verifiable can be verbally communicated or written, making it possible to "know the truth". Thus, "knowledge precedes faith", which means that true faith must believe God on the basis of true knowledge. Anything less is not true Christian faith and—on Schaeffer's principles— cannot be communicated in rational terms approved by Scripture.

The alternative to biblical faith is a mystical leap "without reason" or "with the severe diminishing of reason" (Schaeffer, 1982a:181). Any faith commitment offered as a "probability position" that denies or diminishes reason is a leap of faith. Schaeffer does not say that such apologists (or believers) are not Christians, but their understanding of faith falls below scriptural standards and caters to "relativistic people to whom everything is only probability". Thus, probable positions are relativistic. This is a central axiom in Schaeffer's system that must not be overlooked. Biblical faith, however, is based on "good and adequate reasons" for certain conclusions (1982a:182). Throughout this apologetic, "the biblical concept of faith" is presupposed as the measure by which all other concepts are weighed and criticized. At bottom, the leap of faith is not simply a "no reason" position, though Schaeffer often writes in a way that conveys that impression. A diminished-reason position is also compromised and unbiblical.

In fact, Schaeffer's (1982a:154) view of true faith is the key to his entire critique of modern philosophy and theology. If the true knowledge grounding true faith must be scriptural and verifiable within "a framework of historic truth", then anything less is not true knowledge, making a lesser faith distorted and incommunicable as a biblically rational system. In other words, God must be "there in the historical biblical sense" or his existence and relationship with personal creatures is not properly communicated (1982a:158). This view of knowledge and faith—from my perspective—is the central tenet of Schaeffer's concept of truth. In essence, he takes the revelation of the gospel and its proclamation as the paradigm of true knowledge and faith and then measures all other knowledge and faith claims by it. This is presuppositionalism with a vengeance! The irony of Schaeffer's critics is that most have charged him with being anything but a consistent presuppositionalist when, in fact, his presupposition of the gospel as "open to verification" determines everything. Verifiability is what makes truth "*true truth*" (1982a:163; cf. Baird, 1986:51-53).

For Schaeffer (1982a:154), then, whatever is not open to verification is not open to being communicated, since biblical proclamation and communication is based only on such verifiable knowledge. Verifiability is defined in terms of biblical evidences and tests, not a general ethic of historical research applied in a neutral way. This is the ruler by which even Karl Barth is sized up as a new modernist. Again, one may disagree with Schaeffer on this point, but he cannot be accused of inconsistency on his own terms. The gospel itself is the central presupposition of Schaeffer's positive apologetic. The goal of apologetic evangelism is also its starting point, which explains his strong statement: "only that faith which believes God on the basis of knowledge is true faith". Therefore, any knowledge—philosophical or theological—that is not open to verification in the way the gospel is open fails to qualify as knowledge in the biblical sense. Like Frame, who defines epistemology in terms of the Bible's covenantal structure, Schaeffer does the same in terms of the covenantal gospel of God's redemptive presence—his being there—in space-time history. Anything less is a distortion of truth by abstraction, separating biblical ideas from the Bible's "total concept of life and truth" (1982a:159).

How, then, does one approach the apologetic task with this understanding in mind? Just as presuppositions govern the Christian view of truth, so non-Christians also have "a set of presuppositions" pointing to a logical outworking in thought and life (Schaeffer, 1982a:132). The problem is that the non-Christian cannot change the form of the world as God created it or his own "mannishness", and so he cannot live consistently with his presuppositions. Since "Christianity is the truth of what is there", every person is caught "in a place of tension" between his own thought and life and the world as God made it. One cannot live in a self-constructed universe with respect to either "logic" or "practice" (1982a:133). Nevertheless, apologetics must begin with a person's self-knowledge. On the one hand, the lost person knows something of the world and himself. But on the other hand, "when a man is lost, he is lost against all that there is, including what he is". Every non-Christian, therefore, is in tension within himself between the known and the unknown. This dilemma is experienced as a "pull" in two directions: "Every person has the pull of two consistencies, the pull towards the real world and the pull towards the logic of his system."

What this means is that the more consistent the unbeliever is to his non-Christian position, the further he strays from "the real world" (Schaeffer, 1982a:133). But the more consistent he is to the real world, the more inconsistent he becomes with respect to his presuppositions. This tension is experienced "in differing strengths", each person settling somewhere between the real world and the consistent demands of his belief system (1982a:134). Because there are things within each person that "speak of the real world", tension is inevitable with respect to morality, beauty, significance, rationality, or "fear of nonbeing" (1982a:135). Attempts to "deflect" this stress point are ultimately futile. The apologist, therefore, must find this point: "We, in love, looking to the work of the Holy Spirit, must reach down into that person and try to find where the point of tension is."

Ironically, this very inconsistency is what makes it possible to communicate with the non-Christian (Schaeffer, 1982a:137; cf. 1948:9). Complete logical consistency would leave the believer and unbeliever with no common presuppositions, but "in *practice* you will find a place where you can talk". Thus, apologetics trades on the rationalist-irrationalist dialectic in unbelieving thought. Schaeffer refers to this, not as the "point of contact" as in Van Til, but as the "point of communication". While this is a point of "common ground" with the unbeliever, it is not neutral: "There are no neutral facts, for facts are God's facts." (1982a:138.) But living in God's world forces the non-Christian to confront God's facts as contrary to his own interpretation. Thus, presuppositional apologetics does not stifle conversation. Instead, it obviates the point of communication and makes helping modern people possible. This communication concerns both "the nature of truth and the method of attaining truth". By pushing toward the logical conclusion of an unbelieving position, the apologist exposes the "false balance" at the heart of the position. This must be done gently and with care since it causes pain, so the apologist should push no further than a readiness to receive the gospel requires. The gospel must be made clear in terms of real truth, guilt, and history. Without this understanding, the inquirer "is not ready to become a Christian" (1982a:139). The hearer's "real interests" are the best place to press logical conclusions, and all questions must be allowed. Blind authority should never be a refuge for the Christian or non-Christian in apologetic conversations.

Schaeffer (1982a:140) also describes this strategy as "taking the roof off". Because the point of tension is a point of inconsistency within an unbeliever's system, "a roof is built as a protection against the blows of the real world, both internal and external". In taking the roof off, the apologist allows the truth of the real world in "to beat upon" the unbeliever. In doing so, the non-Christian's need is exposed, and the Scriptures can then be applied as the answer. This is not optional: "It is strictly biblical in its emphasis" (1982a:141). Because the non-Christian is already lost, the point of conversion is "the point of personal antithesis", prior to which "man is dead indeed". While modern people experience their deadness as meaninglessness or guilt feelings and not as true moral guilt before God, this experience calls for a solution that the gospel provides as "a total structure of truth" (1982a:144). The experience of metaphysical death is the point of communication for a Christian answer to both metaphysical and moral deadness. The sober task of providing the Christian answer requires a sympathetic understanding of the darkness of the modern perspective: "Men must know that with integrity we have faced the reality of the dark path they are treading."

The Final Apologetic

Beyond this method, there is also for Schaeffer (1982a:165) a "visible quality" in apologetics: "The final apologetic . . . is what the world sees in the individual Christian and in our corporate relationships together." The world must see "a substantial, corporate exhibition of the logical conclusions of the Christian presuppositions." Unless there is healing and love within the Church, the world will reject the Christian answer. Schaeffer uses the word "substantial" to indicate a real but imperfect exhibition of the Christian answer in the lives of believers. The reality here is a true "communion and community" among God's people "on the basis of true doctrine" (1982a:166). Therefore, the separations that come as a result of sin should be observably healed. Until contemporary people can say what was said of early Christians, "behold, how they love each other", there will be no "realism in exhibition" in the present generation (1982a:166-167). To be present, the holiness and love of God must be "existential", and this is possible only through the Holy Spirit (1982a:167). Thus, the present "existential moment" is what counts in apologetics, not the Church's past victories. This existential dimension is based on the fact that "personality is central" to the Christian worldview because God is fully personal (1982a:168). Therefore, without the "reality of personality" individually and corporately in the Church, the world will not accept the ultimate Personality behind it all (1982a:169). This is nothing less than "*living truthfully* upon what the truth is" (1982a:187; cf. Follis, 2006:135-141).

6 ESCAPE FROM REASON

The second and third books of Schaeffer's trilogy merely elaborate essential themes already presented in *The God Who is There* (Reugsegger, 1986c:28). As mentioned above, *Escape from Reason* details the philosophical development of earlier philosophy leading to Kierkegaard through Kant and Hegel. Given the apologist's responsibility to learn the "thought-forms" of her audience, Schaeffer (1982a:207, 208) wrote this book to explain "the changing existential situation"—the "movements of thought"—faced by Christians today and "how the situation has come about historically". In light of the goals of this section to explain Schaeffer's apologetic method and to analyze the ways in which triperspectivalism is reflected in his trilogy, the second and third books are not as foundational as the first. *The God Who is There* is a comprehensive statement of Schaeffer's position, although some points in the other two books are helpful to insure a correct understanding of his apologetic evangelism and its cogency as a perspectival system. Therefore, only those issues providing clarification or provoking critical responses relevant to these goals will be addressed as qualifications of concepts already summarized on the basis of *The God Who is There*. Many of Schaeffer's examples of the modern dichotomy and leaps of faith, though interesting, are not relevant to further clarifying his apologetic method (cf. 1982a:245-260).

Nash's (1986:53-56) observations on "Schaeffer's method" are especially relevant to a proper understanding and assessment of this second book of the trilogy. His method was "to look at the broad flow of philosophy and culture in the West, and to focus upon the key thinkers at critical points where these problems were most apparent" (1986:53). The "panoramic view of intellectual history and culture" provides only "a broad perspective of the past". While Nash also finds some interpretive problems here, these do not invalidate Schaeffer's basic method. Critics and followers are also guilty of "distortions of Schaeffer's work" (1986:54). As a "generalist", Schaeffer's approach often runs "at cross purposes" with those of the specialist. Both approaches, however, are valid and necessary. Therefore, Schaeffer should be assessed according to his context, audience, and objectives. In Nash's opinion, "anyone who can lead hundreds of thousands of people, as Schaeffer did, to drink even briefly at the waters of philosophy has performed an important service" (1986:54-55). While this opinion does not establish Schaeffer's cogency, it does warrant greater care in assessing his method.

Nature and Grace

Inspired by Dooyeweerd's profound (2012) analysis of Western thought, Schaeffer (1982a:209) begins his account of "the origin of modern man" with Thomas Aquinas (1225-1274). It is notable that Schaeffer affirms that this origin "could be traced back to several periods", but he chooses to begin with Aquinas. Schaeffer undoubtedly knew from his understanding of Dooyeweerd that he could have begun with the form-matter scheme of the Greeks, but he did not choose to do this. Why? It is evident to me that Schaeffer's (1982a:214-216) discussion of universals and particulars in relation to nature and grace accomplishes the same goal. Because of the influence of Greek philosophy on Aquinas and the Renaissance thinkers and artists, the form-matter scheme of the Greeks could be brought into the discussion more easily and with more relevance by starting with Aquinas. In all he writes, Schaeffer is mindful of "the practical aspects of how to communicate", and this likely explains his homiletic analysis of Western thought (1982a:208). To his credit, this approach shows clearly how the dominant ground motives of one age relate to those of a later period.

Schaeffer (1982:209, 211) argues that the higher level of grace (God, the invisible, the soul) was separated from the lower level of nature (creation, the visible, the body), and Aquinas "opened the way" for this. Prior to Aquinas, "there was an overwhelming emphasis on the heavenly things"; with Aquinas, "we have the birth of the humanistic elements of the Renaissance" (1982a:210). Schaeffer points out that Aquinas affirmed "a concept of unity" between nature and grace and would not be pleased with what resulted from his writings over time. But because of his "incomplete view of the biblical fall", the intellect would come to be regarded as autonomous (1982a:211). The development of natural theology is an outworking of this view and is described by Schaeffer as "a theology that could be pursued independently from the Scriptures". Affirming a "correlation" between natural theology and the Scriptures was simply not sufficient; the "autonomous principle" in theology ultimately justifies the same in philosophy and the arts: "as nature was made autonomous, nature began to 'eat up' grace" (1982a:211, 212). While this tendency was present before, "it appears in a more total way from this time on" and reaches its climax by the Renaissance (1982a:211). The very concept of an "autonomous area" is sufficient to allow the lower realm to displace the higher or to separate these into an upper and lower story (cf. Yancy, 1979c:26).

By Leonardo da Vinci's time (1452-1519), Platonic and Aristotelian thought were well established in the form of Neo-Platonism and Thomism, and this is illustrated by Raphael's famous painting, *The School of Athens* (Schaeffer, 1982a:214-215). The philosophical problem of universals and particulars, inherited from Greek philosophy, was correlated with the nature-grace problem of Aquinas. Just as the principle of autonomy leads to the displacement of grace by nature, so without a worldview that provides for the "rational unity" of universals and particulars, the particulars ultimately displace the universals (1982a:216). Neither Aquinas nor the Renaissance thinkers and artists had a sufficient answer to this problem, but the Reformers provided one in their rejection of the "autonomous intellect and the possibility of a natural theology" and in their affirmation of biblical authority as final (1982a:217). The Reformers offered a unified position in contrast to the Roman Church, which held a "divided" position with respect to Scripture, Christ, and salvation (1982a:218). The Reformation *Solas—Sola Scriptura, Solo Christo, Sola Gratia, Sola Fide*—contradicted the "humanistic element" reflected in the Romanist additions. By adding the Church, a natural theology, meritorious works, or moral effort to the authority of the Bible and the finished work of Christ, Romanism undermined unified knowledge upstairs and downstairs. The Reformers' unified position provided a basis for "true freedom within the revealed form" for both art and science: "There is nothing autonomous—nothing independent from the Lordship of Christ and the authority of the Scriptures." (1982a:220, 224.)

Nature and Freedom

The problem of nature and grace in relation to particulars and universals is reflected in the development of modern science. The process of nature eating up grace can be traced through this development beginning with the early modern scientists of the Renaissance and Reformation. Schaeffer (1982a:225) cites Robert Oppenheimer as a contemporary non-Christian scientist who, like Alfred North Whitehead, recognized that "Christianity was needed to give birth to modern science". Sartre's "great philosophic question" as to "why something exists rather than that nothing exists" finds its answer in "the Hebrew-Christian" affirmation of divine creation: "Christianity gives a certainty of objective reality and of cause and effect, a certainty that is strong enough to build on." (1982a:225, 226.) Early modern science was a "religious activity" because it was carried on within the framework of a rational world created to be understood by rational persons (1982a:226). It was natural without being "naturalistic" because God created the world as "an open system", not one that imprisons God and mankind in "the machine of cause and effect" (1982a:227). In other words, "there was not an autonomous situation in the 'lower story.'"

With Kant and Rousseau, however, "the sense of the autonomous was fully developed" (Schaeffer, 1982a:227). In the absence of any remaining concept of revelation, the nature-grace problem shifts to the problem of nature and freedom, freedom replacing grace in the upper story. With respect to particulars and universals, this "titanic" shift introduced an even greater problem than that of the nature-grace scheme. Kant's system, in particular, failed to relate the phenomenal particulars to the noumenal universals. The determinism of nature (physics), of which humans are a part, threatens the alleged freedom of autonomous people: "thus autonomous freedom and the autonomous machine stand facing each other" (1982a:228). As the "weight of the machine" presses in, some counter science in terms of "self-expression" (Rousseau) or practical reason (Kant), while materialists embrace "the uniformity of natural causes in a closed system" (1982a:229). Materialism unifies the upstairs and downstairs in a determinism Schaeffer calls "modern modern science", but it comes at the expense of God, grace, and freedom. The principle of autonomy, then, leads inevitably to an unlivable nihilism: "if man is determined, then what *is*, is right" (1982a:231). Facts and values are destroyed because universals and particulars cannot be meaningfully related; only determined particulars remain. This heightens the tension between the upper and lower stories to the breaking point.

Hegel attempted to release this tension by resolving the antithesis through the introduction of a dialectical methodology that effectively relativizes all things: "truth as truth is gone, and synthesis (the both-and), with its relativism, reigns" (Schaeffer, 1982a:233). This also leaves human autonomy intact—rationalism without rationality. As already noted, Kierkegaard walks through the door (goes below the line of despair) that Hegel opened. In Kierkegaard's thinking, the distinction between nature and grace, which became nature and freedom, becomes a faith-rationality scheme (1982a:234). Noumenal faith, Kant's realm of practical reason, is ultimately non-rational. Those among the middle class who still think in terms of antithesis often "do not understand why they think in the old way", and the rest "have been infiltrated with the new thought-forms in an unanalyzed way" by means of the mass media and the disciplines (1982a:235). Once again, rationalism (as Schaeffer defines it) and autonomy are left intact in this "complete dichotomy of the upper and lower stories" (1982a:237).

Given that this second book of the trilogy details Schaeffer's more controversial interpretations, what is to be made of his generalizations concerning Aquinas, Hegel, and Kierkegaard? Nash (1986:59) believes it is possible "to retain the value of Schaeffer's general approach and basic insights" while strengthening his case "by introducing some qualifications and by refocusing some of his analysis". Nash (1986:61-63) believes that Schaeffer could have begun with the Enlightenment instead of Aquinas, making his argument "much simpler", "more direct", and less controversial with respect to Aquinas. With respect to all three philosophers, Schaeffer might have treated them as "illustrations" or "key figures" rather than as causes of general cultural trends. And would not Nietzsche perhaps be a better key figure of modern nihilism and relativism? Also, Western thought does not flow "in a straight line toward meaninglessness and despair, or toward relativism", but philosophical mistakes are repeated often in history. With respect to Kierkegaard, Nash acknowledges that Schaeffer's interpretation has considerable scholarly support, although his view has been in decline (1986:225; cf. Evans, 2009:151-154). Current scholarship "does not see Kierkegaard has having made a complete separation of faith and reason" (1986:62). On this point, it must be remembered that Schaeffer indicts the "diminishing" of reason as well as its denial, so his view of Kierkegaard's role in modern relativism is not discredited by the current scholarship. Nash rightly says that Schaeffer "was more balanced than he is often given credit" for being. These qualifications are helpful and validate Schaeffer's analysis as pre-evangelistic, homiletic, and reliable but not as academic. And yet, in light of his evangelistic goal, what is more useful than a homiletic analysis?

The Existential Dilemma

The point of this entire analysis is clearly stated by Schaeffer (1982a:259) in one of the most important passages in the trilogy: "If what is placed upstairs is separated from rationality, and the Scriptures (especially where they touch on history and the cosmos) are not discussed as open to verification, why should one then accept the evangelical upstairs any more than the upstairs of the modern radical theology? On what basis is the choice to be made?"

This two-part question is the existential dilemma at the heart of Schaeffer's entire apologetic. In other words, if voluntaristic faith with differing unverifiable content is all that separates the evangelical believer from the liberal theologian or the modern philosopher, then Schaeffer is obviously correct that all three are pragmatic relativists, and the evangelical Christian has no basis—no reason—to call others to believe in the Christ he affirms. Despite serious criticisms of Schaeffer on a number of points, Pinnock (1986:183) agrees with his basic assessment of modern theology: "I happen to agree with Schaeffer that the direction of modern theology since Kant has been in the direction of the fictive upper story."

In fact, Schaeffer would say that the content of the evangelical's faith would be as suspect as the liberal theologian's if it is also not open to verification. Whatever scriptural content might be included, the evangelical's faith—holistically considered—would not be the unified truth of the Bible. Therefore, a pure or probabilistic fideism, which is all that a pragmatic relativism supports, is simply not the Christian gospel. Such a gospel may be personally affirmed, but it may not be authoritatively proclaimed. The modern method of pragmatic relativism is about personal autonomy and freedom, not absolute truth, making any version of it biblically inadequate. One need not judge the personal salvation of those using this method, but the method itself must be judged by Scripture and found wanting. Thus, for Schaeffer, whether faith is a "leap" or a "step" is all-important to commending Christian truth (Brown, 1984:82).

7 HE IS THERE AND HE IS NOT SILENT

The third book in Schaeffer's (1982a:186) trilogy provides what he regarded as "the real answer in regard to epistemology". This is the most philosophical work of the three, presenting a unified answer in the areas of metaphysics, ethics, and epistemology. He begins with metaphysics because "the problem of existence" determines the problem of knowing and morals. Reugsegger (1986c:33) sees this book as presenting "the heart of Schaeffer's apologetic system" and I agree.

The Metaphysical Answer

The area of metaphysics addresses three basic problems, the first two of which were raised by Sartre: (1) something is there rather than nothing; (2) human beings are personal but finite and so cannot be a sufficient self-reference point; (3) humanity is both "noble" and "cruel" (Schaeffer, 1982a:277, 278). In other words, the existence of things "in their present form and complexity" and the twin dilemmas posed by human personality and nobility (greatness) are the problems of metaphysics (1982a:277). Clearly, metaphysical problems are also epistemological and ethical. The manner in which Schaeffer frames these problems implies the interdependence of metaphysics, ethics, and epistemology as perspectival corollaries, but the analysis also includes normative input from the Bible. While the form of the world and human uniqueness are commonly observable realities and raise the same philosophical questions for believers and unbelievers alike, this analysis is also consistent with what the Bible "says" and "explains" (1982a:278). Therefore, the analysis implies the broad circularity of being, knowing, and doing, which implies and requires a unified answer to the problems of philosophy.

If, in fact, these are the true problems of Being that require a sufficient answer, then the Christian must deal with positions that deny one or all of these problems (Schaeffer, 1982a:278-280). Behaviorism, for example, denies human personality, affirming that all things are ultimately the product of "mere chemical or physical properties" (1982a:278). This position, however, is contradictory (test A) and unlivable (test B), determinists contradicting their position by personifying nature (spelling it "with a Capital N"). They also deny "the observation man has made of himself for at least 40,000 years (if we accept the modern dating system)". The Bible also affirms the nobility and cruelty of fallen persons—the ethical dilemma alongside the epistemological dilemma of human personality and finitude. In Schaeffer's terms, philosophy (understood as a "world-view") and religion work with the same problems (1982a:279). Thus, "philosophy is universal in scope. No man can live without a world-view; therefore, there is no man who is not a philosopher" (1982a:279-280).

Schaeffer (1982a:280) argues that there are not many answers to the basic problems of philosophy, although considerable detail surrounds "the basic answers". In fact, there are only two kinds of answers: those that deny a logical and rational answer and those that affirm such an answer. The first class of answer is "dominant" today, and the latter type was dominant in the past. Today's dominant answer is expressed in the "existential world". The problem, of course, is that no one can hold such a position consistently: "It can be held theoretically, but it cannot be held in practice that everything is absolute chaos." In practice, observation reveals a world of "form and order", and life requires conformity to that order. Once "even a little bit of order" is granted, the irrational answer "falls to the ground" (1982a:281). Schaeffer recognizes that the irrational answer is always held "selectively": "they discuss rationally until they are losing the discussion, and then they try to slip over into the answer of irrationality". This is the rationalist-irrationalist dialectic at work: The autonomous thinker determines the boundary line between rationality and mystery from himself, pretending omniscience in the process. The theoretical position founders on the fact that irrationality must be stated in rational terms to be meaningful: "Pockets of order" must be "brought in somewhere along the line".

Rational answers—"answers that can be discussed"—in the area of Being are also few: (1) All that exists has come from "absolutely nothing" or "nothing nothing"; (2) All that exists has come from an impersonal beginning; (3) All that exists comes from a personal beginning (Schaeffer, 1982a:281, 282). The first answer is "unthinkable", since something cannot come from "utter nothing" (1982a:282). The second answer is also inadequate, since everything must be reduced "to the original, impersonal factor or factors" (energy, mass, or motion), thus dissolving any meaning for particulars, personality, morality, and complexity in an impersonal ground (1982a:283). Dualism and polytheism would be expressions of this answer, since "there is a motion back to monism" in these views. Such "pan-*everythingism*" provides "an answer for the need of unity, but none for the needed diversity" (1982a:284). In short, these answers cannot solve the problem of the One and the Many. The "third possible answer" is that of a personal beginning: "In this case, man, being personal, does have mean-ing." (1982a:284, 285.) The Trinity alone provides a basis for everything the impersonal answer dissolves by reduction to the impersonal. Only a God of "personal unity and diversity" is "big enough" to be "a point of reference or a place of residence" for absolutes (1982a:287).

The "philosophic necessity" of this answer is transcendental—not inductive, deductive, or retroductive—since the trinitarian answer is both unique and a uniquely sufficient answer to the problem of meaningful predication in the area of Being: "There is only one philosophy, one religion, that fills this need in all the world's thought, whether the East or West, the ancient, the modern, the new, the old." (Schaeffer, 1982a:287.) Apologists who evaluate Schaeffer's argument here in terms of logical necessity have overlooked the point of his presuppositional argument. Morris (1976:58), Lewis (1986:94), Reugsegger (1986c:34), Harper (1976:139-140), Geehan (1972:18), Edgar (1995a:75), and Follis (2006:99, 114-115) misconstrue Schaeffer on this point, measuring his argument as probable at best based on a neutral view of hypothesis testing. Geisler (1999:685), however, recognizes that Schaeffer is making a "transcendental argument": "Schaeffer, like other presuppositionalists, begins with the Christian starting point of the triune God revealed in Scripture." Contrary to Follis, Hicks (quoted in Follis, 2006:114) was actually correct in describing Schaeffer as "one of Van Til's best-known followers".

The presuppositional argument is holistic and does not proceed from foundational principles from which a logically probable argument is con-structed to support a "tentative" hypothesis (Lewis, 1986:71; cf. Boa & Bowman, 2001:469-470). Schaeffer's argument proceeds from his commit-ment to the Christian system, considering alternatives for the sake of argument. In other words, Scripture plays a normative role in Schaeffer's transcendental argument that it does not play in a retroductive (abductive) argument yielding only probable conclusions. Ironically, Reymond (1976:144-145) accuses Schaeffer of begging the question of God's meta-physical necessity because of the obvious but unacknowledged influence of Scripture on his argument. And yet, scriptural norms are precisely what would be expected in an argument with a transcendental conclusion. While Schaeffer is allegedly in error for not confessing this up front, Frame would say that this acknowledgement is not always required and so says nothing concerning the validity of Schaeffer's argument. Reymond's (1976:145) own view is "confessedly informed by Holy Scripture", and this somehow makes his presuppositionalism valid and Schaeffer's not. But the *practice* of making Scripture normative is actually what counts in a transcendental argument.

In summary, Schaeffer's critics were simply thrown off by his verificational language. Missing it in Van Til, they missed the fact that Schaeffer relied on Van Til's early concept of verification, not the more common approach of neutral hypothesis testing. Even Van Til (1997a, 1997b) failed to recognize himself in Schaeffer's creative adaptation of his system simply because Schaeffer "used evidences and logical tests without first announcing their basis in Scriptural revelation" (Frame, 1995:396). This alleged defect, in turn, led other movement presuppositionalists and critics to disassociate Schaeffer and Van Til. Frame (1995:294; cf. 295-296) points out, however, that Van Til was unfairly critical of those who differed with him on matters of "strategy, formulation, communication, and contextualization", and obviously Schaeffer differed on these matters (as does Frame). Most significant to me is the fact that Schaeffer's rejection of probable answers is the key to identifying his method as transcendental. Christianity alone is "true to what is there" and God has spoken in general and special revelation, speaking "with one voice" (Schaeffer, 1982a:290, 291). Boa and Bowman (2001:473) confirm this interpretation of Schaeffer: "For Schaeffer, the (transcendentally) necessary truth of Christianity is not incompatible with its verifiability." These authors are among the few who recognize that "by 'verify' he means precisely to look and see that Christianity does give the only adequate answers to the big questions".

The Moral Answer

The "second area of philosophic thought" concerns "man and the dilemma of man" (Schaeffer, 1982a:293). The dilemma is two-fold. The first problem of ethics is fundamentally epistemological: humankind is personal and yet finite. Finite persons have "no sufficient integration point" in themselves, which makes them (and their moral choices) "meaningless and absurd" (Sartre). The second problem is that of their nobility and cruelty, which refers to "man's estrangement from himself and other men in the area of morals" (1982a:293-294). A significant transcendental indicator is revealed at this point: Schaeffer does not argue *for* moral distinctions based on human uniqueness; rather, he seeks the "answer" to the *fact* that such distinctions are observed and affirmed in the first place. In other words, greatness and cruelty are part of the universe and its form and call for an answer. While the skeptic would reject this affirmation as an example of the circumstantial species of the *ad hominem* fallacy, Schaeffer would respond that failing to begin with moral distinctions is unlivable (test B) and self-referentially incoherent (test A). After all, the *ad hominem* fallacy is premised on a moral commitment to rational integrity, which means that the skeptic—in practice—must begin with moral distinctions. The problem, however, is that the skeptic cannot be a sufficient reference point to justify his own rational and moral principles.

As in metaphysics, the answers given to the "dilemma of morals" are also limited and are determined by the metaphysical options (Schaeffer, 1982a:294; cf. Reugsegger, 1986b:121-122). The impersonal option ultimately merges finiteness and cruelty in a "motion back to monism" that reduces morals to metaphysics (1982a:284). Since one cannot relate particulars to universals within an impersonal metaphysics, one also cannot make moral distinctions in such a world: "everything is finally equal in the area of morals" (1982a:294). The alienation of society "is now only because of chance", so the human dilemma and tension is not truly moral. Thus, the pantheist redefines this tension as "the failure to accept your impersonality" (1982a:295). Cruelty and non-cruelty become equal, leaving "statistical ethics" as the only option (1982a:296). But the tension still exists because of who people really are—beings with aspirations, including "moral motions" that demand fulfillment and explanation (1982a:295).

With a personal beginning, "there is a possibility of keeping morals and metaphysics separate", making it possible to separate nobility and cruelty as real moral distinctions (Schaeffer, 1982a:297). Cruelty is then no longer reduced to finiteness. Cruelty, however, must also be explained as either intrinsic or acquired (1982a:298). If humanity was created cruel, then the Creator is also cruel (Camus, Baudelaire). It is possible to affirm the goodness of God by an irrational leap of faith (liberal theology), but this is dialectical and arbitrary, reflecting a selective approach to rationality and irrationality (1982a:299). But the rationalist-irrationalist dialectic is itself an expression of tension and is, therefore, not an answer. This dialectical tension accounts for the vacillation of liberalism and Neo-orthodoxy between irrational optimism and rational pessimism with respect to divine goodness. At the extreme of irrationalism, "god words" become meaningless; at the extreme of rationalism, they become hollow.

The personal option leads to a second moral problem, namely, that humanity is either intrinsically cruel, in which case there is no hope of a "qualitative change" for the better, or became cruel, making change a possibility (Schaeffer, 1982a:299). Unless humans became "abnormal" by their own choice, God would still be "a bad God" and there would be no answer to the moral dilemma (1982a:300). According to the Judeo-Christian view, "there was a space-time, historic change in man" through the Fall. Thus, humans are not "programmed" and therefore determined to be evil; rather, "man, at a certain point of history, changed himself, and hence stands in his cruelty, in discontinuity with what he was". This allows for "a true moral situation" in which morals, as morals, exist. The non-Christian, however, is left with reducing human abnormality to the normal condition and explaining it as either an epistemological problem (Plato, Heidegger) or as no problem at all (1982a:301-302). The Christian, on the basis of Christ's substitutionary death, has a basis for fighting evil in the self and the world without fighting against God (Camus) or the self's determined nature. Jesus proved this at the tomb of Lazarus, expressing sorrow and anger against death without being angry at himself as God. Thus, the Christian answer provides a basis "to fight the thing which is abnormal to what God originally made" and to vindicate God as "absolutely good" (1982a:302). Moral evil came into the world because humanity "turned by choice from his proper integration point" and not because he is finite (1982a:300). This is why the Genesis account is vital to Schaeffer and to contemporary evangelicals (1982a:304; cf. Dembski, 2009; Walton, 2009; Sotak, 2017:419-426).

As in metaphysics, "this is not simply the best answer—it is the only answer" (Schaeffer, 1982a:302). But is this, in fact, the only answer? Morris's (1976:58) criticism of Schaeffer is again relevant: "He moves from 'if Christianity is true, then there are answers' to 'therefore, Christianity is true.'" Morris believes that Schaeffer's argument involves an unwarranted "logical gap between possibility and necessary actuality". He also says that Schaeffer has failed to "identify his argumentative direction". In my judgment, Schaeffer's transcendental argument is based on his own version of existential undeniability rather than logical necessity. His use of the word "possibility" is equivalent to an option considered for the sake of argument, not to a probable or tentative hypothesis. But the impossibility of the contrary for Schaeffer is established by existential as well as logical arguments. Morris (1987:35) is correct that the "conclusion of theism which has been reached is not 'necessary' in any deductively logical sense" and is best described as "apparent necessity." Interestingly, this term is roughly equivalent to the existential undeniability principle that I have observed in Schaeffer. The key to his mode of argument is the principle of unified interpretation he took directly from Van Til: "One must always judge a system in its own total structure." (1982a:314; cf. Van Til, 1955:132-

139; Bahnsen, 1998:641-648; Frame, 1995:6-8.) Schaeffer's phrase, "in its own total structure", is simply a rewording of Van Til's original phrase, "as a unit", which goes back to his early apologetics syllabus (cf. Van Til, 1955:113). But Schaeffer also adds to this his own existential perspective.

The Epistemological Answer

Schaeffer (1982a:306) says that the Greek philosophers and Plato in particular were looking for universals to "make the particulars meaning-ful". This move from particulars to universals is "the very substance of how we actually know". The third area of philosophy, then, is concerned with the universals (absolutes) that make predication possible. This may seem to be an unusual way to begin a discussion of epistemology, but the transcendental direction of Schaeffer's philosophy must be kept in mind. Just as moral absolutes are required "to cover all the particulars" in ethics, this "is even more important in the area of knowledge". The universals offered by Plato and the Greeks (the Forms, the polis, the gods, the fates) were simply "not big enough" to bring the particulars together (1982a:307). In fact, without adequate universals, all one is left with are meaningless particulars (1982a:308-309). The history of this problem was covered in *Escape from Reason* and is summarized in this third book (1982a:311-314).

What Schaeffer (1982a:310) adds in this discussion is the idea that positivism, through its "romantic" notion of "total objectivity", affirmed that finite reason could "make universals out of the particulars". Thus, the concept of autonomous freedom took its most arrogant form in modern scientism. The contradiction, of course, is that this postulate represents an upper-story freedom placed over against a lower-story determinism. Positivism is now dead because, as Polanyi argues, "it does not consider the *knower* of what is known", ignoring "the knower's theories or presuppositions" (1982a:314). The ideal of the "objective observer is utterly naïve" and neutrality is a myth (cf. Clouser, 1991).

Schaeffer (1982a:314) detects an even greater problem in positivism based on his principle of unified interpretation. In applying this principle to positivism, "there is no way of saying with certainty that anything exists". Beginning "nakedly with nothing there", positivism as a system provides no reason or universal assuring the knower that "data" or anything else is ultimately there (1982a:315). Also, the knower has no assurance of any correspondence between the subject (the observer) and the object of knowledge. And finally, Popper's falsifiability principle not only denies the possibility of verification but is self-refuting, being accepted as a foundational principle beyond question. The end game of positivism, as the early Wittgenstein discovered, is that "there is only silence in the area of the things man desperately needs most—values, ethics, and meanings" if naked facts and language are all one has in the area of reason (1982a:316). Wittgenstein's choice of the word "silence" to describe what he placed in the upper-story inspired the title of the third book of the trilogy. Thus, at a deeper level, positivism agrees with existentialism with respect to "an 'upstairs' of total silence" (1982a:317). In the final analysis, all language philosophy is "antiphilosophy", since "language leads to language, and that is all"— notwithstanding the later Wittgenstein and the later Heidegger (cf. 1982a:199).

It should be recalled that the Reformers had no problem with language because of their commitment to propositional divine revelation (Schaeffer, 1982a:323; cf. 345-349). Like Wittgenstein and Heidegger, the Reformers understood that something must be spoken in order to know anything, and they also knew that universals were not possible through finite human speaking alone. Only on the presuppositions of "propositional, verbalized revelation" and "the uniformity of natural causes in a *limited* system, open to reordering by God and by man" could one find an answer to the problem of nature and grace (1982a:324, 325). The humanistic presupposition of "the uniformity of natural causes in a closed system" simply makes the Christian presuppositions "unthinkable" (1982a:324). But the humanistic (naturalistic) view leads to "dehumanization", reducing the human being to a mere "verbalizer" (1982a:325). For Schaeffer, a presupposition is "a base, and we can choose it" (1982a:326). Therefore, we can choose between the biblical and humanistic presuppositions about the nature of the universe and language. In doing so, the choice is made between the God who is there and speaks absolutely and there really being "no one there to speak" (1982a:327). Within the "Christian structure", there is nothing "unlikely" or "surprising" about the biblical presuppositions. In fact, a silent God who made verbalizing creatures would obviously be the "unlikely" proposition (1982a:328). Within the humanistic structure, its own presuppositions are irrational and unlivable. At bottom, "it is a question of which of these two sets of presuppositions really and empirically meets the facts as we look about us in the world" (1982a:327). Using tests A and B, the answer is obvious: Only the Christian system meets the coherence and correspondence tests. Thus, the choice of presuppositions is not a leap of faith but is based on good and sufficient reasons—"it is totally reasonable".

The falsification of the humanistic answer is that life in this world cannot be lived consistently on the humanistic base: "we must live in it acting on a correlation of ourselves and the thing that is, even if we have a philosophy that says there is no correlation" (Schaeffer, 1982a: 330). The subject-object and cause-effect correlations challenge "the most consistent concept of unrelatedness" (Hume), and only the Christian system explains these correlations. Language, in turn, is a sufficient tool to accurately embody human knowledge of the world. Though words are used differently based on personal backgrounds and experiences, there is sufficient overlap based on a common world and experience to insure accurate, though not exhaustive, communication (1982a:332). This applies to the Christian's knowledge of God as well. Since "nobody knows anything exhaustively except God", creaturely knowledge is limited but nevertheless true and certain because a reasonable God correlated "the categories of my mind to the universe, simply because I have to live in it" (1982a:333, 335). Even non-Christian philosophers have noted "uniform" mental categories (Kant, Levi-Strauss, Chomsky). The Christian is not surprised at this but asks, "What do you expect?" (1982a:335.) This state of affairs in epistemology applies to external knowledge of the world and to the inward reality of the self—"the real person who is there" (1982a:338).

The Christian's North Star

The conclusion of the third book of the trilogy—and of the trilogy itself—is stated as a transcendental conclusion: "No other system has an apex under which everything fits. That is why I am a Christian and no longer an agnostic." (Schaeffer, 1982a:339.) This gives the Christian and the non-Christian "some way to begin" under "the unity of the same norms, in regard to both values and knowing" (1982a:341). Thus, the Christian system is a "North Star" by which to navigate this world, a "bridge" between the inner and outer worlds, and a basis for "the beauty of creativity" (1982a:341, 343). Why is this conclusion transcendental? Schaeffer's answer is that the Christian's North Star is the *only* star by which to triangulate certain knowledge. Reugsegger (1986c:33) misconstrues the force of Schaeffer's argument by interpreting him as offering a "better" set of presuppositions than the non-Christian offers. But Schaeffer does not contend that Christianity merely "explains more" than unbelieving systems. Like other critics, Reugsegger may think that Van Til rejected verificational tests and evidences, thereby setting Schaeffer off from presuppositionalism by his use of "evidential" tests. But, like Schaeffer, Van

Til also "repeatedly advances evidential considerations" (1986c:34). He simply does this on the basis of biblical presuppositions—an approach already noted in Schaeffer's own words. Like Morris (1976:58), Reugsegger (1986b:110) applies a foundationalist critique to Schaeffer and finds him wanting. Like many others, he does not criticize Schaeffer on his own terms.

8 SCHAEFFER'S PERSPECTIVALISM

Having identified Schaeffer's system, it is now possible to analyze the ways in which triperspectivalism is reflected in Schaeffer's trilogy, especially with respect to the existential perspective. Up to this point, the study has been focused on preparation; from this point on, the study will be focused on fulfilling the goal of viewing Schaeffer through the lens of Frame' triperspectivalism. Given a precise understanding of both Frame and Schaeffer, it is now possible to demonstrate that Schaeffer does, in fact, present a perspectival apologetic that meets the requirements of a cogent presuppositional system. Because both systems have been presented in detail, the analysis may be presented more concisely as a kind of perspectival blueprint of Schaeffer's system.

At the outset of the study, presumptive evidence was offered that Frame provides the best tool for analyzing Schaeffer. It was noted that Boa and Bowman (2001:502) discuss Schaeffer and Frame as representatives of the same integrationist approach to apologetics. Additional evidence of alignment between Frame and Schaeffer is presented by Follis (2006:86, 95-96, 122), though Frame is nowhere mentioned in the context. In an interview with Follis (2006:86), Gavin McGrath, a L'Abri worker, reported "that Schaeffer was adopting the 'perspectibility' approach whereby at certain points certain perspectives need to be emphasized though not given a higher importance". This approach explains why Schaeffer emphasized "the rational faculties" (Frame's normative perspective) in dealing with students influenced by Eastern religions: "Emphasizing certain perspectives and downplaying others was a common approach adopted by Schaeffer." (2006:96.) The prevalence of "irrationalism and an impersonal worldview" elevated the importance of "rational argument" and "human personality" within his system (2006:122). The fact that "some of Schaeffer's L'Abri colleagues" understood him in this way and even used a term roughly synonymous with Frame's terminology provides strong support for the contention that Schaeffer was a perspectival thinker. While an attentive reader may readily see corresponding thought patterns between Frame as a theoretical model and Schaeffer as an illustrative case of triperspectival apologetics, it is necessary to draw those lines of correspondence more clearly.

Because the study focuses primarily on Schaeffer's existential perspective, it is also important to emphasize this perspective in his apologetic above the other two perspectives. It should be recalled that Frame's notion of the identity of perspectives means that each perspective is really the other two from a different vantage point. Therefore, it is impossible to separate the perspectives as isolated categories. They bleed or flow into each other, which means that the perspectives inform and require each other. Therefore, in showing how the existential perspective in Schaeffer is related to his normative and situational perspectives, it will be helpful to recast his apologetic as primarily existential. This is consistent with Schaeffer's own practice of emphasizing certain perspectives over others and Frame's principle of the identity of perspectives. It is also consistent with Schaeffer's principle of the balance of form and freedom (relativity), which allows for the reformulation and rephrasing of Christian truth within biblical boundaries.

Because Frame's existential perspective concerns the self as a locus of divine presence and revelation, how does the human self relate and respond to the divine Self? Answering this question perspectivally suggests the reformulation of Schaeffer's apologetic evangelism in terms of its basic principles in existential form. Four structural themes emerge from Schaeffer's apologetic as it is developed in the trilogy, and these may be stated and developed from the existential perspective. They are listed in the order in which they are presented in *The God Who is There*: (1) The antithesis principle as the radical category; (2) The divine Self as the radical reality; (3) Faith as a "step" not a "leap"; (4) Apologetics as an appeal to personal integrity. Each of these themes reflects Frame's existential perspective, which focuses "on our own inwardness, our personal experience, in which God has chosen to be near us" (Frame, 2010c:11). The subsidiary issues of this perspective are also implied in this formulation: (1) The certainty of faith as "cognitive rest" or confidence; (2) The antithesis of belief and unbelief in terms of personal choice; (3) Faith as an expression of personal rectitude or integrity. Having analyzed and explained the systems of both Frame and Schaeffer, it is now possible to show their corresponding thought patterns and the depth and cogency that Frame's analysis lends to Schaeffer. In doing so, it will be helpful to abbreviate Frame's perspectives because of their familiarity and the need to refer to them frequently and in many contexts: (NP) Normative Perspective; (SP) Situational Perspective; (EP) Existential Perspective.

The Antithesis Principle as the Radical Category

For Schaeffer (1982a:10, 184), the antithesis principle is the radical category of the self with respect to thought and life: While "absolutes imply antithesis" (NP) and antithesis is "rooted in reality" (SP), the human mind was "created to think in the category of antithesis" (EP). Antithesis is the radical or root category of the self because human beings not only think antithetically, but they also feel and act antithetically. It was noted that the disjunction of reason and meaning is an antithetical act of reason that denies reason, but feelings are also experienced in this way. Schaeffer's key concept of the "line of despair" reflects a disappointed *hope* with respect to an existential *need* for unified truth (1982a:8). Optimism and pessimism are the emotional corollaries of an antithetical choice or decision (EP) that is also rational (NP). Moral choice is also governed by this principle, since one's antithetical choice between belief and unbelief will determine moral action. The "basic antithesis is that God objectively exists" as opposed to not existing (NP), but the existential corollary is that humankind subjectively exists according to the same principle. In short, one cannot divide the field of knowledge without dividing the self.

Antithesis is both a personal and interpersonal principle. As a personal principle, antithesis is required for thought communication within the self (Schaeffer, 1982a:58). The principle also provides a necessary basis for communication with other persons (1982a:7). Thus, the antithesis principle is "existentially undeniable" (Geisler, 1976:143-144). In practice, no one can "totally reject the methodology of antithesis" (Schaeffer, 1982a:58). The consequence of rejecting antithesis by an act of antithetical reasoning is self-alienation, which is an existential condition of intellectual, psychological, and moral separation within the self. Taking into account that the meaninglessness experienced in self-alienation is not acceptable to human nature because of the need for unified truth, "the optimistic jump" is the only remedy short of an antithetical act of repentance toward God and faith in Christ (1982a:61).

What is missed by critics like Pinnock (1977:32) is that Schaeffer's existential mode of argument and practical thrust are not simply based on a "utilitarian" concern "with the practical effects of believing one set of presuppositions rather than another". As a perspectival apologist, his normative and situational concerns also determine the argument. The biblical presupposition of human creation in the divine image in a revelational environment provides the norm for Schaeffer's (1982a:61, 179) view of human nature (NP), and so "God shuts everyone up to the fact of reality, and everyone has to deal with the reality that is" (SP). The "fact of reality" as Schaeffer develops this is clearly reality as God interprets it in nature and Scripture—a reality that must, in turn, be interpreted through the faculties of human subjectivity (EP). Thus, the identity of perspectives is clearly illustrated by the antithesis principle as a radical category.

The Divine Self as the Radical Reality

While the antithesis principle comes first in *The God Who is There*, the divine Self is the radical reality in Schaeffer's Christian theism and the basis for the principle of antithesis. The formulation of this principle is inspired by the title of Gonzalez's (2005) work on Ortega y Gasset's philosophy of subjectivity, *Human Existence as Radical Reality*. At many points, Schaeffer's existential philosophy is the Christian mirror image of Ortega's system. Ortega correctly recognized that "radical reality" is a person, not impersonal Being. However, he identified the human self as the radical reality, not the divine Self, as in Schaeffer. Gonzalez (2005:x) agrees with Ortega that "existential concerns have always been those human concerns that are embraced by our own self-conscious subjectivity". He also agrees that "only from such self-awareness of our subjectivity can a vital individuality flow". And like Schaeffer (and Frame), Ortega recognizes that reality, as humans experience it, "is always perspectival" (2005:xi). The problem is that the human self is not the radical reality and is not a sufficient reference point for itself. Therefore, the divine subjectivity is the necessary corollary to human subjectivity and its point of reference (Calvin).

So why is the divine Self as radical reality an existential principle rather than merely a metaphysical or epistemological principle? While for Schaeffer (1982a:9) it is clearly all three, the existential perspective is concerned with a personal choice—a decision—concerning the "integration point" for "all knowledge, meaning and value". More specifically, which self—divine or human—defines the unity of thought and life? Which rational mind draws the line between knowledge and mystery? While unbelief chooses in favor of the human self, Schaeffer affirms with Sartre (and Ortega) that human finitude does not and cannot provide a "sufficient reference point" for certain knowledge (1982a:100; cf. Gonzalez, 2005:72). Schaeffer's definitions of rationalism and humanism reflect the apostate choice of beginning from the finite individual. The "unified rationalistic circle" is the apostate alternative to the unity of thought under God and leads to a rationalist-irrationalist dialectic (1982a:10). In the case of both believer and unbeliever, the unity of thought (NP) is existential because it involves the total personality choosing a self-reference (EP). Thus, the divine Self defines the human self.

The Trinity is obviously a key presupposed norm (NP) in Schaeffer's system, and as radical reality, the triune God defines personal subjectivity (EP). The Trinity is required for a personal integration point, since God must originate what defines the human self and "answers to the basic needs of modern man" (Schaeffer, 1982a:93). In other words, Christianity must provide "an adequate and reasonable explanation for the source and meaning of human personality" (1982a:94). "Basic needs" (EP) define human subjectivity in terms of feelings and aspirations toward hope, purpose, love, moral motions, beauty, communication, and compassion (1982a:93). Of these needs, love especially requires an ultimate personal reference point: "The validity and meaning of love rest upon the reality that love exists between the Father and Son in the Trinity." (1982a:106.)

The normative and situational perspectives with respect to this existential principle are now easy to summarize. The unity of thought in the divine mind is a presupposed norm based on Scripture (NP), and a revelational creation and human being reflect a situation or environment in which facts, proofs, and evidences (SP) bear on human subjectivity (EP). Nature and Scripture are both "certain" witnesses to a holistic truth that is not exhaustive, and certain witnesses are what the self needs for certain knowledge (Schaeffer, 1982a:100). Human needs—whether emotional or intellectual—define the existential perspective in Schaeffer as they do in Frame. Again, the identity of perspectives is reflected in a principle that necessarily combines normative presuppositions, situational proofs, and existential persuasion in an inseparable triad where the existential perspective may be given first priority in apologetic situations where this proves useful.

Faith as a "Step" Not a "Leap"

The exercise of faith is clearly existential since individuals must take this step as whole persons. The manner in which this step is taken is a central issue in Schaeffer (1982a:15), who forbids exercising faith as a non-rational "leap". Since "the whole man" must believe, all three of Frame's perspectives are clearly reflected in the antithetical choice between truth and falsehood as total systems (1982a:61). It is possible, nevertheless, to highlight the existential dimension of belief, showing how the nature of this decision is determined by the human self as divinely created.

Regarding faith, Schaeffer (1982a:182, 16) teaches that one believes on the basis of "good and sufficient reasons" without "the absolute separation of the rational and logical from faith". In other words, individuals believe that which "answers to the basic needs of modern man" with certainty (1982a:93). "Good" reasons are those that appeal to individuals as valuable in warranting faith, thus reflecting a virtue epistemology that is consistent with an existential perspective. Certain answers are those that rise above a mere "probability" position, and "sufficient" reasons are those able to satisfy the subjective need for adequate proof (1982a:181). Such needs reveal the personal motives at the heart of faith. Thus, while reason (NP) and proof (SP) are necessary conditions of Christian faith, the self in its rational and moral makeup must be enabled to respond to proofs and evidences in order to be fully persuaded (EP). "Knowledge precedes faith" (NP) because anything less cannot be communicated in the rational terms approved by Scripture and appropriate to the makeup of the human self (1982a:154). And yet, the personal presence of the Holy Spirit (EP) is also necessary to enable persuasion (1982a:185).

It is not necessary to belabor the relationship of the existential perspective to the other two perspectives with respect to the principle of faith as a step (Schaeffer, 1982a:24, 178). The promises of God (NP) and biblical evidences (SP) play a necessary part in taking the step of faith (1982a:15, 153-154). The unity of believing thought (NP) is grounded in revelation and creation (SP). "God shuts us up to reality", which forces the self to respond to its created environment according to divine revelation within (EP) and without (SP) the self (1982a:178, 341). These dynamics enable a "living orthodoxy" of the whole person in which the step of faith can be taken only in the unity of truth (1982a:61).

Given the importance of verification in Schaeffer's system, it is also necessary to analyze this concept in relation to the existential perspective. Verification is normative with respect to the "total rationale" of the Christian system, situational with respect to proofs and evidences, and existential with respect to the antithetical choice between truth and falsehood as total systems (Schaeffer, 1982a:65). It has been noted that Schaeffer's qualifications of the coherence and correspondence tests appeal to the existential perspective. Explanatory adequacy and livability (experiential fit) reflect the existential demands (needs) of the human self, which is why any theology declaring "immunity from proof" (SP) undermines the certainty of faith (EP) and denies the verificational structure of Scripture (1982a:101). The principle of antithesis enters at this point also, implying a single system that rises to the top as *uniquely* sufficient (1982a:185-186). In the final analysis, there is no pluralism at the worldview level to poison

Christian certainty with agnosticism. Thus, the believer's holistic or unified interpretation (NP) serves the cognitive rest of faith (EP).

Hypothesis testing and the transcendental argument also reflect the existential perspective. While hypothesis testing is based on the presupposition of "the God who is there according to the Scriptures" (NP), the goal of such testing is to verify the Christian hypothesis as uniquely sufficient (Schaeffer, 1982a:101). Again, the need to verify a system of truth over against inadequate systems reveals the existential motivation of Christian hypothesis testing. The goal is the truth, not the testing, so one begins with the expectation that the need for truth as a guide for life will not be disappointed. Because worldviews are adjudicated as wholes, one must use a transcendental argument (SP), presupposing the Christian God and the non-Christian's position for the sake of argument (NP). The holistic approach of the transcendental argument is not simply an arbitrary subjective choice. It not only reflects the integration of metaphysics, epistemology, and ethics in all reasoning (NP), but it also reflects the unity of the whole person (EP). It also provides for the certainty of faith (EP), rising above induction and retroduction, which yield only probability positions.

Deduction, while providing for logical certainty, also falls short of a transcendental method, since the biblical worldview is not a deductive system in the first place and must be formalized as an analogical system that includes paradoxical doctrines (Frame, 1976:295-330). Like Frame, Schaeffer understands the Bible's teaching as an "ectypal" or creaturely system (1976:312). An ectypal system is a finite replica of God's "archetypal" thought, a receptive reconstruction of God's revelation reflecting both interdependent and paradoxical doctrines. Interdependent doctrines are "somehow in tension with one another" due to limitations of "our created status and by God's sovereign limitation of revelation" (1976:320, 321). Schaeffer (1982b:166-167) affirms this view in popular terms by rejecting a deductive system in favor of a balance of form and freedom in theology. His view of doctrine as "a circle and not a point" and his reference to "the swings of the pendulum in church history" are metaphorical descriptions of biblical doctrines that are interdependent and yet in tension (1982b:166, 167). No other conception of theological system fits Schaeffer, and his rejection of both scholastic orthodoxy and Neo-orthodoxy is further evidence that he agreed with Van Til and Frame on this point. Thus, the unity of the person (EP) and the unity of truth (NP)—analogically understood—demand a presuppositional mode of argument (SP). However, rationality provides only "a form" for knowing; it is clearly not the sole basis for faith (1982a:124).

Reymond (1976:142-143) criticizes Schaeffer for violating his presuppositional principles by inviting both the Christian and the non-Christian "to judge Christianity with an apostate epistemology". Because Schaeffer allows Christian teaching to be measured by "what we observe", and because the unbeliever does not interpret what he observes by Christian teaching, Schaeffer is therefore allegedly offering grounds by which the unbeliever "can conclude that Christianity is false" (1982a:142, 143). What is worse, according to Reymond, is that Schaeffer grants the Christian the right, as a matter of "integrity", to question whether or not God exists and whether the Christian system is true (1982a:143). In a private conversation, Reymond confirmed Schaeffer's belief that "the Christian himself should always be willing sincerely to reexamine these questions as to the possibility of his having been 'taken in' by his Christian commitment".

Reymond's criticism falls short for two reasons. First, Schaeffer's commitment to holistic interpretation means that he cannot bring an apostate epistemology to bear on the question of the truth of the Christian faith, since all systems must be judged by their own criteria. A set of commonly recognized philosophical problems may be brought to all systems for solutions, but this is not the same as starting with an apostate epistemology. Moreover, Schaeffer's own truth tests, as already noted, are scriptural tests—not neutral tests. Second, questioning God's existence and the truth of the Christian system is existentially inescapable since the human mind is designed to think presuppositionally. Given the variety of worldviews, one must hypothesize on the basis of different presuppositional sets in an attempt to understand why Christian commitment is superior to all others. One need not begin in unbelief or suspend belief in any absolute sense to do this. Indeed, an honest answer to those who claim that Christians have been taken in by their own beliefs requires a demonstration of integrity, and this assumes that one has looked at this "possibility" for the sake of argument. Questioning oneself is an acknowledgement of personal finitude and fallibility, not a program for reasoning hypothetically on the basis of an apostate epistemology. Because humans lack omniscience as presuppositional thinkers, they will inevitably question their thoughts and beliefs. In theory, one can conceive a state of affairs in which God created the world but did not reveal himself adequately to provide the necessary conditions for human knowledge. Thus, agnosticism is a valid option to be entertained for the sake of argument.

Apologetics as an Appeal to Personal Integrity

The fourth structural theme in Schaeffer's apologetic gets to the heart of the rationale for this study. Personal rectitude concerns the judicial sentiment or "imperative essence" of human beings (Carnell, 2007b:17). While this term relates primarily to moral "uprightness" (2007b:16), it applies to the whole person as an *ought*: What ought one to think, feel, and do? As a judicial sentiment, it is the impulse to judge between systems of belief, moral options, and ways of feeling. It reveals itself as a concern for personal consistency, an attraction to harmony, and an aversion to tension. While human sinfulness frustrates this drive, it is nevertheless universal. Even intellectual consistency, which is often considered more a matter of formal logic than personal integrity, demands that one honor the principle of antithesis at the heart of reality and oneself as a moral commitment to honesty and truth. Without the "imperative essence", rationality becomes a utilitarian tool or an optional convention. Given both the "imperative essence" of human beings and the frustration of that essence by sin, apologetics proceeds on the basis of an existential tension at the heart of the self.

It is noteworthy that presuppositionalists generally and Schaeffer especially have developed an apologetic strategy on this existential foundation. Traditional apologetics sometimes reflects a narrow intellectualism, treating belief and unbelief almost purely in terms of the adequacy of arguments and proportions of evidence with respect to Christian certainty. Schaeffer's (1982a:132-133) apologetic strategy, however, capitalizes on the created form of the world and human nature, which prevents consistent living on the basis of apostate presuppositions. Since "Christianity is the truth of what is there", every person is caught "in a place of tension" between his own thought life and the world as God created it (1982a:132). For this reason, the non-Christian's experience is described as "the pull of two consistencies, the pull towards the real world and the pull toward the logic of his system" (1982a:133). Without the existential drive for personal integrity, wholeness, and consistency, there would simply be no tension, no pull to be addressed by apologetics. Thus, the relevance and appeal of the Christian gospel are based on its ability to address an existential condition, not just its power to solve intellectual problems of belief and unbelief.

The perspectival consistency of Schaeffer's (1982a:140) existential method is reflected in the dynamics of "taking the roof off" to expose the unbeliever's "point of tension" or inconsistency. This operation exposes the need (EP) for a uniquely sufficient answer or proof (SP), which is also scriptural (NP). Perspectively speaking, the Christian answer is biblically normative and provides a proof sufficient to the situation, allowing the appeal to be maximally persuasive if it addresses the individual's true point of tension in the power of the Holy Spirit. The point of conversion becomes "the point of personal antithesis" (1982a:141), the point at which the basic choice between belief and unbelief is put before the hearer in the preaching of the gospel (EP). Thus, for Schaeffer (1982a:144), the gospel provides a solution serving as "a total structure of truth" (NP) as it seeks to "press" the hearer "in the direction of honesty" (EP). Exposing the "false balance" of non-Christians also appeals to the integrity and sympathy of the apologist, who must understand "with integrity . . . the reality of the dark path they are treading" (1982a:138, 144). Clearly, triperspectivalism illuminates this apologetic strategy in a profound way without forcing Frame's categories in the process of applying them to Schaeffer's apologetic.

What Schaeffer (1982a:165) calls the "visible quality" in apologetics is likely his most celebrated contribution to apologetics and reflects his existential perspective: "The final apologetic . . . is what the world sees in the individual Christian and in our corporate relationships together." In what may be the most succinct triperspectival summary of his apologetic, Schaeffer links this "final apologetic" (EP) with "the rational [NP], logical [SP] defense and presentation" of the Christian faith—all within a single sentence! Schaeffer (1982a:167) even credits to the existentialists on this point: "Demonstrating God's character must be existential. The existentialists are right at this place, though they are wrong when they say history is not going anywhere." This existential quality is based on Schaeffer's point that "personality is central" to the Christian worldview because God is fully personal (1982a:168). Because the divine Self is the radical reality, the human self of the apologist is also central to apologetic practice. Without the "reality of personality" individually and corporately in the Church, the world simply will not accept the ultimate Personality behind it all (1982a:169). Thus, *living truthfully* upon the truth of what is" should be the goal of apologetic evangelism for those who preach and those who hear (1982a:187). And yet, living truthfully has no urgency, no appeal, no "pull" without the "imperative essence" of human nature. Personal integrity, then, is at the heart of the gospel's appeal and the world's expectation that Christians will practice what they preach consistently and substantially.

Existential Certainty and Necessity

The value of a perspectival meta-apologetic for the analysis of a popular apologist like Schaeffer is that it allows for a more subtle analysis of concepts usually treated too narrowly. Schaeffer's concepts of certainty and necessity illustrate this point, since they are typically viewed only from the perspective of epistemic (logical) certainty and necessity. It should now be evident that Schaeffer's system is a perspectival and analogical system, not a deductive system with categories exhausted by reason alone. As an existential system, Schaeffer's apologetic must be assessed by how well it explains the dynamics of the self in relation to God. On the issue of certainty and necessity especially, Schaeffer has offered a sound analysis, which most of his critics have missed entirely.

Christian certainty has been problematic in apologetics because of the lack of a normative perspective. It should be recalled that Frame's primary problem with other Christian apologists is their lack of acknowledged biblical norms for fear of begging the question, or reasoning in a circle. It will also be recalled that Schaeffer nowhere falls into the trap of pretending or granting neutrality but openly acknowledges the dependence of his analysis on Scripture. Approaching truth holistically, Schaeffer—like Frame—was able to analyze the certainty of faith and the necessity of the Christian answer from epistemic (SP), psychological (EP), and biblical (NP) perspectives, rather than assessing these concepts from the epistemic and psychological perspectives alone. Among apologists lacking the normative perspective, the analysis of these concepts typically yields some mixture of logical probability (SP) and psychological certitude (EP). Depending on the method of argument used, Christian certainty is defined on a continuum ranging from deductive certainty to various inductive levels in descending order from moral and practical certitude to "rational believability" as possibly the weakest form of certainty (Frame, 2000:308).

The problem with separating epistemic and psychological certainty is stated by Frame (2006a:142): "Whatever level of warrant is required for epistemic certainty, it must be a level that gives psychological confidence." In essence, "epistemic certainty is reducible to psychological certainty", although the two may be perspectivally distinguished. Frame notes that our "psychological feelings of certainty" should conform to "objective principles of knowledge", making psychological and epistemic certainty "mutually dependent". Frame also recognizes that the Bible affirms that Christians "can, should, and do know God and the truths of revelation" in a non-tentative way (2006a:143). According to the Bible, "God's special revelation is certain, and we ought to be certain about it." (cf. Mat 9:6, 11:27, 13:11; Luk 1:4; Joh 7:17, 8:32, 10:4-5, 14:17, 17:3; Act 1:3; 2Ti 3:16-17; Heb 6:13, 18-19; 2Pe 1:19-21.) Doubt, however, is "the opposite of faith" and is "a spiritual impediment" (cf. MAT 14:31, 21:21, 28:17; ACT 10:20, 11:12; ROM 14:23; 1TI 2:8; JAM 1:6). Doubt "in the face of clear special revelation" is sinful, but doubt due to ignorance is not. In much of life, confidence rather than certainty must be our goal, but absolute certainty is the ideal response to special revelation. Since God's Word is the normative criterion of Christian certainty (NP), "what God says *must* be true, for . . . it is impossible for God to lie" (2006a:143; cf. JOH 17:17; PSA 33:4, 119:160; HEB 6:18; TIT 1:2; 1JO 2:27). Frame's "must" in this context conveys the biblical sense of Schaeffer's concept of necessity. Such certainty requires "an act of God, through the testimony of his Spirit" and "often accompanies a human process of reasoning". Thus, absolute certainty "is essentially supernatural".

Schaeffer takes these biblical norms into account, which explains in part his rejection of probability as an adequate standard for Christian certainty. His employment of transcendental reasoning also reflects his commitment to the goal of absolute certainty with respect to God's special revelation, for transcendental coherence does aim at epistemic certainty, not probability. While particular issues within the Christian system may be doubtful or held with confidence only and not absolute certainty, commitment to the Christian system as a whole should not be viewed as probable or tentative given the scriptural account of certainty. While Schaeffer is not as explicit as Frame concerning the biblical account of certainty, at the very least he recognizes that the biblical account does not warrant a probability position with respect to the Christian worldview as a system of belief.

Schaeffer's account of epistemic certainty is consistent with and dependent upon his account of psychological certainty, which expresses the existential perspective. It is possible to read Schaeffer's philosophical apologetic in *He is There and He is Not Silent* from the existential perspective, noting how the needs of the self (EP) require the presuppositional form of argument he uses (SP). These perspectives—in turn—depend on the biblical norms of Christian certainty and necessity (NP). The three philosophic necessities he considers reflect an infrastructure of personal faith that is existentially powerful precisely because it lines up with biblical norms. Because existential motives are validated by Scripture, they may not be dismissed simply as Schaeffer's own idiosyncratic or utilitarian preferences (Pinnock). They reflect the certainty of faith and the necessity of Christian truth as the Bible presents these concepts.

Given that Schaeffer's unified argument has already been elaborated, it will be helpful to highlight the existential qualities of the argument. By narrowing down the philosophic possibilities to what amounts to only two alternatives, he allows for a binary decision based on explanatory adequacy. This is a very effective strategy and has also been used persuasively by Pascal (1995:6, 19, 37), notably in his fragments on life without God as a diversionary project (24, 70, 132, 134). The strategy employs a binary decision where each fork in the road leads to another fork requiring another binary decision. It is this strategy that gives the argument its feel of necessity—the word *feel* being used here for its existential import and without apology. Pascal's logical progression is not the unbreakable logic of a metaphysical system or a rigorous proof; rather, it is the inescapable logic of humanity's existential situation. In Pascal's strategy, one cannot escape the argument because one cannot escape the situation. The premises in his disjunctive syllogism (fragment 134) are not indubitable propositions; they are inescapable and undeniable conditions. This is what makes his approach powerful and profound; it is the logic of lived experience, not merely the logic of systematic reason. Like Schaeffer's method, Pascal's approach to making Christianity attractive is fundamentally simple: (1) Explain the existential problem at the heart of human nature; (2) Show how Christianity alone solves that problem; (3) Provide the proof from the Bible's own witness to Jesus Christ through prophecy and miracles.

In the realm of metaphysics, Schaeffer's personal answer to the form of the world and human uniqueness reflects the existential perspective, the monistic alternatives being unlivable. No pantheist or naturalist lives consistently with the idea that personality is either an illusion or determined: "human consensus and the existential impossibility of living consistently with this theory discredit such a proposal" (Burson & Walls, 1998:185). While the transcendental thrust of Schaeffer's argument implies logical necessity, he clearly underscores existential necessity. For him, a position that cannot be lived imposes an existential choice or decision, so logical necessity is not the only way to explain how and why human beings choose positions as truth. For Schaeffer, an existential choice is one that involves the whole person, which is why both lived consistency and logical consistency are necessary conditions of belief. If an impersonal worldview cannot endow life with purpose or significance, then it fails to meet existential demands and is discredited.

In the realm of ethics, the uniqueness of humanity requires an answer to the dilemma of finitude and cruelty as two separate problems that may not be collapsed into one metaphysical problem. Naturalists, pantheists, and liberal theologians commit this error, thereby reducing morality "to different forms of sociological, statistical or situational relativism" (Burson

& Walls, 1998:187). The problem with this state of affairs is that "humans cannot rid themselves of the nagging notion that some things are truly right and others are truly wrong". One can attempt to stifle this moral sense, but in doing so, "moral motions are entirely abnormal, thoroughly absurd and finally futile". Again, the problem with an impersonal solution is that persons simply cannot live with the logical consequences of such a world as it relates to ethics. Thus, to account for the uniqueness of humanity, one must account for the "moral motions" of human beings as well, and only a personal answer provides what the self needs. Burson and Walls confirm this interpretation of Schaeffer: "by starting with a personal origin we can keep the metaphysical and moral issues separate, because a personal beginning provides the possibility of an ultimate ethical standard". Again, existential demands (EP), logical demands (SP), and an ultimate standard (NP) point to a "final option" that is "the only rationally defensible and existentially satisfying explanation to the human dilemma of finitude and cruelty" (1998:188). What is rationally defensible must also be existentially satisfying or it is not the truth.

In the realm of epistemology, there are also only two options to consider, the impersonal and the Christian personal answers. The problem of knowledge is simply Plato's old problem of universals and particulars. Given an impersonal interpretation of the universe and mankind, one has no universals to provide meaning and values. Even Plato's system failed to provide for values, since his Forms were not ordered by an infinite intelligence. The universals must somehow be related to one another, which requires a higher level universal to relate all universals. The problem in Western philosophy is that philosophers like Plato and Aristotle provided an account of universals over against an impersonal backdrop. In the end, there must be "one universal umbrella under which all the vast levels of diverse particulars and universals can fit" (Burson & Walls, 1998:191). Again, "Schaeffer contends that the infinite-personal, triune God of Christianity is the only universal that can rise above the rubble" of Western thought on the subject. Neither naturalistic nor idealistic monism provides "a fully integrated, holistic solution" (1998:190). Only a "verbal, propositional revelation" solves the problem of knowledge: "In Scripture, God speaks about himself (grace) and history and the cosmos (nature), providing a unified body of knowledge and meaning." (1998:195.) What is existentially significant here is the need for unified knowledge and meaning. Like moral motions—the "nagging notion" that some things are truly right or wrong—a unified body of knowledge is also a nagging existential need human beings were created to satisfy.

The Cogency of the Schaefferian Apologetic

The lack of a perspectival meta-apologetic, in my judgment, is the single greatest problem with Schaeffer's critics. Unlike his critics, Schaeffer reflects a perspectival consistency appropriate to an analogical system. Frame (1982) is clear that the problem of modern apologetics is its lack of biblical norms, and Schaeffer—unlike his critics—does not have this problem. His position on certainty and necessity illustrates this point: Each perspective agrees with the others concerning the biblical standard of certainty and the necessity of the Christian system (NP), the mode of argument that meets that standard (SP), and the experience of confidence or "cognitive rest" commensurate with that standard (EP). The perspectivalism that Frame developed and the perspectibility that Schaeffer intuited are clearly congruent, based on the comparison of these two theories and Frame's (2010a) own assessment of Schaeffer.

In the introduction to this study it was indicated that the cogency of Schaeffer's apologetic would derive from Frame's perspectival method, Schaeffer demonstrating the explanatory power of Frame's method and Frame demonstrating the consistency of Schaeffer's apologetic. Based on the presentation of each apologetic theory and the parallel thought patterns observed, I consider the argument of this study to be sound and compelling. It only remains to confirm this contention, and Frame's own assessment of Schaeffer provides the most important confirmation. In examining Frame's evaluation of Schaeffer, it will become evident that no major criticisms are offered touching the cogency of Schaeffer's system as a perspectival apologetic.

As a student at Westminster Seminary from 1961 to 1964, Frame was influenced by Schaeffer's (1948) *Bible Today* article, which reflected the influence of both Van Til and Buswell on Schaeffer (see Appendix). Frame (2010a:1) admits that Schaeffer's argument influenced him: "from then on I believed that the differences between Van Til's and the 'traditional' apologetic were somewhat less than Van Til understood them to be". By the time he completed his studies at Westminster, Frame "emerged fully convinced of biblical authority and presuppositional epistemology, modified a bit in Schaeffer's direction" (2010a:2). The specific modifications Frame mentions are two: (1) He agrees with Schaeffer that alternative hypotheses concerning God should be considered "for the sake of argument"; (2) He thought Schaeffer "very insightful" concerning his analysis "of the non-Christian's (and the Christian's) inconsistency and the fruitfulness of this inconsistency". Specifically, Frame says he "came out agreeing with Schaeffer, and not with Van Til, that it is legitimate to use the unbeliever's inconsistencies as a positive point of contact". It is noteworthy that Frame's agreements with Schaeffer did not inspire Frame's perspectivalism, but they are critical to arguing for the consistency of Schaeffer's method on the basis of Frame's principles.

Frame (2010a:3) also believes that Schaeffer's "emphasis on *both* presuppositions *and* verification is important; possibly even an advance over Van Til in emphasis". As was shown previously, Schaeffer's presuppositional verification was actually inspired by what Schaeffer learned from Van Til, but it appears that Schaeffer developed fully an insight that Van Til defined more narrowly. Frame also notes Schaeffer's emphasis on being able to live consistently on one's own presuppositions as an important apologetic insight, a realization that the rationalist-irrationalist dialectic "appears in practical life, not just in theory". Frame also affirms that "Schaeffer's apologetic is transcendental in a more explicit way than either Butler's or Carnell's" (2010a:5). With respect to the proper use of *ad hominem* arguments in apologetics, Frame says that Schaeffer challenges "the unbeliever's right to speak (and especially to live) as he does" (2010a:6). Frame identifies this as "perhaps the most persuasive element of Schaeffer's apologetic".

However, Frame (2010a:3) faults Schaeffer for his interpretation of modern philosophy and for recommending a return to the Greek view of "truth as antithesis". Hegel was "not the first to abandon true objectivity", and "Kant is more important than Hegel to the distinctively modern form of the dialecticism". Frame also believes that Schaeffer's writings convey the "impression" that he advocates "a neutral notion of truth apart from Scripture", even though Schaeffer told him in a private conversation that "he didn't mean to suggest this". Frame also thinks that requiring a commitment to antithesis as a condition for hearing the gospel represents "a sort of pre-preparationism" that contradicts Frame's view that "there is no preparation for grace". Rather, hearers should be educated about the truth from Scripture, which is evangelism, not pre-evangelism. Perhaps Frame's strongest criticism is that "Schaeffer does not make explicit the natural man's rejection of all legitimate standards of verification."

In Schaeffer's defense, it has already been made clear that he did not advocate a Greek notion of antithesis. Schaeffer (1982a:8) bases his concept on the scriptural teaching of God's existence: The objective existence of God, as opposed to his not existing, is "the basic antithesis". In our view, Frame has overlooked the point that Schaeffer was very careful to distinguish his view of truth and antithesis as based on Scripture, not the Greeks. Nor does Schaeffer believe that Hegel was the first to deny rational objectivity. He refers to the unity of non-Christian thought post-Hegel as essentially irrational, while the unity of thought prior to Hegel was essentially rational. This does not mean that Schaeffer viewed all apostate thought prior to Hegel as purely objective and rational. While Frame's analysis of the history of philosophy is more precise than Schaeffer's and his point about Kant well taken, Schaeffer's homiletic analysis is not discredited by this criticism. Schaeffer was concerned with the historical point at which modern irrationality began to shift the cultural consensus as a whole, and he saw this take place with Hegel and Kierkegaard, not with Kant. Despite Frame's (2010a:5) differences with Schaeffer on the history of philosophy, he affirms that these are "differences in detail and historical perspective, not differences in underlying commitment".

With respect to Frame's (2010a:3) more serious criticism that "Schaeffer does not make explicit the natural man's rejection of all legitimate standards of verification", I am left wondering why this is necessary in light of Frame's commitment to a "presuppositionalism of the heart". If Schaeffer's verificational tests are used in a broadly circular fashion—and the study has shown they are and Frame (2010a:4) agrees they are—then how does making the natural man's rejection of legitimate standards explicit improve Schaeffer's apologetic—or any apologetic for that matter? If apologetics is conveying the Christian rationale by broadly circular arguments, then affirming the non-Christian's rejection of all standards seems to imply that the natural man must reject all apologetic arguments, since all arguments are based on some method of verification. Apologetics calls the non-Christian to embrace scriptural tests for truth along with the gospel, so it hardly seems necessary to make explicit what— according to Frame—goes without saying. Indeed, Frame himself advocates the *practice* of presuppositional principles above their explicit statement, which makes this criticism of Schaeffer seem completely out of character. Frame's system does not stipulate that evidences and logical tests may be used only if their basis in scriptural revelation is announced at the outset. On this point of criticism, Frame's argument seems frankly inconsistent with his own principles.

In canvassing Frame's collected thoughts on Schaeffer's apologetic, it is important to insure that the author of the theoretical model of this study finds nothing fundamentally incompatible between Schaeffer's views and his own. The points of commendation and criticism above demonstrate to my satisfaction that Schaeffer's apologetic evangelism is consistent with Frame's modified presuppositionalism and represents a creative illustrative case of a triperspectival apologetic. By focusing on Schaeffer's existential perspective, an even more profound and illuminating view of Schaeffer is possible—a perspective that gets to the heart of his greatest contributions as an evangelical apologist.

Schaeffer's Christian Existentialism

It was established at the outset that one goal of this study is to confirm and extend Frame's perspectival theory through its application to Schaeffer, establishing Schaeffer's cogency in a new way. Given the prominence of existential themes in Schaeffer's trilogy as his best contributions to apologetics, it was assumed that this perspective provides the best vantage point from which to illustrate the power of Frame's theory and the cogency of Schaeffer. By carefully identifying Schaeffer's method in light of the criticism of his work and projecting it through the prism of Frame's theory, my original contention should now be evident: Frame's triperspectival Christian epistemology provides possibly the best available tool for understanding Schaeffer's apologetic in general and the existential perspective of his apologetic in particular.

The study has also taken note of the fact that Schaeffer's existential themes are not only his most valuable contributions; they are also a source of scholarly criticism. In elaborating these themes perspectivally, it should now be evident that these are developed within the larger context of a presuppositional and perspectival theory that strengthens and establishes their crucial role in a creative Christian apologetic. Schaeffer has been both praised and blamed for the existential perspective of his apologetic. It is praiseworthy, in my view, that Schaeffer fought secular existential fire with a Christian existentialism of his own—a strategy attempted by few contemporary evangelical apologists other than Schaeffer. In further confirming the cogency of Schaeffer's apologetic, it will be helpful to enlist the support of one highly-respected apologist whose existential apologetic resonates with Schaeffer's at many points and further illustrates the value and validity of his contributions.

SCHAEFFER, CARNELL & EXISTENTIALISM

9 CARNELL'S EXISTENTIAL CRITIQUE

In supporting Schaeffer's credibility, it is helpful to compare and contrast Schaeffer's existential perspective with those of Edward Carnell and secular existentialism, which both apologists opposed. Carnell (1919-1967) was a leading figure in the evangelical renaissance of the second half of the 20th Century, a popular teacher and productive writer who spent his postdoctoral career at Fuller Theological Seminary (Marsden, 1987:97). The relevance of Carnell to Schaeffer has already been established on the basis of their close association in the literature of apologetics. Boa and Bowman (2001:453-476) present them back-to-back as representatives of the integrationist approach, and Lewis (1976:300; 1986:93, 102; 1999) and Follis (2006:114-121) argue in favor of a verificational classification of both apologists. While it is evident that Schaeffer (1948:9) was influenced by Carnell's (1948:217) first work on apologetics—having quoted it—there is no evidence from Schaeffer's unpublished work or recorded lectures that he was following Carnell's approach (Follis, 2006:120).

It is evident that the formal similarities between Schaeffer and Carnell have led some apologists to attribute to them the same apologetic method. Clearly, Schaeffer and Carnell were presuppositional in the sense that both assumed the Christian system at the outset as the best explanation of the observed facts and the most existentially viable worldview. Both were willing to subject the trinitarian theistic presupposition or hypothesis to truth tests roughly equivalent to coherence, correspondence, and viability (cf. Carnell, 1948:56-64; Schaeffer, 1982a:121-123). Both also stressed the importance of the law of contradiction, Schaeffer doing so more in terms of the concept of antithesis. Based on these similarities, it has been argued that both are members of the verificationalist school.

There are, however, significant differences as well. Schaeffer's mode of argument is clearly transcendental, while Carnell's is retroductive or abductive (cf. Lewis, 1993:334; Montgomery, 1998:274). As already indicated, the transcendental argument infers a conclusion that is logically certain, while a retroductive argument infers a probable conclusion (cf. Carnell, 1948:113). This difference with respect to epistemic certainty is significant and may explain why Schaeffer preferred the language of presupposition to the language of hypothesis. In speaking of the application of his tests, Schaeffer (1982a:121) refers to "a theory" to be tested rather than a hypothesis. While the non-Christian may engage with the Christian worldview as a tentative hypothesis, the Christian believer does not present it as such. In considering answers that do not require a leap of faith, Schaeffer applies verificational tests to them as theories, not as tentative hypotheses. The issue for Schaeffer is not how these theories are held but how they fare with respect to the tests. They are "possible answers" as postulates that submit to testing according to the law of contradiction, the relevant phenomenon, and a broad consideration of human nature. Considering postulates as theories rather than as hypotheses may seem to be a distinction without a difference, but we believe that Schaeffer chose terminology that was more neutral with respect to how a worldview proposal is held at the outset by believers or unbelievers. Instead, theoretical proposals are tested without this concern, making it possible to simply look at worldview options for the sake of argument.

Given these differences, it is nevertheless evident that Schaeffer and Carnell share as much in common as Schaeffer and Van Til, although we believe that Schaeffer is best classified as presuppositional rather than verificational. Verificationalism is retroductive rather than transcendental, even though both methods reason from a set of conditions back to the preconditions that account for them (Knudsen, 1986:228). Thus, the retroductive and transcendental methods are formally similar in the same way that Carnell and Schaeffer are formally similar. Viewed according to the typology of Boa and Bowman, both are integrationist, presuppositional and verificational, but according to a typology of apologetic schools, Schaeffer is a presuppositionalist and Carnell a verificationalist.

The formal similarity between these two apologists is what makes Edward Carnell possibly Schaeffer's best scholarly ally. Both shared similar concerns over existentialism and Neo-orthodoxy, Carnell being an expert in both these areas, having done doctoral dissertations on Kierkegaard (Ph.D., Boston University) and Reinhold Niebuhr (Th.D., Harvard Divinity School). The fruits of this work were eventually published for a broader audience (Carnell, 2006, 2007d). Both apologists also shared the existential concern for the viability (Carnell) or livability (Schaeffer) of the Christian faith. Even more important, both Schaeffer and Carnell saw similar problems in existentialism and Neo-orthodoxy, Carnell providing the detailed analysis lacking in Schaeffer. While Carnell (2007b:73-79; 2006) was also concerned to develop Kierkegaard's spiritual legacy of inwardness, which Schaeffer (1982a:15) merely acknowledges, Carnell's criticisms of Kierkegaard resonate with Schaeffer's and develop them in more detail. For these reasons, Carnell provides scholarly support for and confirmation of Schaeffer's critique of existentialism and Neo-orthodoxy. At the same time, Carnell's great appreciation for Kierkegaard led him to develop an existential apologetic that also resonates with Schaeffer's own existential perspective. While it is not the goal of this study to critically evaluate Carnell's understanding of Kierkegaard, we are aware that some interpreters would differ from Carnell on the same grounds they would differ from Schaeffer (cf. Evans, 1981).

Carnell's (2007b:73) great appreciation for the existential perspective and for Kierkegaard in particular is best stated in his own words: "Without the stimulation of the Danish gadfly, I probably would never have learned to ask questions from the perspective of inwardness." Given this high praise, it is evident that Carnell's criticisms of Kierkegaard and his philosophical and theological legacy are balanced with the greatest respect for this spiritual genius and a desire to learn from him. This kind of balance is evident throughout Carnell's treatment, reflecting a level of scholarly accuracy and care that justified his reputation as one of the foremost scholars of contemporary evangelicalism (Marsden, 1987:180-181). Carnell embodies Ramm's (2000:109) "dialectical" approach to modern theologians, which appropriates their truth while also criticizing their errors.

Truth as Inwardness

Carnell (2007a:449) recognizes the importance of truth as inwardness, but inwardness alone is not the whole truth. The problem with the idea of truth as inwardness embraced by faith is that without an objective authority it degenerates into an unstable inwardness. Christian truth must be understood in terms of three "loci": (1) Reality itself—truth by acquaintance; (2) Judgments or propositions corresponding to reality—truth by inference; and (3) "Truth in the heart"—truth as subjectivity (2007a:453). This third locus is truth as inwardness, which Carnell defines as a character quality that expresses itself in love. These three loci require each other and represent the inner and outer experience of human consciousness (2007a:451). Interestingly, Carnell's three loci correspond to Frame's situational, normative, and existential perspectives respectively, and—like Schaeffer—Carnell's view of truth requires a connection to the facts of reality, evidence, rational propositions, and sincere faith in Christ (2007a:450, 449). If truth is defined in terms of the third locus alone, faith becomes a subjective leap that allegedly compensates for the lack of an objective authority. However, rejecting objective authority and evidence on the ground that they subvert spiritual potential, the individual masks autonomy under the pretense of spiritual freedom (2007a:449).

Truth as inwardness is personal truth (Carnell, 2007a:452). Jesus himself is "the way and the truth and the life" (JOH 14:6), which explains why the Christian faith "places a premium" on personal truth. Since God cannot be pleased apart from faith (HEB 11:6), truth cannot be defined purely on the basis of acquaintance or inference. However, truth as inwardness requires a rational system of truth for guidance (2007a:453). Reasoning from Scripture, Carnell (2007a:450) recognizes that the spirit and the mind must be engaged for understanding (1CO 14:14-15). Thus, the heart cannot believe the gospel unless its propositions are understood (2007a:454). This is equivalent to Schaeffer's view of faith and reason (cf. Lewis, 1993:322).

Existentialism went wrong by rejecting this understanding of faith and reason, attempting instead to interpret life in terms of "the existing, passionate individual himself" (Carnell, 2007a: 454). Like Schaeffer, Carnell recognized the faith-rationality split at the heart of existentialism. In theory, existential truth comes through a self-validating "inward concern" requiring no "propositional correspondence" to the world (2007a:455). If this is not an outright denial of reason, it certainly reflects the diminishing of reason that Schaeffer criticized. For Kierkegaard, a logical system can only anticipate reality and truth, whereas the existential system is about "*being* the truth" (2007a:456). Carnell (2007a:457) quotes Swenson, who describes this theory of existential truth as "a veritable Copernican revolution". Clearly, Schaeffer was not the only one to recognize the pivotal significance of Kierkegaard in the flow of Western thought (cf. Bretall, 1946:192).

Spirit as Freedom

In defining the essence of human nature, Kierkegaard turns from the physical and rational to freedom as the essential quality: "Spirit is freedom, and freedom is choice." (Carnell, 2007a:458.) Only freedom can take hold of the "rule of duty" in order to reflect the eternal in the temporal. When the individual chooses eternal values in time, at that instant passionate inwardness—truth—comes into existence. This translation or mediation of the eternal in time overcomes temporal necessity, synthesizing soul and body through spirit. Thus, truth comes into being through free choices in "moments of temporal decision" (2007a:460). In this way truth is existentially mediated, not rationally mediated (Hegel), committing the individual to continual striving through ethical decisions to become a self. This "existential assignment" cannot be completed, but passionate decision and self-becoming are fueled by its continual demand. Sin (untruth) is refusing to witness to one's eternal duty (truth) through lack of humility, resolve, or effort in the face of "self-despair" (2007a:461). Thus, truth is determined existentially, not epistemologically (cf. Bretall, 1946:153-161).

For Kierkegaard, then, freedom inevitably brings sinfulness, revealing both the responsibility to "be the truth" and its simultaneous impossibility (Carnell, 2007a:461). The tension of this paradoxical faith defines truth as "subjectivity" and is intensified by the biblical concept of *agape* love as its content. Love links time and eternity and makes the spirit dizzy with dread in the face of its impossible responsibility (2007a:464). One's "limitless duty" to God and the neighbor reflects an impossible duty since time and eternity are not transmutable (2007a:465). In this way, the dialectic becomes "absolutely strenuous".

Inwardness and Reason

Clearly, if Kierkegaard's goal was to make inwardness "absolutely strenuous", then anything that lessens or removes the strain becomes an obstacle to subjectivity (Carnell, 2007a:466). Reason is a stumbling block because it brings complacency into the person, a feeling of completeness that dissipates or dampens passionate inwardness. Carnell is careful to point out that Kierkegaard did not disparage "reason *per se*". However, Carnell is congruent with Schaeffer in his judgment of Kierkegaard's strategy: "Nevertheless, by restricting reason's domain, Kierkegaard *in fact* turned aside from reason. Reason reads off the implications of logical relations in order that spirit (for that reason) might not believe them."

Carnell (2007a:467) recognized that this strategy "reversed the order" of previous Christian thinkers who grounded faith in "the reasonable". Instead, Kierkegaard demanded that faith derive its impetus and strength from the passion of objective uncertainty. In effect, he so defined human faith that reason must be a stumbling block because faith is a paradoxical passion in which its strength is inversely proportional to its objective uncertainty. Contrary to Carnell's evidentialist proportionality principle is what we would call Kierkegaard's inverse proportionality principle: "set the subjective witness in opposition to the objective, proportioning the certainty of the former to the uncertainty of the latter" (2007a:505). Thus, the faith-rationality split complained of by Schaeffer is the function of this new proportionality principle. Formal truth is simply too easy, allowing for a calm assent that cools rather than fuels the passion of faith (cf. Bretall, 1946:216-218).

Carnell (2007a:467) is careful again to qualify his interpretation, recognizing that Kierkegaard's "believing against understanding" is also an understanding at a higher level. But this higher understanding cannot be "logically necessary" if it is to reflect the historical transition and transcendence of becoming, which is centered in the will. Indeed, belief must embrace "the most thinkably offensive paradox" juxtaposing time and eternity (2007a:469). Such is the paradox of Christ's incarnation, "an absolute contradiction in the strictest sense of the term". Rather than seeking to remove the offense of the incarnation through attempting to make it reasonable, easy and painless, the Christian apologist should adorn and magnify the paradox by showing the high cost of faith (2007a:470). Taken to its logical conclusion, this view justifies the creation of one's own object of faith depending on the passion it inspires, since the object merely provides an opportunity to exercise inwardness (2007a:472). Thus, existential validity replaces systematic consistency in apologetics since personal knowledge has no systematic finality (cf. Bretall, 1946:203-214).

It is noteworthy that Carnell (2007a:473) praises Kierkegaard for establishing "the supremacy of truth as inwardness", but such truth cannot be secured by passionate inwardness alone. Scripture presents Christ as the rationality (*logos*) of God, "the true light that gives light to every man" (JOH 1:9). Carnell (2007a:474) quotes in full 1 Corinthians 14:13-17 as the biblical basis for his criticism of Kierkegaard, showing that Paul coordinates spirit and mind rather than opposing them. Carnell also recognizes that Kierkegaard respects the authority of reason except at points where "time and eternity intersect" and paradox results (2007a:475). So what is Kierkegaard's precise error? Carnell (2007a:478) answers with pinpoint accuracy: "Worthy passion is aroused by the nature of the value in question, not the strength or weakness of the evidences which support it." In other words, Kierkegaard's passion mistakes risk for value, for value is the true passion generator of the human spirit. Passionate concern simply does not increase in proportion to objective uncertainty (2007a:494). It is this psychological mistake that led Kierkegaard to affirm that a passionate idol worshipper has more truth than a complacent Christian (2007a:479). This mistake also led to atheistic existentialism.

Like Schaeffer (1982a:76-79), Carnell (2007a:481) affirms that it is simply not prudent to live by commitment alone, since rejecting reason can have fatal results. While commitment is necessary to learning the truth, how does one test commitment on the basis of Kierkegaard's inverse proportionality principle? As Carnell (2007a:482) puts it, "how can one determine that this expression of the dialectic, rather than another, best yields the unfrustrated life of tension?" This is simply an interrogative form of Schaeffer's (1982a:164) statement, "Christianity is not just a better dialectic." On the inverse proportionality principle, truth increases as the risk of faith increases (Carnell, 2007a:483). So the more absurd and offensive one's faith, the more commitment is warranted. This raises the question: Is the incarnation truly the greatest objective absurdity? While Kierkegaard would say so, there is no rational basis on which to establish this belief. Furthermore, the incarnation has been presented in rational terms, certainly more rational than a number of speculative philosophies and cults (cf. Green & Baker, 2000). What then prevents commitment to other equally or more absurd beliefs? "If one is able to rest his happiness in a God-man myth of a pagan religion, for example, the only test one must meet is the barometric reading of passion." (Carnell, 2007a:487.) This echoes Schaeffer's point quoted above that the evangelical gospel and the radical liberal gospel are practically of no different appeal without rational verification. Certainly, Schaeffer has not gone too far in characterizing this epistemology as pragmatic relativism. Carnell is making essentially the same point on the basis of more extensive analysis and criticism.

Neo-orthodoxy and Existentialism

Despite variations within Neo-orthodoxy, Carnell (2007a:490) recognizes a common "denominator" stemming from Kierkegaard's influence: "the real man is the existential man, and the relation between time and eternity is dialectical" (cf. Bretall, 1946:108-109; 409-410). The implication of the dialectic is that eternal revelation entering time "*must* offend rational categories", thus perpetuating Kierkegaard's rejection of classical logic. This is why Barth denies that dogmatics must be justified in the light of philosophy. Brunner is not only less dialectical than Barth but also views revelational and rational knowledge as qualitatively different (Carnell, 2007a:491). This effectively separates theological knowledge from rational verification. Both Carnell and Schaeffer fault Kierkegaard and Neo-orthodoxy for violating logic (antithesis) and forbidding truth tests. For Schaeffer, antithesis involves the law of noncontradiction but is more explicitly informed and normed by Scripture than Carnell's view. However, the two apologists offer essentially the same criticism. Schaeffer's tests are not simply philosophical, for they are biblical and philosophical with respect to the questions they answer. Carnell would also agree with this view and often cites Scripture to justify his analysis.

While Schaeffer often cites Barth, Carnell (2007a:493) cites Niebuhr, who criticized Kierkegaard for going too far in affirming the absurdity of final truth. Therefore, Niebuhr retains "an area of rational congeniality" that leaves only some room for paradox. Among Neo-orthodox theologians, then, theological knowledge is more or less rational depending on their personal consistency with the dialectical method and Kierkegaard's proportionality principle, but all effectively put such knowledge beyond rational verification. This is the material point of agreement between Schaeffer and Carnell as allies against a common expression of error in Neo-orthodoxy.

There is in all this criticism one point of agreement among all parties: Revelational knowledge is not a deductive system and is not, therefore, exhaustively penetrable by human reason. While Kierkegaard and Barth may reflect one end of the spectrum on this point, Carnell (2007a:494) certainly represents the opposite end: "There is no convincing reason why time-eternity relations should stand outside of the conventional connections of rational coherence." Though Schaeffer might agree with this statement, it requires qualification according to biblical norms and the "mystery" Carnell acknowledges surrounding time-eternity relations (2007a:485). The biblical rationale must inform rational coherence, which is not defined by a neutral application of conventional laws of logic.

It should be evident at this point in the study that Schaeffer's presuppositionalism viewed in light of Frame's strikes a biblically-normed balance between the fideism of Kierkegaard and the rationalism of Carnell. It should also be evident that three proportionality principles have been represented in the study thus far: (1) the inverse proportionality principle of Kierkegaard; (2) the transcendental proportionality principle of Schaeffer, Frame, and Van Til; and (3) the evidential proportionality principle of Carnell. Three standards of certainty correspond to these proportionality principles: (1) passionate faith; (2) logical and psychological certainty; (3) logical probability with psychological certitude. The specific doctrine of analogical knowledge shared by Schaeffer and Frame creates a middle path between the fideism of Kierkegaard and Neo-orthodoxy and the coherentism of Carnell. Frame (2002:209; cf. 1995:89-95) defines analogy in relation to God's revelation "as the source and authority" for human knowledge, unlike other definitions built on a false application of divine transcendence, the empiricist principle, or theistic nativism or innatism (Bunting, 2006:69, 72-73).

The traditional Roman Catholic and recent Radical Orthodox doctrine of analogy are based on a "participation ontology", which extrapolates the knowledge of God from that of his creatures (Smith, 2004:277, 83-84; Frame, 2002:208-209). Frame argues against this approach for two reasons: (1) God created human language to refer to him and to finite things in the world, so a chain-of-being metaphysics is not necessary to forge the link between God and creatures; (2) the revelation of God is required to know creatures in the first place, so "the process of analogizing can go either way: from God to the world or vice versa". Thus, creation and revelation work in tandem to support the doctrine of analogy reflected in Frame and Schaeffer. These nuanced distinctions must be noted in order to acknowledge the complexities underlying the criticisms of Neo-orthodoxy and existentialism shared by Schaeffer and Carnell. At bottom, both apologists agree that putting theological knowledge beyond verification violates both Scripture and reason. Carnell (2007a:495) concisely states their mutual agreement: "There is no 'leap' in faith. While faith may involve a cordial commitment of the whole man to Jesus Christ, it is a passion . . . drawn out by objectively measurable evidences."

Kierkegaard's inverse proportionality principle, "like Rebekah, gave birth to two struggling children: theistic theology and atheistic philosophy" (Carnell, 2007a:495). The key to atheistic existentialism is Kierkegaard's thesis that inwardness increases as outwardness decreases. This thesis allows for a complete pragmatic relativism. By taking "anti-objectivity" to the extreme, the sovereign individual becomes the radical reality, the autonomous center without any "outside reference points" (2007a:496). Carnell thus explains Schaeffer's central argument about the faith-rationality split logically eventuating in atheistic existentialism: It gives license to pure subjectivity. Individuality and freedom are maximized as the individual "leaps beyond the universal to behold himself transparently in God". Carnell observes that—following Kierkegaard's principle—atheistic existentialists simply viewed God as just another form of objectivity that blocks creativity and freedom. Why not throw this "metaphysical crutch" away, taking individuality to its logical conclusion? The choice between God and no-God is simply a matter of individual choice. But would not creativity and passion be maximized with no God at all? Carnell states this aptly: "If Kierkegaard's magical leap of freedom can bring God into existence, presto, Sartre's leap can cancel that existence out." (2007a:497.)

At the heart of atheistic existentialism is the recognition that the existence of God, truth, or morality represents "a return to objectivity"

(Carnell, 2007a:500). Thus, Kierkegaard was not fully consistent with his own theory of inwardness based on individual freedom. His spiritual writings (*Works of Love*) assume "an objective theory of morals", and yet he also believed that the good exists only by willing it (2007a:501; cf. Bretall, 1946:107). This implies that the central issue of morality is not "willing the good" but "choosing to will" (Carnell, 2007a:501). The freedom conscious knower realizes that personally choosing to be good is more fundamentally a personal choice of the good itself. Thus, inwardness opposed to metaphysical objectivity might lead to either "an arbitrary individualism" (Sartre) or "an arbitrary collectivism" (Heidegger) (2007a:502). In the end, neither is livable since the pluralism of individual freedom can only be reconciled to a subjective collectivism by force and revolution. No objective justification can be given for an individual or collective choice, leaving only bare acts of will to compete for power in this nihilistic worldview (Nietzsche). The collective ego must establish itself by attacking the individual ego, and yet individual freedom is the basis for all choice. This tension extends not only to the social and political realms, but language and logic also represent "objective rights" that limit personal freedom (2007a:504). Existence itself is a limit to existing. Carnell uses the example of a compass to represent a "form of objectivity" that—on existentialist principles—would justify one's remaining "lost at every moment" in the interest of personal freedom. Thus, existentialism is freedom without form, not freedom within form (Schaeffer).

Evidences and Inwardness

This critique of existentialism by Carnell tracks well with Schaeffer's critique. For Carnell (2007a:505) and Schaeffer (1982a:119-120), truth and value must be discovered, not created by an act of will. This requires inwardness, but not free-spirited inwardness reasoning according to the inverse proportionality principle and leading to pragmatic relativism. Rather, "a healthy inwardness must be guided by, and proportioned to, objective evidences". While the respective proportionality principles of Carnell and Schaeffer have a significant difference, both apologists agree that objective evidences guide existential inwardness to embrace the truth, goodness, and beauty revealed by the triune God in nature, Scripture, and the self. If Schaeffer has not defended this point adequately with respect to Kierkegaard, Carnell certainly has done so on Schaeffer's behalf.

I n approaching modern theologians dialectically, Carnell does not settle for mere criticism; with Kierkegaard especially, criticism is also balanced by a positive appropriation of his profound insights on inwardness. In using Carnell in support of Schaeffer, this study capitalizes on Kierkegaard's love of irony: The very scholar who provides the best support for Schaeffer's criticism of Kierkegaard also draws from that philosopher the strongest support for Schaeffer's own existential perspective. Such ironies are common in the world of scholarship where opponents often shape the thinking of their critics far beyond what the critic recognizes or acknowledges. Carnell, however, openly confessed the life-changing influence of Kierkegaard on his thinking, taking the scholar's right to criticize as an obligation to receive the undeniable truth that remains after the criticism. Though Schaeffer does not acknowledge a personal debt to Kierkegaard, it is clear that his own study of existentialism was sympathetic, and he was also willing to acknowledge his debts (cf. Schaeffer, 1982a:167). But Carnell is the model of dialectical Christian scholarship. Following his example and guidance, we cannot resist the irony of supporting Schaeffer's existential apologetic using insights derived from one of his greatest opponents, thus paying tribute to these three great existential apologists.

Truth as Personal Rectitude

In developing Kierkegaard's "third kind of truth", Carnell (2007b:16, 3)—like Kierkegaard—resorted to a "semiautobiographical" method. This method is necessary because personal truth is learned only within the experiential context of the "moral and spiritual environment . . . as one acquaints himself with the realities that already hold him from existence itself" (2007b:2). There is a "reciprocal relation between rectitude and the perception of objective reality", meaning that one may not separate fact and value (2007b:6). Moral freedom is the source of personal rectitude, which Carnell (2007b:17) calls "the imperative essence". Personal rectitude is the third kind of truth alongside the "ontological" (truth by acquaintance) and the "propositional" (truth by inference). Thus, knowledge comes through direct experience, indirect inference, and moral command—all three mutually necessary to apprehend the truth in its fullness. Once again,

Frame's situational, normative, and existential perspectives are evident in Carnell's ordering of knowledge. Knowledge breaks down when these three are separated, especially when the imperative essence is separated from the rational faculty. One is free to ask why rational self-consistency matters, but unless one is "already held" by a sense that rationality is a moral duty, a mere statement of that duty is powerless to convey the sense (2007b:21). As Carnell (2007b:20) put it, "nothing is a duty unless it captures the heart as a command".

This "moral compulsion to be logical" is critical in supporting Schaeffer's existential apologetic, which also assumes that the moral precedes the mental—both faculties together motivating the individual to belief and action (Carnell, 2007b:21). While Schaeffer affirms this compulsion or "pull" as an inescapable characteristic of human nature, Carnell explains in more detail why this is so and how it is often circumvented through freedom. Human beings are "free to decide" to be rational or not, but the command to be rational—in itself—is only a moral claim. One must be controlled by a sense of duty for the imperative essence to function, and Carnell (2007b:22) refers to this as "moral self-acceptance", which is the self's acceptance of "the sum of those duties that already hold him". Thus, the imperative essence functions *through* acquaintance and inference but is not identified with those methods of knowing (2007b:23). Knowing is "systematic contact with the real" through all three modalities or perspectives—acquaintance, inference, and personal rectitude (2007b:24).

If Carnell's existential epistemology is to effectively support and explain Schaeffer's existential apologetic, a key question must be answered at this point: How does one activate the imperative essence, which is so easily put out of gear by the rational faculty? Carnell's (2007b:27) answer is simple: Existence itself commits the individual to certain moral realities; by acquainting himself with those, "he may discover, to his surprise that he is already in possession of the rough outline of a coherent view of God and the world". In other words, by analyzing common human experience, the imperative essence will be revealed in the natural moral reactions of individuals to these experiences. While Carnell appeals to John 15:22 for his concept of epistemological obligation, he switches to "the power of moral and rational self transcendence to acquaint the mind with consequences that flow from freely motivated conduct" (2007b:26). Had Jesus not spoken, his hearers would not have been "guilty of sin", but since God also speaks imperatively in experience, refusing to listen to existential consequences also establishes moral guilt and responsibility. Romans 1:19-20 also agrees with this idea of existential accountability (cf. ROM 2; Shinn, 1958:278; Zetterholm, 1958:241). Thus, the moral responsibility to know is part of knowing—biblically and existentially (Carnell, 2007b:36).

The universal existential starting point for Carnell (2007b:36) is simple: "All men must act." The validity of this principle is established by inference, not rectitude. The problem with a moral starting point is that one must be "honest" enough to acknowledge that moral obligation is as basic to knowledge as is reason. Many skeptics ignore this connection, sensing no moral breach in using the law of noncontradiction to deny the law of noncontradiction (2007b:40-43). Unless the skeptic is honest enough to acknowledge that the law of noncontradiction is a reality to which existence commits him, he will accept no moral duty to conform to the logic of language or nature. Such a position is unlivable, however, and the relativist will often betray his dishonesty (contradiction) by acting contrary to his expressed view of reality. As Carnell (2007b:44) put it, "the real Pyrrho was Pyrrho in the act". This is Carnell's existential viability principle, which is congruent with Schaeffer's livability principle. If philosophers would only "stand in the center of their own commitments", they would recognize that rectitude is at the heart of knowledge, and the violation of that obligation is an affront to personal dignity, for "dignity *consists* in rectitude" (2007b:46, 48). This is evident in the fact that even skeptics reflect "morally inspired conduct" or, in Schaeffer's terms, moral motions (2007b:49).

So how does God fit into this existential analysis? Further examination of "routine conduct" reveals distinctions that point to God (Carnell, 2007b:49). Moral conduct is revealed in personal relations, especially where personal dignity is violated: "The sheer presence of others alerts us to the issues of justice and injustice." (2007b:54.) While Carnell appeals to scriptural support (MAT 5:8; ROM 1:19, 32) and theological language (the creation of mankind in the divine image) to support his analysis, he also believes that the realities of existence require commitment "to the laws of our dignity" as ultimately personal (2007b:51-58, 56). These laws point to an ultimate Lawgiver to account for the spiritual and moral environment, even as Paul argued in Acts 17:28: "For in him we live and move and have our being." (2007b:58, 138.) Since human beings "participate in, but do not devise, the terms of fellowship", this calls for a personal account of these relations (2007b:61). Carnell is using a transcendental argument supplemented by Scripture to guide his existential analysis. The goal of this analysis is to show that the relativist cannot escape the use of moral absolutes any more than the skeptic can escape the law of noncontradiction (2007b:66). Like Schaeffer, Carnell offers submission to reality as the only viable alternative (2007b:64). As one submits to the moral-spiritual environment, "God graciously meets our humility by creating right affections in us; and these affections, in turn, excite a spontaneous desire to be upright" (2007b:69).

Kierkegaard's Virtue Epistemology

The problem with classical philosophy is that it did not correctly appraise the greater power of human freedom to command reason and the weakness of rational form to inspire duty (Carnell, 2007b:72). Carnell identifies Socrates, Pascal, and Kierkegaard as the only philosophers who integrated this moral sense with philosophy (2007b:73). Carnell is indebted to Kierkegaard for his insight that the individual mediates eternity in time through passionate moral decisions that express and transform the true self. Kierkegaard's problem, however, is that he failed to recognize that the intellect is required to define personal rectitude. By attempting to insure that thinking about duty will not replace doing one's duty, Kierkegaard created a "polarity tension between objective reality and subjective faith" (2007b:75). Faith, then, must defy the intellect to embrace the risk of faith. Carnell (2007b:77) builds on his previous criticism, namely that Kierkegaard mistakes risk for value, now expressing this mistake in terms of an attitude: "Passion should be guided by the seriousness and truth of the object, and not by its rational offensiveness." Once this mistake is recognized and corrected, one can affirm Kierkegaard's virtue epistemology of passionate faith aided by—not threatened by—the contribution of the intellect, which defends the faith rationally and defines ethical duties. The passion of faith is fueled by the "seriousness" of its issues, which reflect eternal values mediated in time. Carnell cites Romans 10:2 and 1 John 4:1 in support of this position, showing that "zeal" must be "based on knowledge" and supported by sufficient evidences and truth testing. God's command to "test the spirits" of the prophets assumes the importance of sufficient evidence in both testaments (2007b:78; cf. DEU 13:1-3). Carnell (2007b:83) clearly reflects a proper concern to be "consistent with"—if not normed by—Scripture.

Carnell's reference to a "polarity tension" at the heart of Kierkegaard's thinking raises the question of theological hypocrisy on the part of Frame, Schaeffer, and Carnell. Is it fair to fault Kierkegaard for affirming tension and paradox in theology with respect to time-eternity relations when these evangelical thinkers do the same? It should be recalled that Frame (1976:310) refers to the necessity and freedom of God's will as "paradoxically related". Why is this polarity tension valid and Kierkegaard's not? The answer to this question is all-important to clarifying the difference between evangelicalism and existentialism in theology. In evangelical thinking (and some Neo-orthodoxy), a polarity tension does not imply ultimate irrationality in the mind of God; on the contrary, God's freedom and necessity are viewed as complementary rather than contradictory. While their precise relationship cannot be explained, both poles are required to explain the other. So, for example, God's sovereignty is necessary to human freedom, providing a context in which moral action and responsibility become intelligible (cf. Van Til, 1971:34-37). The language of absurdity with respect to time-eternity relations is simply inappropriate, being useful only as a description of the non-Christian's view of theological paradoxes (cf. Evans, 1981:325). Above all, the evangelical view of paradox does not become a justification for the rejection of antithesis (the law of noncontradiction). Truth is logical to the extent of the limits of human reason and God's revelation. Thus, some truth may be beyond human reason (subjective paradox), but it is not against reason as an "objective paradox" (Carnell, 2007b:269). In Schaeffer's terms, the evangelical position neither denies nor diminishes reason, even though it affirms tension and paradox in theology. There is no faith-rationality split, and "faith is not based on risk" (2007b:77).

The Existential Analysis

Carnell (2007b:83) offers an ingenious analysis of the moral sense: "When we stand in the presence of others, do we sense an obligation to regard their dignity?" Most of what follows in *Christian Commitment* is offered in support of an affirmative answer to this one question. For Carnell, moral obligation—the moral sense—is revealed through close relationship with others: "To what moral duties am I committed when others enter the circle of nearness?" (2007b:85.) As one humbly submits to "the duties that already hold us", the imperative essence is revealed with undeniable force, especially when one's personal rights are violated. Those who remain outside this circle are "people in the abstract" and therefore do not arouse moral claims in the heart (2007b:219). Thus, Kierkegaard's principle of inwardness leads to an immediate experience of human dignity "that is known only as it is felt" and not by mere inferential knowledge (2007b:86). The rational development of this "direct experience" is expressed in legal and social systems. Human dignity is expressed in terms of human rights, promises, oaths, shame, and other "socially measurable terms" (2007b:87, 179). Thus, the true self is not the rational self of Plato and classical philosophy but the moral self, which unites intellect, emotion, and will in spiritual freedom (2007b:88; cf. Boa & Bowman, 2001:461-462; Harper, 1977:141).

Human nature, then, is committed to moral absolutes, which—when violated—evoke judicial sentiments (Carnell, 2007b:92). This observation is confirmed by Paul, who affirmed that "no one ever hated his own body, but he feeds and cares for it" (EPH 5:29; cf. GEN 9:6; 2007b:214). The "judicial sentiment" is aroused whenever we become "judicially irked", whenever the "divinely implanted sense of personal sanctity" is violated by those who enter the circle of nearness (2007b:178, 92). Judicial sentiment is the negative counterpart of personal rectitude as love, and both are based on personal sanctity. Thus, personal dignity and judicial feelings define the "complementary claims" of the existential environment. This explains why both self-love and duty must be combined in a consistent ethic: Both are revealed in social experiences, contrary to philosophers who reject either self-love (Kant) or moral duty (James) on rational grounds (2007b:97, 100).

This moral environment puts those who humbly submit to it in contact with God: "Man subsists in God from the first moment of moral self-consciousness, for God completes the moral cycle by answering to the judicial sentiment." (Carnell, 2007b:101.) Scripture and the moral sense witness to a God consciousness activated by moral self-acceptance. Carnell (2007b:102) lists four existential realities that hold those who humbly accept them. Human beings are (1) contingent with respect to their existence, (2) conscious of a sense of duty in the presence of others, (3) committed to the real guilt of those who violate personal dignity, and (4) confronted by the "judicial predicament" that those who judge by the law have no inherent right to enforce it (2007b:103; 234). From these realities, God completes the moral cycle of "law, transgression, and accountability before a duly authorized moral tribunal" (2007b:104). The concept of authorized or delegated authority requires a higher power, a morally perfect Being, to whom all must give an account. Nowhere is this more evident than in the use of oaths, which are founded on the name and power of God (2007b:108). Because this moral knowledge is activated through a free will—not reason—it constitutes a mere "procedure" or analysis consistent with Scripture, not a rational proof for God's existence

(2007b:109, 141; cf. 1948:159; Lewis, 1976:261). Nevertheless, Carnell's (2007b:109) mode of reasoning sounds like a transcendental proof, since the moral conditions he describes are "indispensable" and cannot be denied by those who live within the conditions. For all his emphasis on logical probability, Carnell employs the language of necessity in the moral realm, even though he denies offering a rational proof in doing so (cf. Lewis, 1993:325, 327).

It is now possible to forge the connection between Carnell's existential "procedure" and Schaeffer's apologetic. Carnell (2007b:110) identifies the conscience as "the subjective principle of responsibility for one's deeds before the divine tribunal". This "voice of accusation" judges the free actions of the accused within the self and may be altered by conditioning but not reduced to it (2007b:112). To judge the faculty of conscience as the product of mere conditioning would be to refuse moral self-acceptance by rejecting the inescapable conditions of all moral action. Within the circle of nearness, this is impossible anyway since moral relativists defend their relativism only until their own personal dignity is attacked (2007b:113). One cannot honestly refuse the demands of the moral and spiritual environment. As the non-Christian refuses the knowledge of God (ROM 1:28), "the result is unremitting moral anxiety" (2007b:236).

This moral anxiety is what Schaeffer appeals to in apologetics—the pull toward personal integrity, which Carnell (2007b:237) calls "harmony with rectitude". While Schaeffer does not offer a detailed existential analysis, he recognizes the inner claims of duty as a demand for moral integrity or consistency within the self. Thus, Carnell explains the existential complex that justifies Schaeffer's own apologetic appeal to existential realities that hold in personal relationships. What Carnell (2007b:119) learned from Kierkegaard is that "the real man is not the rational man; the real man is the moral and loving man". It is through this imperative essence and the conscience in particular that the moral Lawgiver presses his claims upon those who accept the realities that hold them. Furthermore, personal rectitude compels integrity through love, since love "rejoices with the truth" (1Co 13:6; 2007b:210). Without this existential analysis or something close to it, Schaeffer's apologetic method lacks full explanation and support. Schaeffer capitalizes on the non-Christian's tension within himself between the known and the unknown, but the "pull" between the real world and the logic of one's system is morally grounded. An inner voice of accusation with respect to moral and intellectual hypocrisy must be awakened by the apologist, and Schaeffer (1982a:140) seeks to do this by "taking the roof off". Schaeffer (1982a:68, 115-118) often presses the moral implications of the non-Christian's worldview, showing that what the unbeliever claims to value in personal relationships is inconsistent with his own unbelieving worldview. Such appeals attempt to awaken the unbeliever to moral self-acceptance and his own conscience, which "accuses" him of violating the inner law of God and his own word (ROM 2:15). Thus, moral anxiety is the key to an existential apologetic.

Personal rectitude is not only the basis for Schaeffer's (1982a:165) appeal to moral integrity in the non-Christian but governs his "final apologetic" as well. The non-Christian must see a "visible quality" of integrity or consistency in believers as well as in themselves. When the Christian enters the non-Christian's "circle of nearness", the imperative essence will evoke judicial sentiments in the unbeliever if the Christian either violates the unbeliever's dignity or the believer's own professed standards. Personal rectitude expressed as spiritual integrity is critical to showing that a Christian existential analysis accounts for the facts of reality. Schaeffer's (1982a:167) "realism in exhibition" in the "existential moment" reflects the Christian personalism explained so profoundly by Carnell and inspired by Kierkegaard.

Carnell's Eristic Apologetic

Ironically, Carnell speaks most like Schaeffer when presenting an existential apologetic. While Carnell (2007b:109, 286; cf. Holmes, 1959:3) repeatedly claims that he is not offering a proof for the Christian faith, his language betrays him: "Existence itself raises a question to which the righteousness of Christ is the only critically acceptable answer." The transcendental direction of his existential "procedure" has already been noted, and Carnell often grafts his analysis to the scriptural testimony and rationale and—like Schaeffer—speaks the language of "spiritual necessity" (2007b:162, 208; cf. 248-265). Sounding like Frame, Carnell (2007b:210) also refers to "the normative teaching of the apostle Paul" on love to support his analysis. However, a close analysis of Carnell (2007b:235) reveals a distinction between the merits of argument and the certitude of faith: "having found God, we believe that sufficient evidence exists to show that the accusing power of conscience originates with the divine tribunal" (cf. Lewis, 1993:328). Using a variation of Paley's Watchmaker argument, Carnell says that one may not argue from a specific pair of shoes to a specific shoemaker's trademark until one knows the shoemaker. He is even more explicit in his *Introduction to Christian Apologetics*: "One may be morally certain God exists, and pray with full assurance, though the objective evidence is but rationally probable." (Carnell, 1948:120; quoted in Boa & Bowman, 2001:455.) This clearly separates Carnell's transcendental reasoning in the existential analysis from his commitment to probable evidences in argument. The moral certitude of faith reflects a transcendental orientation that evidences and arguments do not.

This reveals the weakness of Carnell's (2007b:267) evidentialist proportionality principle: The merits of argument are not truly proportional to the certainty of faith—faith must "leap" from objective probability to subjective certainty. This flaw also explains the defection of modern philosophers like Kierkegaard from the evidentialist proportionality principle and the consequent separation of faith and reason. The presuppositionalist's proportionality principle does not have this defect, reflecting an equal proportionality between the certainty of the transcendental argument and the certainty of faith. With respect to Christian certainty, then, Carnell is dialectical—just not as dialectical as Kierkegaard or Niebuhr. Therefore, he does not fully challenge the dialecticism of existentialism, since he builds on the principle that precipitated it. It is to Schaeffer's credit that he did not fall into this error.

The flaw in Carnell's epistemology, however, does not overshadow the genius of his analysis or its relevance to Schaeffer's apologetic. It is not going too far, in my judgment, to place Carnell's work on par with the great confrontational or "eristic" apologetic systems of Pascal and Kierkegaard (Patrick, 1947a:219; 1947b). In terms of the depth of his analysis, Carnell's work is equally impressive, contrary to Harper (1977:145), who sees a "lack of creativity" in Carnell's work, and Fowler (1958:315), who does not believe that *Christian Commitment* "will live as one of the great apologia". While not sufficiently transcendental, Carnell (2007b:286) argues—as Schaeffer does—that "Christianity is true because its major elements are consistent with one another and with the broad facts of history and culture" (cf. Lewis, 1993:325, 335). If one did not know that Carnell had penned these words, one might think Schaeffer had written them. For Carnell, Christ is the answer to the moral predicament; for Schaeffer, Christ is the answer to personal integrity, which is saying the same thing.

AN APOLOGIST FOR POSTMODERNS

11 THE MODERN-POSTMODERN DIALECTIC

The final side or strut of the frame captures the ways in which Schaeffer's apologetic of personal rectitude addresses the postmodern situation he anticipated. To reach this goal, it will be necessary to first summarize the development of postmodernism from its roots in modernism beginning with Kant. In assessing Schaeffer's anticipation of postmodernism and his response to it, it is important to recognize that Schaeffer understood the dialectical nature of modern thought. It was noted that Frame (2010a:3) criticized Schaeffer for not giving priority to Kant over Hegel in accounting for modern dialecticism. But Schaeffer (1982a:227-229; 1982c:174-180) acknowledged Kant's role in modern dialecticism, along with Rousseau, Hegel, and Kierkegaard. "Modern man is a man of dichotomy" especially because of these four philosophers (1982c:180). Schaeffer's understanding of the interplay of rationality and irrationality in all non-Christian philosophy enabled him to anticipate the trajectory of the postmodern from the modern. Therefore, the following summary of postmodernism, which provides a context for an assessment of Schaeffer's response, is purposely focused on the dialectical character of modernity and postmodernity.

In an attempt to assess the extent to which Schaeffer's apologetic provides an apt apologetic for postmoderns, we will enlist the support of three scholars who have evaluated Schaeffer's position on this issue. Erickson (1998:63-80), Tinker and Tinker (2005) provide competent studies of Schaeffer's apologetic evangelism in relation to postmodernism, and their focus—like that of this study—is primarily on his trilogy. In addition to our own conclusions, these studies provide ample evidence of the continuing relevance of Schaeffer's apologetic of personal rectitude.

With respect to the terminology of postmodernism, there is considerable variation. Erickson (2001:9) distinguishes postmodernism as the "intellectual beliefs of a specific period" from postmodernity as the "cultural phenomenon" stemming from those beliefs. Benson (2006:561), however, prefers the term postmodernity to postmodernism, "since the 'ism' implies a uniformity that postmodern thinkers do not share". While more detailed studies of postmodernism may find it useful to distinguish the terms, this study will treat them as synonymous.

The "odd alliance" between the rational and the irrational in non-Christian thought has been central to the philosophical analysis of Schaeffer, Frame, Van Til, and Dooyeweerd (Jones, 2009:592; cf. Edgar, 1995b:361; Dooyeweerd, 1975; Singer, 1979). While many Christian thinkers, including Schaeffer, emphasize the importance of key transitions in intellectual history, Van Til stressed only one as all-important: the Fall (Frame, 2008b:886). The result of this turning point is that history reflects a continual "replay" of simultaneous rationalism and irrationalism in thought and life. As Frame puts it, "Eve was rationalist and irrationalist, modern and postmodern . . . an idolater of value and a destroyer of it, all at the same time." Edgar (1995b:362) defines the rationalist pole similarly to Schaeffer, stressing that the facts of the world are legislated by human thought operating scientifically or empirically and autonomously. This is equivalent to Kant's phenomenal realm. The irrationalist pole is that of "subjective freedom", which comprehends the realm of "religion, morals, and meaning" and equates to Kant's noumenal realm. This dialectical approach to philosophical analysis is critical to understanding Schaeffer's anticipation of postmodernism and his response to it, for modernity and postmodernity are symbiotically related, reflecting both the rationalism and irrationalism of modern thought beginning with Kant. More current philosophers, such as Derrida, Foucault, Lyotard, and Rorty, are labeled postmodern, but they are preceded by Nietzsche, Kierkegaard, and Heidegger who were postmodern (or anti-modern) before the term became common (cf. Singer, 1979:152-159, 261-267, 270-275).

Modern Rationalism

While not employing the rationalist-irrationalist dialectic as an interpretive lens, Benson's (2006:561-564) treatment of postmodernity is consistent with Edgar's (1995b:359-382; cf. Benson, 2002). Edgar purposely sets out to demonstrate the dialectic in the historical development of postmodernism. Benson (2006:561) recognizes that postmodern thinkers are united in their reaction to modern (Enlightenment) thought, but he also sees that "postmodern thinkers both criticize and continue modernity" because modernity contains the seeds of postmodernism. In fact, neither modernity nor postmodernity were ever fully unified. Benson recognizes three "connected elements" in modernity that provided the impetus for postmodernism: (1) a commitment to individual autonomy as a way to replace tradition and authority with individual judgment concerning truth and morality; (2) a commitment to reason as a basis to make decisions; (3) a commitment to rational methods as objective means to provide universal conclusions, "at least in theory". These three elements are evident in Kant's (2010) essay, "What is Enlightenment?" While Kant's directive to think for oneself is qualified by his description of the limits of reason and the role of faith, his seminal description of modernism clearly exalts individual autonomy by exalting reason.

Benson (2006:561) notes the contradiction at the heart of Kant's "Copernican revolution", which "has exactly the opposite effect of making the human self become the center of the universe". Instead of the mind mirroring the world, the world mirrors the mind, which interprets the world "through concepts the mind creates". Thus, individual thought becomes transcendentally necessary to all experience, and Kant simply universalizes (absolutizes) the categorical structure he created. The price for this reorientation is Kant's phenomenal-noumenal distinction, which separates the world as it is in itself from the world as it is to the self-contained knower. As Benson states it, "knowledge for Kant is objective in the sense of being universal but not objective in the sense of existing apart from the subject". Thus, Kant's objective rationalism is contaminated by subjective irrationalism, which comes to fruition in anti-modern and post-modern thinkers who eventually undermine universal truth through his principle of autonomous freedom (cf. Singer, 1979:86-115). Benson (2006:562) observes that within Kant's own lifetime, Fichte was employing Kant's doctrine of radical freedom to subvert universal truth, arguing that "our minds organize the world on the basis of our personal needs, so that many different ways of viewing the world are possible, no one being truly 'correct'". Hegel develops this further, presenting worldviews as perspectival truths that constitute truth only in the aggregate. Religiously speaking, "the human horizon replaces the divine as the basic ordering principle" (Edgar, 1995b:368).

Postmodern Irrationalism

This progression makes Nietzsche's rejection of all Western notions of universal truth unsurprising (Benson, 2006:562). Nietzsche attacks Platonism and Christianity, which he viewed as a version of Platonism, as examples of "static" conceptions of truth, affirming that truth is perspectival, historical, and contextual. However, Nietzsche embodies the modern mentality in his affirmation of individual autonomy and the self as the ultimate reference point. Heidegger amplified Nietzsche's point that truth is historical and contextual, rejecting "basic philosophical dualisms" that assume the objectivity of truth. For example, the realism-idealism dualism is undermined by the fact that the "interconnection" of the two terms places an objective world (realism) and our subjective creation of that world (idealism) in tension. This leads Heidegger to an anti-realism that undermines reason and the central self, thus reducing philosophy to "a kind of poetry that attempts to think about being and truth without making pretentious claims to know it". Gadamer also attacks the central self, arguing that tradition and authority are legitimate and indispensable to individual thought. The ideal of pure reason (Kant), then, is simply impossible, since thinking is bound to one's historical and cultural context (Benson, 2006:563). Clearly, these anti-modernists are both modern and postmodern, giving rational accounts of reason's fallibility and oscillating between a centered (Nietzsche) and de-centered (Heidegger) self and an individual (Nietzsche) and collective (Gadamer) autonomy. The dialectic is obvious, for as Edgar (1995b:363) points out, "irrationalism is always a reasoned articulation" (cf. Nietzsche, 1968:421-422; 2005; Heidegger, 1996:191-193; Gadamer, 2004:278-285).

Derrida develops the idea of deconstruction, which also provides an interesting illustration of the rationalist-irrationalist dialectic. According to Benson (2006:563), "deconstruction is the idea of unbuilding in order to examine a text or a theory, which can be used for good or ill". While deconstruction might be used to justify relativism, Derrida employs the term to show that concepts and language are inadequate to provide more than a "trace" of that to which they refer. This means that language about justice or God will always fall short as a description of either the phenomena or noumena. Therefore, philosophy should center on "the true 'otherness' of the other", not on totalizing claims for "dominating the other". Philosophy is not merely about thinking for oneself (Kant) but about allowing one's thinking "to be put into question by the other". The instability of this dialectical relationship between the self and the other allows for the modernist "imperative of thinking for oneself" (Nietzsche, Foucault) and the postmodern imperative of submitting one's thought to the other (Derrida, Levinas). Thus, philosophy oscillates between domination by the self (individualism) and the other (collectivism). It is simultaneously rationalist and irrationalist (cf. Derrida, 1996:48-59, 1998:61; Levinas, 1979:46-47, 82-101; Foucault 1994, 1995).

Benson (2006:563) provides a contemporary example of postmodern relativism in Rorty, who holds personal beliefs while acknowledging that they are only pragmatically useful. With the demise of modernist foundationalism, philosophy must content itself with poetic "redescriptions" rather than arguments. Benson sees this as a reaffirmation of Nietzsche's "poetization of the self". By this account, faith becomes a mere pragmatic belief that serves individual interest but makes no claim to universality. Again, modernist freedom and autonomy come to full expression in this conception of truth. And yet, Rorty reflects the same dialecticism of his predecessors, since he states his philosophy in rational terms while denying it any status above a "redescription" of reality—rationalism and irrationality in tandem (cf. Rorty, 1989:78, 90-91; 1981). Thus, the modernist conception of objective truth ultimately gives way to the postmodern conception of subjective truth, and individual philosophers autonomously decide where they settle on the continuum between the two. In academic terms, modernists "major in rationalism and minor in irrationalism" and postmodernists major in irrationalism and minor in rationalism, but all non-Christian philosophers fall into the dialectic (Edgar, 1995b:362).

The Biblical Response to Postmodernity

Edgar (1995b:374) describes postmodernity as a period of "fragmentation" involving "an infinite plurality of language games" (Wittgenstein), an era of mere "linguistic doing" in which grand or macro narratives have been replaced by petite or micro narratives (Lyotard). Despite this postmodern situation, several features of modernity are likely here to stay, such as individualism, capitalism, consumerism, technology, racism, and urbanization (1995b:376). The extent of the social and economic damage resulting from these modernist conceptions will be determined by the extent to which the Enlightenment program of progress, education, and "the exaggerated power of the self" continues to govern modern-postmodern societies (1995b:377). Unless reason and freedom become grounded in God's revelation, the unstable dialectic of rationalism and irrationalism will continue to oscillate between oppressive expressions of individualism and collectivism (1995b:378). The benefits of modernity require the Protestant Reformation as an underpinning, and without at least some "funding by Protestant capital", modernism degenerates into an oppressive capitalism, an oppressive communism, or something in between. Reason and freedom cannot be negotiated within an autonomous worldview—not even with the aid of a natural theology. Only a "radically biblical way" will do. Neither modernism nor postmodernism will be transcended by a post-postmodernism unless the Christian worldview is accepted as the answer to this dialectical phase of intellectual history.

Therefore, the postmodern idea of moving beyond modernism is simply impossible given that postmodernism is firmly based on modernism. The postmodernist stands on modernist ground in the attempt to leap to something new, but the modernist law of gravity within the system will continue to pull him back down to his modernist platform. The "ground motive of reason and autonomous freedom" requires postmodernists to continue "appealing to the very standards they reject" (Edgar, 1995a:379). Postmodernism, then, is philosophy on a pogo stick. The reason-freedom dialectic can be overcome only through a "transcendental approach": "Because God is fully rational, and because human knowledge is revelatory of that God, dependent rather than independent, our knowledge has meaning, and we can properly understand the world without falling into the dialectical labyrinth."

Edgar's (1995b:380) helpful summary of postmodernism explains why Schaeffer anticipated this movement: As a student of Van Til, Schaeffer understood that "there has always been a certain challenge to modernity within the camp" because all non-Christian thought is dialectical. The nature-grace and nature-freedom schemes that Schaeffer explains are a reflection of his understanding of the dialectical nature of all unbelieving thought. Applying this basic principle of Van Til and Dooyeweerd, Schaeffer did not need to read a great deal about postmodernism to understand where modernity must inevitably go. The anti-modern is inevitably the ultra-modern (cf. Erickson, 1998:43-62). The problem is not the modernist belief in the "emancipated self", since Protestantism also seeks to free the individual from traditional authority to stand before God in the freedom of conscience (Edgar, 1995b:381). Rather, the emancipated self must be "properly understood as the image of God". The problem is also not the modernist belief in the importance of reason; rather, reason must be "properly subjected to the norms of revelation". Thus, the revelation that reason requires and the good that freedom requires must be transcendental notions. Schaeffer understood this clearly, and it explains why he articulated an appropriate apologetic for postmoderns.

12 AN APOLOGETIC FOR POSTMODERNS

I t has already been noted that Erickson (1998:63-64) recognized the relevance of Schaeffer to postmodernism. Tinker and Tinker (2005:201) agree, contending that Schaeffer offers both a "framework" for understanding postmodernism and an apologetic "eminently suited" to it. While the previous chapter provides an understanding of postmodernism compatible with Schaeffer and his apologetic, it will be helpful to provide more testimony confirming his relevance to the current postmodern situation as a conclusion to the study.

Erickson's Evaluation

Erickson (1998:63) believes that Schaeffer was ahead of his time because he worked among the "forerunners" of postmodernism in Europe before these influences were established in North America. Schaeffer (1982a:253-254; 1982b:11) does refer to Foucault as an example of autonomous freedom in opposition to the authority of reason, but he does not refer to any of the other contemporary postmodernists mentioned above. Nevertheless, according to Erickson (1998:63), there is sufficient interaction with postmodern ideas in Schaeffer's work to warrant consideration of his apologetic as a relevant response to the movement. For example, in connection with Schaeffer's assessment of musique concrète, Erickson (1998:64) recognizes the "basics" of postmodernism: "the loss of logical antithesis, a thoroughgoing relativism, and the impossibility of any holoscopic metaphysical synthesis, or metanarrative". Specifically, Schaeffer's demand for antithesis represents the key principle beneath all his examples, and Erickson (1998:68) agrees that this demand must be maintained by Christians engaging with postmoderns.

Another critical point for postmodern engagement, which Erickson recognizes in Schaeffer, is the existential tension between the unbeliever's thought and life caused by the image of God. While Erickson does not mention the environment of divine revelation and the imperative essence in connection with the divine image, these should be included in the discussion. This aspect of Schaeffer's apologetic, which was elaborated in a previous chapter with support from Carnell, is clearly central to the existential perspective at the heart of this study. Personal rectitude is the basis upon which the demand for rational and moral integrity may be impressed upon the non-Christian, and Erickson has recognized the importance of this component of Schaeffer's apologetic as a vital point of postmodern engagement. While postmoderns may profess to have moved beyond modern rationalism, they cannot live without rationality. Even if one majors in freedom and minors in reason, a commitment to reason is inescapable and integral unless one is willing to live with Foucault's idea that insanity expresses the ultimate freedom.

Erickson (1998:78) recognizes in Schaeffer "a pioneering effort to give an evangelical response to postmodernism". While he does observe some weaknesses in Schaeffer's approach, he recognizes several strengths as well. Notably, he believes that Schaeffer has done "a great service by recognizing and flagging the postmodern phenomenon early", even though he would have benefitted from the later development of postmodern categories. Erickson (1998:79) also commends Schaeffer for having recognized the roots of postmodern thinking in the anti-modern philosophers of the 19th Century and for seeing how cultural trends stemming from those ideas spread to the disciplines, theology, and the culture at large. Erickson also appreciates that Schaeffer did not attempt to commend the Christian faith in postmodern terms but recognized that ideas have consequences that must be addressed. The faithful Christian witness pushes the unbeliever toward the logical consequences of his position, understanding—but not accommodating—the position.

Like other scholars, Erickson (1998:79) recognizes weaknesses in Schaeffer as well. He recognizes "some oversimplification of analysis", but he also understands that Schaeffer was a generalist and not a specialist in any area to which he applies his thought. Like Frame, Erickson also recognizes that Kant, rather than Hegel, is the origin of modern and postmodern dialecticism. Erickson (1998:80) also faults Schaeffer for seeming to assume "that Christianity is really the only viable alternative" to the irrationalism he describes without adequately showing how other religious alternatives fail to meet the demands of rationality. Finally, Erickson criticizes Schaeffer for "a basically rationalist assumption" that overlooks the role "non-rational factors play in belief and behavior". In other words, Erickson thinks that Schaeffer's apologetic assumes that merely exposing non-Christian irrationality in light of the Christian worldview is sufficient to lead others to Christ. But the distasteful demands of Christian morality and the difficulties of rearranging one's life along Christian lines also complicate the apologetic appeal.

In my view, Erickson's last two criticisms fail to consider the richness of Schaeffer's apologetic, especially with respect to the existential perspective at the heart of this study. It is true that Schaeffer does not engage with religious worldviews as individual alternatives but tends to deal with them in the aggregate. Unitarian theisms are refuted in connection with the argument for trinitarian theism, and the inadequacies of pantheism are presented to cover all the monistic religions. In this respect, Schaeffer was following the general strategy of the presuppositional thinkers who influenced him, particularly Van Til and Dooyeweerd. There is also an obvious practical advantage to this strategy provided one's analysis is sufficiently comprehensive and not over-generalized.

Erickson's last criticism seems completely off the mark given that Schaeffer clearly stresses non-rational factors in apologetic evangelism. Schaeffer refers to prayer, the work of the Holy Spirit, and the evangelist's own personal rectitude as vital factors involved in leading others to Christ. Erickson has simply focused too narrowly on Schaeffer's use of the rationalist-irrationalist dialectic in the methodological chapters of his trilogy and has ignored the equal emphasis he places on non-rational factors throughout his writings. In fact, given the argument of this study, Schaeffer qualifies as one of the truly balanced evangelical apologists of recent times, and his success was arguably based on the balance of rational and non-rational factors in his apologetic. Schaeffer's existential perspective, which has been elaborated in this study, has been recognized and praised by followers and critics alike.

The Tinkers' Testimony

The Tinkers (2005:201) also recognize the importance of Schaeffer's work to the postmodern context. While recognizing that Schaeffer has been criticized as too rationalistic for postmoderns, these authors contend that his approach "still provides a valuable resource for the way in which Christians might engage with the postmodern mind". Moreover, Schaeffer's ideas provide a "framework" for understanding postmodernism and "the present postmodern scene". The "apologetic suspicion" that characterizes the postmodern context and some evangelical circles requires a person-centered and dialogical approach (cf. Clark, 1993:99; cited in Tinker & Tinker, 2005:202). Schaeffer (1982a:175-187) clearly articulated and practiced this approach.

The Tinkers (2005:202) point first to Schaeffer's upper and lower story distinction as a relevant analysis that explains the postmodern response to modernism. In separating reason from faith, the postmodern thinker makes faith attainable only by a "gigantic leap" (2005:203). Postmodernism takes the split between faith and reason a step further, also casting doubt on the modernist's confidence in reason: "The result is either solipsism or epistemological anarchism." The Tinkers call attention to Schaeffer's (1982a:253-254) reference to Stephen Marcus's review of Foucault's book, *Madness and Civilization*, in which Marcus uses the term "post-modern" to describe what Schaeffer called anti-philosophy. This is all the more interesting because Schaeffer commented on Foucault in 1968, long before the term "post-modern" became common currency. Schaeffer (1982a:254) recognized in Foucault what Marcus described as "the reality of the intellectual situation of the present moment" and summarized Foucault as follows: "So we find that Foucault follows Rousseau's thought to its conclusion: the ultimate in autonomous freedom is being crazy. It is a fine thing to be crazy for then you are free."

The Tinkers (2005:204) also recognize the importance of Schaeffer's "pre-suppositional apologetic technique" as relevant to postmodern engagement. Erickson (2001:190) agrees that "some form of presuppositionalism would be a more effective strategy" for communicating with postmoderns. The Tinkers (2005:204) observe that Schaeffer's requirement to "lovingly push people to the limits of their presuppositions" is an exercise that postmoderns have already performed with respect to modernism. Schaeffer offers a Christian method of deconstruction that shows that postmoderns have taken refuge in the upper story of autonomous freedom. However, neither the nature-grace nor the nature-freedom schemes can be overcome by the postmodern leap. Rather, the postmodern solution simply collapses "the objective into the subjective", replacing "truth out there" with "truth we create" (2005:206). Only the Reformation solution heals the split between nature and grace and nature and freedom, thereby coordinating both objective and subjective truth in a unity under God. The incentive for postmoderns to heed this solution is their own intellectual and moral inconsistency and an inner drive for integrity. Schaeffer's approach is not "rationalistic", for he recognizes that only this inner drive for integrity and honesty (personal rectitude) will pull the unbeliever toward consistency in Christ, and spiritual conditions are required to awaken that drive. If prayer, the Holy Spirit, and the personal rectitude of the evangelist and the church are necessary conditions for effective apologetic evangelism, it is unfair to accuse Schaeffer of being rationalistic just because he insists on the importance of reason and uses it in engaging unbelief.

The Tinkers (2005:206) further recognize that the search for human significance explains the postmodern retreat to the upper story. Because modernity leads only to despair, postmoderns seek meaning in the irrational. Schaeffer agreed with postmodernists that modernism reduces the individual to a meaningless machine through its tendency to determinism: "all decisions, actions and personality could be explained exclusively in terms of naturalistic causation" (2005:207). Schaeffer directly challenged this conclusion of modernism with a biblical view of humanity rather than with the notion of autonomous freedom. In essence, Schaeffer agrees with postmoderns concerning the problem of modernity but not with the solution. For Schaeffer, "the explanatory power of the *imago dei* is not to be underestimated". While truth is not "value free" and "wholly objective", as modernists claim, there is no need to go to the opposite extreme of reducing objectivity to pure subjectivity.

Schaeffer offers an apologetic for postmoderns because he recognized that "the doctrine of creation of man is vital" (Tinker & Tinker, 2005:208). The search for significance is "basic to the human condition, including the postmodern condition". The postmodernist seeks meaning in rejecting the modernist error of omni-causality and embracing personal freedom. Thus, what the postmodern seeks in an irrational upper story, the biblical faith provides in a "true upper level" that provides for "the significance of each individual life in relationship and action". Schaeffer's affirmation of the importance of personal freedom in the face of a deadening determinism is, in my view, one of his strongest points of communication with postmodern thinkers. The biblical view is both rational and existential in providing a basis for "true truth", and it is the only answer to the pragmatic relativism that has resulted from the modernist-postmodernist dialectic (2005:211). Because one must use antithesis to deny antithesis, postmodernism must collapse on itself thereby showing that reason is undeniable and inescapable. Even better, however, is that Christianity actually works. It is not true because it works, "but rather it works because it is true and it all flows from a personal knowledge of God" (2005:213; cf. Lundin, 1995).

Authenticity in Action

A final "point of contact" between Schaeffer's apologetic and postmodernism is his "concern for authenticity in *action*" (Tinker & Tinker, 2005:213). In one of the best summaries of Schaeffer's apologetic, the Tinkers capture this point of contact: "Schaeffer's apologetic and concern for propositional truth was undergirded and surrounded by his concern for authentic

Christian living." If Christians will "exhibit" true truth in practice, they can appeal to postmoderns for whom "actions speak louder than words" and "truth is something to be experienced" (2005:213, 214). Christian practice, "transposed into the postmodern world", is the best means to show the soundness of the Christian argument as a live option for postmoderns. As long as Christian practice—individually and corporately—does not reflect the oppression allegedly at the heart of all meta-narratives, it may be able to rise above the apologetic suspicion of postmodern times. For some, it may be viewed as a valid micro-narrative before it becomes the grand narrative that combines upper and lower stories. But authentic Christian living provides the best access to the personal rectitude or imperative essence of human nature. This supports the Tinker's (2005:215) judgment that Schaeffer offered the "ultimate" apologetic for the postmodern world because of his emphasis on "truth in living" (cf. Stackhouse, 1995).

13 AN APOLOGIST FOR ALL SEASONS

The perspectival nature of Schaeffer's apologetic—understood in terms of Frame's triperspectivalism—is, in my view, the greatest epistemological asset of his approach to apologetic evangelism today. Postmodernism is committed to the perspectival nature of human knowing as a core belief. Middleton and Walsh (1995a:133) refer to this in terms of two variations: a "perspectival realism" and a "radical perspectivalism" that "epitomizes the postmodern shift" (cf. Middleton & Walsh, 1995b:165-171). A perspectival realist acknowledges that judgments concerning knowledge are affected by personal perception. Thus, "the external world is always mediated by the perspective of the knower". It is possible, however, to know a world that exists "out there" provided that the limitations of finite knowers can be overcome. This is precisely Schaeffer's point with respect to the Christian worldview. God has solved the problem of human finitude by revealing himself in nature, Scripture, and the self, providing normative revelation to guide fallible, perspectival knowers. Such truth may not be exhaustive, but it is true nevertheless, for there is now a correlation between the knower and the known (Schaeffer, 1982a:329).

Based on the results of this study, I view Schaeffer's apologetic legacy primarily in terms of the Christian epistemology he represents and the existential perspective of his apologetic. Perspectival realism is an apt term to describe Schaeffer's theory of knowledge since it reflects the perspectival analysis presented in this study. Schaeffer was as committed to the perspectival nature of human knowing as are postmoderns and, having been inspired by the Bible and Van Til, he was able to recognize the implications of human finitude and the necessity of a revelational environment. Perspectival realism also takes in the presuppositional method undergirding Schaeffer's apologetic evangelism—a method greatly enriched and clarified by the insights of John Frame. The existential perspective of Schaeffer's apologetic, in my view, represents his greatest strength and the most relevant point of communication for apologetic evangelists in postmodern times. Schaeffer's perspectival realism and existential apologetic provide relevant guidance and a valuable legacy for future generations of Christian apologists.

Schaeffer's Apologetic Legacy

Schaeffer's apologetic legacy will be presented in terms of five significant contributions that warrant imitation and development by future apologists: He provides an alternative to contemporary dialecticism, richer apologetic resources, an appeal to personal rectitude, a validation of existential apologetics, and a viable proportionality principle. I am persuaded that Schaeffer represents a significant example—if not a prototype—of the effective apologetic evangelist. While the heart of this study is Schaeffer's existential perspective, the heart of his legacy is his normative perspective—the acknowledgement that God's revelation is necessary to apologetic evangelism at every point. This judgment has been born out by the study, leaving us with only a few criticisms of his work.

As a Christian epistemology, Schaeffer's perspectival realism provides a powerful alternative to the modern-postmodern dialectic that dominates non-Christian thought at the present time. The beauty of this alternative is that it is both modern and postmodern without the tension of the rationalist-irrationalist dialectic. By setting biblical controls (norms) on human reason and freedom, the gains of both modernism and postmodernism may be maximized, balancing the modernist's concern for correspondent knowledge with the postmodernist's concern for perspectival knowledge. The present goal of philosophical apologists should not be to determine what comes after postmodernism; rather, the goal should be to maximize the gains of both modernism and postmodernism by the application of God's normative revelation in a clear articulation of a Christian perspectival realism. Schaeffer exemplifies this goal in a creative and compelling way.

As evident in the study, a perspectival approach also expands the resources of Christian apologetics rather than contracting them. By viewing this approach as a meta-apologetic (Frame), all the traditional resources of apologetics may be brought to bear on the task. Christian theistic evidences and arguments may be combined with an existential focus on personal inwardness and the experience of God's presence. The only requirement is that such arguments and evidences not be offered as neutral criteria requiring no prior normative input from God's revelation. Interestingly, most evangelical apologists observe this requirement to some extent, although most are not sufficiently biblical (transcendental) on this point. Like Schaeffer, both Carnell (2007a:450) and Williams (2011:38-39) offer scriptural support for key principles from which they construct their existential arguments, but unlike Schaeffer they offer this support as merely confirmatory, not as normative. Fearing the fallacy of begging the question, they understate the importance of normative Christian revelation as a legitimate basis from which to argue with non-Christians.

Schaeffer, however, recognized the importance of biblical presuppositions, framing his arguments with a transcendental goal or direction. If all human thinkers must beg the question with respect to their ultimate criterion, the Christian thinker should be honest about this, pointing to the coherence of the evidence and the correspondence between the Christian worldview and our situation in the world. By taking in more details, the stigma of a narrow circularity is overcome through a broader circularity of being and knowing that submits to coherence, correspondence, and pragmatic tests. Such tests are not mere neutral criteria; rather, the Christian worldview justifies their use as well. Schaeffer exemplifies this perspectival and presuppositional approach well, using biblical and extrabiblical evidences, theistic arguments, truth tests, and existential appeals throughout his trilogy—all in dependence on God's revelation as normative. For Schaeffer, arguments confirm revelation, but revelation does not merely confirm arguments, as in Carnell (2007b, 2007c) and Williams (2011). As Frame would put it, Christian evidence is certain and arguments are constructed to convey the certainty of the evidence.

Schaeffer's appeal to personal rectitude, which is grounded in human creation in the divine image within a revelational environment, is clearly the centerpiece of this study and the heart of his apologetic method or strategy. While the significance of this portion of Schaeffer's legacy has been explained, what bears repeating is that the flywheel of his method also demonstrates the radically biblical cast of his entire system of thought. In Frame's terms, the center of Schaeffer's method is normed by God's revelation, which explains why the appeal to personal rectitude works in apologetics. Schaeffer recognized that the law of God and the Spirit of God "pulls" and tugs on all human hearts and built his apologetic strategy on this biblical truth. Interestingly, Schaeffer is not criticized but praised for his insight in this area—even by non-presuppositionalists—despite the fact that he acknowledges this component of his apologetic as firmly based on Scripture. In my judgment, those who praise Schaeffer on this point ought also to question their own fear of begging the question in apologetics and consider the importance of the normative perspective in all apologetic evangelism. Schaeffer's legacy in this area reflects another demand for a consistent acknowledgment of the normative perspective. On this point,

Schaeffer is one of very few prominent evangelical apologists who are perspectivally consistent.

By formalizing a Christian perspectival realism as Schaeffer did, the existential perspective may come into its own in apologetics. Existential subjectivity is an integral part of the postmodern commitment to perspectival knowledge, and Christian apologists do well to follow Schaeffer's example in this area. In a recent offering on existential apologetics, Williams (2011:12) provides an impressive example of a need-based apologetic defending "the legitimacy of acquiring faith through need, emotion, and reason". Inspired by Pascal and Kierkegaard, Williams (2011:35) identifies thirteen needs that are satisfied by the Christian God "better than any other means". Cosmic security, life beyond the grave, heavenly existence, goodness, a larger life, and needs for love, meaning, and forgiveness comprise the "self-directed" human needs (2011:21-24). These are combined with "other-directed" needs, such as the need to love others, to experience awe, to delight in goodness, to be present with others, and to live in justice and fairness (2011:24-27). While not everyone senses all of these, this constellation of needs and the human tendency to adopt beliefs that satisfy these needs provides a powerful point of contact for apologetic engagement. While Williams also diminishes the normative perspective in developing his apologetic, he nevertheless offers a valuable and impressive work in existential apologetics that furthers Schaeffer's vision of an apologetic of personal integrity. The existential apologist can only hope for more such works—a prospect made more likely by the continued interest in Schaeffer's apologetic legacy.

The problem of Christian certainty was noted often throughout the study as a point of conflict among evangelical apologists, and Schaeffer's answer to this problem was offered as the only biblical alternative on the issue. A Christian perspectival realism must also engage this issue with biblical norms in mind. It was noted that several features of modernity are likely to stay, and in my judgment, the proportionality principle is one of them. While evangelicals tend to consider a moral or practical certainty as proportional to the psychological certitude of the Christian believer, Schaeffer calls this into question. The certainty of the evidence and the certainty of faith should be truly equivalent since methods of argument imply differing levels of certainty. Probable evidence simply does not warrant full certainty. Schaeffer understood this problem clearly and affirmed a true proportionality between faith and its evidence—a position no doubt inspired by the influence of Van Til. Frame provides a more nuanced treatment of this issue than Schaeffer, enabling the believer to distinguish between certainty of the Christian faith as a whole-hearted commitment and individual Christian beliefs for which full certainty is not warranted or possible. While not all Christian beliefs share the same level of certainty, one's certainty that Christ is the Way, Truth and Life may be fully certain. Thus, there is a place for probability within the Christian system, but it must be carefully delimited. On this issue especially, Schaeffer's stand represents an urgent demand for continued biblical (normative) reflection among apologetic evangelists.

Schaeffer's Unclarities

While my appreciation for Schaeffer has been evident throughout, there are a few legitimate criticisms of his approach. Since specific criticisms of Schaeffer from other scholars have been noted throughout the study, I will restrict criticism to only those problems arising from my own analysis. Interestingly, Schaeffer's weaknesses are best revealed by comparison with Frame's strengths, and three weaknesses in particular were revealed through the study, each reflecting a lack of clarity: on certainty, on reason and non-reason, and on pragmatic relativism.

While Schaeffer has been praised for his stand against the evidentialist proportionality principle, his opposition to probability as a basis for Christian certainty lacks sufficient development in his trilogy. As noted above, Frame recognizes that one's certainty of the Christian system as a whole must be distinguished from one's certainty regarding individual issues of belief. Christian beliefs are not all held the same way, as any honest and self-reflective believer would admit. Certitude or confidence attaches to many beliefs for which one lacks sufficient evidence for complete certainty. For the basic truth of the gospel, however, the certainty of faith is full and complete, and the argument Schaeffer offers is meant to show that such confidence is warranted by the certainty of the evidence. While I agree with Schaeffer that psychological certitude on the basis of probable evidence does not reflect the biblical view of Christian certainty, the kind of development that Frame provides is necessary to overcome the polarization among evangelical apologists on this point. The notion of psychological certitude is really not a problem among apologists unless it is used to indicate a disproportion between the certainty of faith and probable evidence. Schaeffer might have developed this point in the trilogy and pointed the way to a more nuanced view that nevertheless supports his very important stand on Christian certainty.

It was noted often that Schaeffer criticized both the denial and the diminishing of reason in modern philosophy and theology. For the most part, however, Schaeffer (1982a:64) treated modern thought as a denial of reason with respect to God, meaning, and morals—the issues of the upper story. The dichotomy is presented as a "contentless faith" with "no rationality" in the upper story and "rationality" with meaning in the lower story. Since reason is restricted to the lower story, the upper story must be reached by an experiential or non-rational leap. This reflects a divided field of knowledge and a divided self based on an antithetical act of reason that denies reason. While this characterization is sometimes correct, I think that Schaeffer would have been clearer had he stressed the diminishing of reason more than the denial of reason in modern thought. The rationalist-irrationalist dialectic, as Schaeffer presents it, is not always exemplified in a strict split between the rational and the non-rational. While the denial of reason in the upper story is more evident in theologians like Bultmann and Tillich, this certainly would not be a fitting characterization of Barth. Barth tends to reflect more the diminishing of reason than the denial of reason. Schaeffer was not precise on this distinction and invited criticism from scholars who would have appreciated more clarity on this point. That being said, I am very thankful for the phrase "the severe diminishing of reason" in Schaeffer's (1982a:181) trilogy, since it is truer to the realities of most modern philosophy and theology and to the rationalist-irrationalist dialectic.

In fact, the relationship between the rational and the non-rational must be guided by biblical teaching (Frame, 1976). Reason goes as far as God designed it to go, and faith embraces mystery and ignorance beyond what God has revealed (cf. DEU 29:29; 1CO 13:9-10). The problem with contemporary philosophy and theology is that the autonomous knower draws the line between reason and mystery or ignorance and does so by maximizing the irrational (non-rational) and minimizing the rational. In most cases, contemporary thought diminishes reason rather than denying it altogether. This is consistent with Edgar's point that contemporary thought majors in irrationalism and minors in rationalism. Thus, Schaeffer would have been clearer had he put the diminishing of reason before the denial of reason in his characterization of modern and postmodern thought. Again, Frame is very clear on this point whereas Schaeffer is not.

One of the profoundly important points that Schaeffer (1982a:11) makes is that a leap of faith based on an objective uncertainty and one's own judgment is—in essence—pragmatic relativism. This position sacrifices the biblical concept of unified knowing for a divided concept of knowing and a divided self. This is significant because Schaeffer recognized that once one is caught in this divided and dialectical situation, the different philosophical choices individuals make must be governed by personal and pragmatic considerations. If the evangelical agrees to these terms, he is then faced with the dilemma of deciding between his own evangelical position and a modern radical philosophy or theology (1982a:259). In the end, he will simply have to choose what he wants—what works for him.

Schaeffer (1982b:166-175) also articulates a principle of biblically-bounded relativity within the scriptural teaching. The balance of form and freedom within the biblical revelation is a balance between absolute truth and bounded freedom. It was noted that Schaeffer's principle reflects his own popular form of Van Til's notion of limiting concepts in theology. Thus, the balance of form and freedom is really the balance of reason and freedom within the biblical teaching. This balance is—interestingly—the alternative to the tension of reason and freedom within the rationalist-irrationalist dialectic, which was presented in general as an inability to balance reason and freedom without biblical norms. Schaeffer's insights on pragmatic relativism and biblical relativity are both correct, so what is the problem?

The problem is one of clarity. Schaeffer's desire to avoid unnecessary complications in presenting his ideas in popular form does not mean that his work lacks subtle distinctions and complications. In my view, Schaeffer's point concerning pragmatic relativism would have been clearer and more persuasive had his view of biblical relativity been presented along with it. From the standpoint of Schaeffer's epistemology, we see these two principles as the foci around which his analysis revolves. One either oscillates between an unbounded exercise of reason and freedom (pragmatic relativism), or one freely reasons within the boundaries of God's revelation (biblical relativity). However, these principles are separated in Schaeffer's work, the latter principle being tucked away in an appendix outside the trilogy. While one cannot blame him for not including everything in his trilogy, his principle of biblical relativity is his alternative to the pragmatic relativism of unbelieving thought. Unless one discerns the relationship between these two principles in Schaeffer's work, it is unlikely that one will appreciate the truly profound understanding of this remarkable man. Instead, many see only a lack of clarity on this point. Frame, conversely, is unmistakably clear.

Future Applications

Future applications beyond the scope of this study point in two directions, one related to Frame and the other to Schaeffer. With respect to Frame, further applications of his perspectival meta-apologetic to other apologetic systems might have tremendous ecumenical potential among evangelical apologists. Frame demonstrates a willingness to employ all available arguments and evidences in apologetics—if only they conform to the normative requirements of Scripture. Frame makes this much easier to achieve than Van Til, since Frame affirms the validity of positive or direct arguments as potentially transcendental in direction, thus taking in most of the contributions of traditional apologetics. Frame's (1982) seminal work on epistemological perspectives in relation to apologetics and his contributions in Cowen (2000) provide valuable insight into how his meta-theory might be applied to other apologetic systems, but focused studies could be done. The current study is offered as a prototypical example, showing how the "instrumental" case study may be used to structure the application of Frame's work to other apologetic systems (Grandy, 2010). Such studies would raise all the thorny issues that separate presuppositionalists from other apologetic schools, but the normative status of divine revelation in a Christian epistemology has yet to be settled once and for all and deserves further reflection among evangelical apologists.

With respect to Schaeffer, I would welcome more focused studies on the actual system operating behind the scenes of his work. As indicated in the third criticism above, Schaeffer did not systematize his approach, and related ideas are often dispersed throughout his books. While one might consider Frame's perspectivalism very close to the system underlying Schaeffer's work, a broader consideration of his entire corpus would be helpful in confirming this or in developing a more accurate understanding of the basic Christian epistemology he applies so creatively to apologetics. This study also makes an important contribution to that endeavor, but it offers only a beginning because it is restricted to the trilogy. Schaeffer was a very intuitive thinker, and often the coherence of such thinkers must be discovered beneath the surface of their rich and varied writings. This seems to be the case with Schaeffer, since practical concerns are usually evident on the surface, and theoretical complications are often summarized or avoided for the sake of more effective communication adapted to the needs of individuals and non-specialists in philosophy and apologetics.

Even though Schaeffer did not consider himself a systematic apologist or philosopher, a systematic account of his epistemology and apologetic—

regardless of its similarity to Frame's—would provide a useful tool for preserving the principles of his thought and passing them on to future generations of apologetic evangelists. While much of what Schaeffer wrote is still relevant—some more relevant today than when it was first published—yet his work will become outdated, and his significance will be memorialized by historians of the evangelical movement in the late 20th Century. Therefore, further research would guarantee the perpetuation of his legacy and contributions to apologetic evangelism long after his own writings no longer serve this purpose.

A final direction for future applications was suggested above in describing Schaeffer's validation of existential apologetics. Existential apologetic systems have had significant representation since Pascal's seminal work. Current interest in Pascal and Kierkegaard reflects the relevance of Christian existential thinkers to the apologetic task today. Schaeffer represents one of the most important existential apologists of recent times, despite his seeming antipathy to existentialism. The works of Carnell and Williams noted above also represent important contemporary contributions. The perspectival analysis provided in the current study is meant to inspire a method for not only appreciating the contributions of other existential apologists but for evaluating them in light of a perspectival epistemology. With better tools, it is hoped that further reflection on the existential dimensions of Christian belief will become even more useful in demonstrating the gospel's relevance to the common needs of those seeking a belief system to meet those needs.

Personal Applications

The primary scholarly agenda of my adult life has been to discover a way to justify the use of a rich variety of evidences and arguments within a presuppositional apologetic. The work of Francis Schaeffer was an early influence in forming that agenda by virtue of his creative use of evidences and a form of presuppositional argument that seemed easier to articulate and apply than the more complex and philosophical argument of Van Til. Over time, the importance of existential appeals in apologetics became more personally relevant, especially after studying Pascal and Kierkegaard in depth (Sotak, 2017:145-257). Pascal's approach especially resonated with my path to Christian faith in the late teenage years. Pascal's use of messianic prophecy as proof in connection with his appeal to basic psychological and spiritual needs seemed to mirror my experience of coming to faith in Christ. But how does one put it all together?

The work of John Frame provided the answer to my desire for an ecumenical approach that might take in all the major contributions of Christian apologists that have stood the test of time, especially those reflecting combinational approaches. Through a perspectival analysis, rather than simply a presuppositional analysis, Frame seemed to provide the key to analyzing individual apologists and validating their best contributions. Thus, the way was opened to a better understanding of the one apologist who was most personally inspiring to me. Perhaps the apologetic of Schaeffer, which had always seemed intuitively correct, could be analyzed and justified in the face of a large body of praise and criticism. Through the discovery and use of the "instrumental" case study, I finally found a method to proceed with this analysis in a disciplined and scholarly way (Grandy, 2010; cf. Sotak, 2008).

The results have more than exceeded my original expectations. Not only has the power and utility of Frame's perspectival meta-theory as a tool for apologetic analysis been personally confirmed, but the cogency and relevance of Schaeffer's apologetic is now much more than merely an intuitive conviction. It is now clear that the apologist who first inspired my apologetic calling is a worthy model and mentor for the many evangelical apologists who have been inspired by him to proclaim and defend the gospel of Christ in their own time.

Francis Schaeffer's apologetic is based on a conception of truth that is perspectival and existential as well as propositional, and these qualities are clearly relevant in postmodern times. The presuppositional structure of Schaeffer's apologetic is possibly more relevant today than in the 1970's and 80's, presenting as it does a method of Christian deconstruction that challenges minds already practiced in analyzing the presuppositions behind worldviews. It has already been noted that Erickson (2001:190) recommends "some form of presuppositionalism" as "a more effective strategy" for communicating with postmoderns. But he also believes that some form of "soft foundationalism" is needed in order to find common ground for this communication. Schaeffer, however, understood that common ground was already available in the non-Christian's search for meaning and in a personal integrity grounded in the divine image and a revelational environment. No "soft foundationalism" is needed to appeal to postmoderns. In fact, for postmodern thinkers, a soft foundationalism is likely too close to the classical foundationalism that postmodernists have rejected to be seriously considered. Only an apologetic affirming truth as subjective and personal has any prospect of persuading postmoderns that truth is also objective in the Christian sense.

Employing a Christian perspectival realism, the apologist may offer the postmodern thinker an alternative to the radical perspectivalism of most postmodern thought. Perspectival realism is not a mere epistemology, for it incorporates a metaphysics that affirms the triune God who is there and an ethics that acknowledges that God has not been silent but has revealed himself decisively in Jesus Christ for the salvation of the world. Through repentant faith in what Christ has done, one may be restored as a whole person to live within the unity of truth under God, thus ending one's escape from reason. The postmodern challenge, then, is best met by a renewed call to truth, which is the very thing postmodernism calls into question and the apologetic evangelist must affirm: "Our primary calling is to truth as it is rooted in God, His acts and revelation; and, if it is indeed truth, it touches all of reality and all of life—including an adequate basis for, and some practice of, the reality of community." (Schaeffer, 1982a:187.)

APPENDIX

Presuppositionalism, *THE BIBLE TODAY*, May, 1948

By the REV. FRANCIS A. SCHAEFFER

Considerable interest in the question of Presuppositionalism and traditional Christian evidence in evangelism has been created by recent
book reviews and articles in *The Bible Today*. We are delighted to present
this article by the Rev. Francis Schaeffer, a former student and a friend and
admirer of Dr. Van Til's. Ed.

The material which has appeared in *The Bible Today* dealing with what
Dr. Buswell calls "Presuppositionalism" has interested me greatly. I have
before me these articles in *The Bible Today*, and on the other hand I remember vividly the good things I received from Dr. Van Til's courses. It
seems to me, as I understand it, that the problem is not unsolable.

1. Both sides agree that the unregenerate man cannot be argued into
heaven apart from the Sovereign Call of God. (*The Bible Today*, May 1948,
page 242, "Certainly the Scriptural doctrine of the Sovereignty of God
forbids the elimination of compulsion, ... " Page 244 "The distinction between Presuppositionalism and the philosophy of traditional Christian
evidence is not by any means that the one recognizes the power of the Holy
Spirit more than the other. It is agreed that arguments, inductive and deductive, are never sufficient to work the work of regeneration." "Nothing
but the specific work of the Holy Spirit in conviction and regeneration can
be regarded as the efficient cause of individual salvation."

2. From the human viewpoint, neither side would say, I am sure, that it
is possible for a man (remembering the fall) to simply reason from nature
to a saving knowledge of nature's God without an act of personal faith. Bare
knowledge without faith cannot save. (Page 244, "one may be intellectually
convinced that Christianity is true and yet may reject Jesus Christ.")

3. Neither side, I am sure, would say that it is no use talking or preaching to the unsaved man. Both sides do. Neither would either side say that
the Holy Spirit does not use Christian apologetics when it pleases him to do
so. Both sides certainly use apologetics in dealing with the intellectual
unbeliever.

4. As I remember Dr. Van Til's practical approach, it was to show the
non-Christian that his world view, *en toto*, and in all its parts, must
logically lead back to full irrationalism and then to show him that the

Christian system provides the universal which gives avowed explanation of the universe. It is Christianity or nothing.

5. Dr. Buswell says in considering improvements on Thomas Aquinas's arguments, page 241, that he, Dr. Buswell, would set forth certain logical conclusions to the unsaved man, based on these arguments, and then show him that "Among many hypotheses of eternal existence, the God of the Bible is the most reasonable, the most probable eternal Being."

6. Both sides say, *in their own field*, "See where your position leads, now see where Christianity leads. In the light of this comparison, Christianity is the right one." I am convinced that neither side would say that Christianity could be wrong, except "for the sake of the argument." (Page 244, "The Philosophy of the Christian evidences, which I am advocating does not differ from Presuppositionalism in that I am ever willing to admit or assume anything whatsoever contrary to Christian theism, *except* in the well-known logical form of an admission "for the sake of the argument'.")

7. Therefore, it seems to me, that the problem is reduced to what apologetics is valid, and especially whether there is any room for inductive evidences being used with a common starting point. Dr. Buswell says this himself on page 244, "The distinction between the two schools is that the one denies, and the other recognizes, that the Holy Spirit uses inductive evidence and arguments from probability as instruments in the practice of evangelization and conviction, these arguments being transitive to the minds of unbelievers."

8. My suggested answer to this problem is as follows:

A. The unsaved man is seldom consistent.

B. If the unsaved man was consistent he would be an atheist in religion, and irrationalist in philosophy (including a complete uncertainty concerning "natural laws"), and completely a-moral in the widest sense.

C. However, most unsaved men are not atheists, irrationalists, or completely a-moral. Inconsistently, most unsaved men do have a part of the world-view which logically can only belong to Bible-believing Christianity.

I personally believe this very inconsistency is a result of common grace. The sun shines on the just and on the unjust, and illogically the unsaved man accepts some of the world as it really is, just as the Christian Scientists own good restaurants and have funeral directors.

D. Therefore, the average unsaved man has two parts to his world-view.

(1.) In as far as he is logical in his unbelief his "system" is hopeless and has no contact with the Christian system. This would include, if completely logical, a complete cynicism (or skepticism) to the natural world so that he could not be sure that the atoms which constitute the chair he sits on will not suddenly arrange themselves into a table, or even that the atoms may not disappear entirely. If logical he would have no contact with reality and I believe suicide would be the only logical answer. It would be completely "other" to the true world, which God has made.

(2.) Some men have come to the above state, but very few. The rest have much in their thinking which only logically belongs in the Christian system. There are all degrees of this intellectual "cheating." The modernistic Christian is the greatest cheater. The cynic, who is just short of suicide but continues to bring more life into this world by his, to him, a-moral actions when logically he should be erasing all life possible from this, again to him, hopeless world, cheats the least.

E. Notice that those who cheat the least have least of that which belongs logically only to the Bible-believing Christian, those who cheat the most have the most.

F. Thus, illogically men have in their accepted world-views, various amounts of that which is ours. But, illogical though it may be, it is there and we can appeal to it.

G. The Lord uses this degree of illogical reality the unsaved man has in his false world. The Lord shows some men their bankruptcy as they use a microscope, some as they fall in love, and some as they fear to die. When the bankruptcy is perceived then Christ may be seen as the answer. No man can accept Christ as Saviour until his need at some level is apparent to him. Certainly in this the Holy Spirit has used the illogical in the unsaved man's world-view.

It is not apart from the Holy Spirit, nor could it be possible without the predestination of the Sovereign God. Many look at the beauty of the moon at night and do not want eradication, fall in love and do not want it to end in blackness, or fear to die, without by these things being brought to Christ, but God can and does use these illogical things in unsaved men to bring some of them to salvation.

As a matter of fact, no one who has ever been saved has failed to have such an experience. Christ told the woman at the well of her sin before she was ready to hear of Him as Messiah. But if she had been completely logical in her unsaved condition she would not have cared about her sin. There can be no doubt that, first, she was of the elect, and second, the Holy Spirit used this which was illogical in her. Election includes the means as well as the end.

H. Now if God does so use, certainly we may also in our preaching and apologetics, pray that the Holy Spirit will use them. To the extent that the individual is illogical we have a point of contact. Therefore, to a certain type we preach of sin and point out to him that by his sin he has been brought down to the gutter. To some we give Dr. Machen's book, *The Virgin Birth*. To some we appeal to fulfilled prophecy. To some we use the classical arguments. To some we use the philosophical approach. We show them the alternatives, whether it is the man in the gutter or the philosophically minded unbeliever. We use what point of contact we can get. If they flee from the nearer contacts into the distant we pursue them there. In either case it is Christ or death. It is Christ or Diana, Christ or Modernism, Christ or irrationality, Christ or suicide. So it goes. The last step back to which we press them is into the blackness of irrationality, and if they are already there we ask them why they haven't committed suicide.

As a matter of fact we could preach or testify to no one without touching some point of common contact which is there because of his illogical double position. If the un-saved man were completely logical, and so had no point of common contact, we could not reach him for he would have taken his life and so be out of our reach.

I. In conclusion then, I do not think the problem is impossible. The answer rests in the fact that the unsaved man is not logical and therefore I can agree to both the statements that (1) the un-Christian system* and the Christian system "have absolutely no common ground whatever on any level, for, when the world view is seen as a whole, it necessarily evinces metaphysics, a metaphysics which governs every level of meaning." (Page 247, *The*

Bible Today, May, 1948, quoting Dr. Carnell); and also (2) that there is a point of contact with the unsaved man.

Incidentally, I think it is worthwhile also to call attention to the fact that after we are converted we do not hold the whole Christian world view consistently either. Many people are Christians with very little of a full Christian world view. I remember Dr. Machen saying "no one knows how little a man has to know to be saved." I agree, and we should never forget either that none of us will be completely consistent until we are fully glorified.

To the unsaved man that which is present which is Christian is inconsistent, and to the saved man that which is present which is un-Christian in thinking or life is inconsistent too.

---

*Note that Mr. Schaeffer here uses the word "system" as implying a consistent organization of thought, whereas sometimes a "system of philosophy" even as a "system", itself contains inconsistencies. Ed.

REFERENCES

Adler, M. 1990. *Intellect: Mind Over Matter*. New York: Macmillan Publishing Company. 205 p.

AHCD (The American Heritage College Dictionary.) 1993. 3rd ed. Boston, MA: Houghton Mifflin Company. 1630 p.

Anderson, J.N. 2009. Presuppositionalism and Frame's Epistemology. (*In* Hughes, J.J., ed. *Speaking the Truth in Love: The Theology of John M. Frame*. Phillipsburg, NJ: P&R Publishing. p. 431-459.)

Bahnsen, G.L. 1998. *Van Til's Apologetic: Readings and Analysis*. Phillipsburg, NJ: P&R Publishing. 764 p.

Baird, F. 1986. Schaeffer's Intellectual Roots. (*In* Reugsegger, R.W., ed. *Reflections on Francis Schaeffer*. Grand Rapids, MI: Zondervan. p. 45-67.)

Benson, B.E. 2002. *Graven Ideologies: Nietzsche, Derrida & Marion on Modern Idolatry*. Downers Grove, IL: InterVarsity Press. 243 p.

Benson, B.E. 2006. Postmodernity. (*In* Campbell-Jack, W.C., McGrath, G. & Evans, C.S., eds. *New Dictionary of Christian Apologetics*. Downers Grove, IL: InterVarsity Press. p. 561-564.)

Bible. 1984 [1973, 1978]. The Holy Bible: New International Version. Grand Rapids, MI: Zondervan Publishing House.

Blomberg, D.G. 1975. Apologetic Education: Francis Schaeffer and L'Abri. *Journal of Christian Education*, 54:5-20.

Boa, K.D. & Bowman, R.M. 2001. *Faith Has its Reasons: An Integrative Approach to Defending Christianity*. Colorado Springs, CO: NavPress. 608 p.

Bretall, R., ed. 1946. *A Kierkegaard Anthology*. Princeton, NJ: Princeton University Press. 528 p.

Brown, C. 1968. *Philosophy and the Christian Faith*. Downers Grove, IL: InterVarsity Press. 320 p.

Brown, H.O.J. 1984. Kierkegaard's Leap or Schaeffer's Step? *Christianity Today*, 28:82, Dec.

Brown, H.O.J. 1986. Standing Against the World. (*In* Dennis, L.T., *ed. Francis Schaeffer: Portraits of the Man and His Work.* Westchester, IL: Crossway Books. p. 13-26.)

Bunting, H. 2006. Principle of Analogy. (*In* Campbell-Jack, W.C., McGrath, G. & Evans, C.S., eds. *New Dictionary of Christian Apologetics.* Downers Grove, IL: InterVarsity Press. p. 69-73.)

Burson, S.R & Walls, J.L. 1998. *C.S. Lewis & Francis Schaeffer: Lessons for a New Century from the Most Influential Apologists of our Time.* Downers Grove, IL: InterVarsity Press. 308 p.

Calvin, J. 2008 [1559]. *Institutes of the Christian Religion.* Translated from the Latin by H. Beveridge. Peabody, MA: Hendrickson Publishers. 1059 p. http://books.google.com/books?id=RYHL_tt3EFoC&dq Date of access: 04 Feb. 2012.

Carnell, E.J. 1948. *An Introduction to Christian Apologetics: A Philosophical Defense of the Trinitarian-Theistic Christian Faith.* Grand Rapids, MI: Eerdmans. 379 p.

Carnell, E.J. 2006 [1965]. *The Burden of Soren Kierkegaard.* Eugene, OR: Wipf & Stock. 174 p.

Carnell, E.J. 2007a [1952]. *A Christian Philosophy of Religion.* Eugene, OR: Wipf & Stock. 523 p.

Carnell, E.J. 2007b [1957]. *Christian Commitment: An Apologetic.* Eugene, OR: Wipf & Stock. 314 p.

Carnell, E.J. 2007c [1960]. *The Kingdom of Love and the Pride of Life.* Eugene, OR: Wipf & Stock. 164 p.

Carnell, E.J. 2007d [1960]. *The Theology of Reinhold Niebuhr.* Eugene, OR: Wipf & Stock. 250 p.

Clark, D.K. 1993. *Dialogical Apologetics: A Person-Centered Approach to Christian Defense.* Grand Rapids, MI: Baker Book House. 245 p.

Clark, G.H. 1982. A Semi-Defense of Francis Schaeffer. *Christian Scholar's Review*, 11:148-149.

Clark, K.J. 2000. Reformed Epistemology Apologetics. (*In* Cowan, S.B., *ed. Five Views of Apologetics.* Grand Rapids, MI: Zondervan. p. 266-284.)

Clouser, R.A. 1991. *The Myth of Religious Neutrality: An Essay on the Hidden Role of Religious Belief in Theories*. Notre Dame, IN: University of Notre Dame Press. 330p.

Collett, D. 2009. Van Til and Transcendental Argument Revisited. (*In* Hughes, J.J., ed. *Speaking the Truth in Love: The Theology of John M. Frame*. Phillipsburg, NJ: P&R Publishing. p. 489-524.)

Cowen, S.B., ed. 2000. *Five Views of Apologetics*. Grand Rapids, MI: Zondervan. 400 p.

Craig, W.L. 2000. Classical Apologetics. (*In* Cowan, S.B., ed. *Five Views of Apologetics*. Grand Rapids, MI: Zondervan. p. 26-55.)

Davis, S.T. 1978. How Should We Then Live? by Francis A. Schaeffer. (Reviewed in *The Evangelical Quarterly*, 50:109-112.)

Davis, W.C. 2009. Frame in the Context of Recent Apologetics. (*In* Hughes, J.J., ed. *Speaking the Truth in Love: The Theology of John M. Frame*. Phillipsburg, NJ: P&R Publishing. p. 431-459.)

Dembski, W. 2009. *The End of Christianity: Finding a Good God in an Evil World*. Nashville, TN: B&H Academic. 254 p.

Dennis, L.T., ed. 1986a. *Francis Schaeffer: Portraits of the Man and His Work*. Westchester, IL: Crossway Books. 237 p.

Dennis, L.T. 1986b. Schaeffer and His Critics. (*In* Dennis, L.T., ed. *Francis Schaeffer: Portraits of the Man and His Work*. Westchester, IL: Crossway Books. p. 99-126.)

Derrida, J. 1996 [1973]. *Speech and Phenomena and Other Essays on Husserl's Theory of Signs*. Translated from the French by D.B. Allison. Chicago: Northwestern University Press. 166 p. http://books.google.com/books?id=N4v2AkGMnqcC&dq Date of access: 04 Feb. 2012.

Derrida, J. 1998 [1994]. *Of Grammatology*. Translated from the French by G.C. Spivak. Baltimore, MD:Johns Hopkins University Press . 360 p. http://books.google.com/books?id=95ZyM7vujG0C Date of access: 04 Feb. 2012.

Dooyeweerd, H. 1975 [1960]. *In the Twilight of Western Thought: Studies in the Pretended Autonomy of Philosophical Thought*. Nutley, NJ: Craig Press. 195 p.

Dooyeweerd, H. 2012 [1979]. *The Roots of Western Culture: Pagan, Secular, and Christian Options*. Grand Rapids: Paideia Press/Reformational Publishing Project. 258 p.

Duriez, C. Francis Schaeffer. 1993. (*In* Elwell, W.A., ed. *Handbook of Evangelical Theologians*. Grand Rapids, MI: Baker Book House. p. 245-259.)

Duriez, C. 2008. *Francis A. Schaeffer: An Authentic Life*. Wheaton: Crossway Books. 240 p.

Edgar, W. 1995a. Two Christian Warriors: Cornelius Van Til and Francis A. Schaeffer. *Westminster Theological Journal*, 57:57-80.

Edgar, W. 1995b. No News is Good News: Modernity, the Postmodern, and Apologetics. *Westminster Theological Journal*, 57:359-382.

Edgar, W. 2009. Frame the Apologist. (*In* Hughes, J.J., ed. *Speaking the Truth in Love: The Theology of John M. Frame*. Phillipsburg, NJ: P&R Publishing. p. 399-430.)

Edwards, M. 1998. How Should We Then Think?: A Study of Francis Schaeffer's Lordship Principle. *Westminster Theological Journal*, 60:193-223.

Erickson, M.J. 1983. *Christian Theology, Volume 1*. Grand Rapids, MI: Baker Book House. 477 p.

Erickson, M.J. 1998. *Postmodernizing the Faith: Evangelical Responses to the Challenge of Postmodernism*. Grand Rapids, MI: Baker Book House. 163 p.

Erickson, M.J. 2001. *Truth or Consequences: The Promise and Perils of Postmodernism*. Downers Grove, IL: InterVarsity Press. 335 p.

Evans, C.S. 1981. Kierkegaard's Attack on Apologetics. *Christian Scholar's Review*, 10(4):322-332.

Evans, C.S. 1998. *Faith beyond reason: A Kierkegaardian account*. Grand Rapids, MI: Eerdmans. 176 p.

Evans, C.S. 2006. *Kierkegaard on faith and the self: Collected essays*. Waco, TX: Baylor University Press. 408 p.

Evans, C.S. 2009. *Kierkegaard: An Introduction*. Cambridge: Cambridge University Press. 206 p.

Feinberg, P.D. 2000. Cumulative Case Apologetics. (*In* Cowan, S.B., *ed. Five Views of Apologetics*. Grand Rapids, MI: Zondervan. p. 148-172.)

Follis, B.A. 2006. *Truth With Love: The Apologetics of Francis Schaeffer*. Wheaton, IL: Crossway Books. 208 p.

Foucault, M. 1994 [1970]. *The Order of Things: An Archeology of the Human Sciences*. Translated from the French by Les Mots et les choses. New York: Vintage Books. 416 p.

Foucault, M. 1995 [1975]. *Discipline and Punish: The Birth of the Prison*. Translated from the French by A. Sheridan. New York: Vintage Books. 352 p.

Fowler, H.T. 1958. Christian Commitment, by Edward John Carnell. (Reviewed in *Religion in Life*, 27(2):314-315, Spr. Available: ATLA Religion Database. Date of access: 8-Mar. 2011.)

Frame, J.M. 1976. The Problem of Theological Paradox. (*In* North, G., *ed. Foundations of Christian Scholarship*. Vallecito, CA: Ross House. p. 295-330.)

Frame, J.M. 1982. Epistemological Perspectives and Evangelical Apologetics. (Paper delivered to ETS, Far West, Biola University on 23 Apr 1982.) http://www.frame-poythress.org/frame_articles/1982Epistemological.html Date of access: 12 Dec. 2010.

Frame, J.M. 1987. *The Doctrine of the Knowledge of God*. Phillipsburg, NJ: P&R Publishing. 437 p.

Frame, J.M. 1988. Essence of Christianity. http://www.frame-poythress.org/frame_articles/1988Essence.html Date of access: 13 Dec. 2010

Frame, J.M. 1994. *Apologetics to the Glory of God*. Phillipsburg, NJ: P&R Publishing. 265 p.

Frame, J.M. 1995. *Cornelius Van Til: An Analysis of His Thought*. Phillipsburg, NJ: P&R Publishing. 463 p.

Frame, J.M. 1999 [1990]. *Perspectives on the Word of God: An Introduction to Christian Ethics*. Eugene, OR: Wipf & Stock Publishers. 66 p.

Frame, J.M. 2000. Presuppositional Apologetics. (*In* Cowan, S.B., *ed. Five Views of Apologetics*. Grand Rapids, MI: Zondervan. p. 74-89, 132-137, 194-199, 207-264, 307-312, 350-363.)

Frame, J.M. 2002. *The Doctrine of God*. Phillipsburg, NJ: P&R Publishing. 992 p.

Frame, J.M. 2006a. Certainty. (*In* Campbell-Jack, W.C., McGrath, G. & Evans, C.S., *eds. New Dictionary of Christian Apologetics*. Downers Grove, IL: InterVarsity Press. p. 141-145.)

Frame, J.M. 2006b. Transcendental Arguments. (*In* Campbell-Jack, W.C., McGrath, G. & Evans, C.S., *eds. New Dictionary of Christian Apologetics*. Downers Grove, IL: InterVarsity Press. p. 716-717.)

Frame, J.M. 2006c. *Salvation Belongs to the Lord: An Introduction to Systematic Theology*. Phillipsburg, NJ: P&R Publishing. 382 p.

Frame, J.M. 2008a. A Primer on Perspectivalism. http://www.frame-poythress.org/frame_articles/2008Primer.html Date of access: 13 Dec. 2010.

Frame, J.M. 2008b. *The Doctrine of the Christian Life*. Phillipsburg, NJ: P&R Publishing. 1104 p.

Frame, J.M. 2009. Responses to Some Articles. (*In* Hughes, J.J., *ed. Speaking the Truth in Love: The Theology of John M. Frame*. Phillipsburg, NJ: P&R Publishing. p. 961-976.)

Frame, J.M. 2010a. Some Thoughts on Schaeffer's Apologetics. http://www.frame-poythress.org/frame_articles/2010ScrivenerInterview.html Date of access: 26 Nov. 2010.

Frame, J.M. 2010b. (jframe@rts.edu) 07 Dec. 2010. Discussion of Frame's Perspectivalism in relation to Francis Schaeffer. Email to: Sotak, M.H. (msotak@regis.edu).

Frame, J.M. 2010c. *The Doctrine of the Word of God*. Phillipsburg, NJ: P&R Publishing. 684 p.

Frame, J.M. 2011a. (jframe@rts.edu) 03 May. 2011. A Revolutionary Idea in Your Essay. Email to: Sotak, M.H. (msotak@regis.edu).

Frame, J.M. 2011b. (jframe@rts.edu) 04 May. 2011. A Revolutionary Idea in Your Essay. Email to: Sotak, M.H. (msotak@regis.edu).

Franz, H.J. 1969. Review of The God Who is There. *Westminster Theological Journal*, 32:114-116.

Gadamer, H.G. 2004 [1975]. *Truth and Method.* New York: Continuum. 601 p. http://books.google.com/books?id=ScG5YqYcsEcC&dq Date of access: 04 Feb. 2012.

Geehan, E.R. 1972. The "Presuppositional" Apologetic of Francis Schaeffer. *Themelios*, 8(1): 10-18.

Geisler, N.L. 1976. *Christian Apologetics.* Grand Rapids, MI: Baker Book House. 393 p.

Geisler, N.L. 1999. *Baker's Encyclopedia of Christian Apologetics.* Grand Rapids, MI: Baker Book House. 841 p.

Giacumakis, G. & Tiffin, G.C. 1977. How Should We Then Live? The Rise and Decline of Western Thought and Culture, by Francis A. Schaeffer. (Reviewed in *Fides Et Historia*, 9:52-58.)

Gill, D.W. 1981. Jacques Ellul and Francis Schaeffer: Two Views of Western Civilization. *Fides Et Historia*, 13(2):23-37.

Gonzalez, P.B. 2005. *Human Existence as Radical Reality: Ortega y Gasset's Philosophy of Subjectivity.* St. Paul, MN: Paragon House. 198 p.

Grandy, G. 2010. Instrumental Case Study. (*In* Mills, A.J., Durepos, G. & Wiebe, E., eds. *Encyclopedia of Case Study Research, Volume 1.* Los Angeles: Sage Publications, Inc. p. 473-475.)

Green, J.B. & Baker, M.D. 2000. *Recovering the Scandal of the Cross: Atonement in the New Testament and Contemporary Contexts.* Downers Grove, IL: InterVarsity Press. 232 p.

Groothuis, D. 2000. *Truth Decay: Defending Christianity Against the Challenges of Postmodernism.* Downers Grove, IL: InterVarsity Press. 303 p.

Grounds, V.C. 1984. A Friend of Many Years Remembers Francis Schaeffer. *Christianity Today*, 28(9):61-62.

Habermas, G.R. 2000. Evidential Apologetics. (*In* Cowan, S.B., ed. *Five Views of Apologetics.* Grand Rapids, MI: Zondervan. p. 92-121.)

Hackett, S.C. 1984. *The Reconstruction of the Christian Revelation Claim: A Philosophical and Critical Apologetic.* Grand Rapids: Baker Book House. 349 p.

Hankins, B. 2008. *Francis Schaeffer and the Shaping of Evangelical America*. Grand Rapids, MI: Eerdmans. 272 p.

Harper, K.C. 1976. Francis Schaeffer: An Evaluation. *Bibliotheca Sacra*, 133:130-142, Apr.

Harper, K.C. 1977. Edward John Carnell: An Evaluation of His Apologetics. *Journal of the Evangelical Theological Society*, 20(2):133-145, Jun.

Heidegger, M. 1996 [1953]. *Being and Time*. Translated from the German by J. Stambaugh. Albany, NY: State University of New York. 487 p. http://books.google.com/books?id=9oc2BnZMCZgC Date of access: 04 Feb. 2012.

Hill, K.R. 1985. Francis Schaeffer (1912-1984): An Evaluation of His Life and Thought. (*In* Fitch, N.R. & Etulain, R.W., eds. *Faith and Imagination: Essays on Evangelicals and Literature*. Albuquerque, NM: Far West Books. p. 137-171.)

Hoitenga, D.J. 1991. *Faith and Reason from Plato to Plantinga: An Introduction to Reformed Epistemology*. Albany, NY: State University of New York Press. 263 p.

Holmes, A.F. 1959. The Nature of Theistic Apologetics. (Paper delivered to Mid-Western Section Meeting held in Chicago, Illinois, on 09 Feb 1959.)

Holmes, A.F 1969. The God Who is There, by Francis A. Schaeffer. (Reviewed in *HIS*, 29:26, Feb.)

Hughes, J.J., ed. 2009. *Speaking the Truth in Love: The Theology of John M. Frame*. Phillipsburg, NJ: P&R Publishing. 1118 p.

Jones, P.R. 2009. Neopaganism: Stepchild of Secular Humanism. (*In* Hughes, J.J., ed. *Speaking the Truth in Love: The Theology of John M. Frame*. Phillipsburg, NJ: P&R Publishing. p. 575-610.)

Jones, W.T. 1986. Philosophical Disagreements and World Views. *Proceedings and Addresses of the American Philosophical Association*, 48:223-239.

Kant, I. 2010 [1784]. *An Answer to the Question: 'What is Enlightenment?'* Translated from the German by H.B. Nisbet. New York: Penguin Books. 120 p. http://books.google.com/books?id=8alzRAAACAAJ&dq Date of access: 04 Feb. 2012.

Kline, M.G. 1972. *The Structure of Biblical Authority*. Grand Rapids, MI: Eerdmans. 218 p.

Knudsen, R.D. 1971. Progressive and Regressive Tendencies in Christian Apologetics. (*In* Geehan, E.R., ed. *Jerusalem and Athens: Critical Discussions on the Theology and Apologetics of Cornelius Van Til*. Phillipsburg, NJ: P&R Publishing. p. 275-298.)

Knudsen, R.D. 1986. The Transcendental Perspective of Westminster's Apologetic. *Westminster Theological Journal*, 48:223-239.

Ladd, G.E. 1959. *The Gospel of the Kingdom*. Grand Rapids, MI: Eerdmans. 144 p.

Lakey, P. 1969. The God Who is There, by Francis A. Schaeffer. (Reviewed in *Gordon Review*, 11(4):241-245.)

Leigh, D.R. 1990. Two Apologists: Cornelius Van Til and Francis Schaeffer. Worcester, MA: Wheaton College Graduate School. (Thesis – M.A.) 205 p.

Levinas, E. 1979. *Totality and Infinity*. Norwell, MA: Kluwer Academic Publishers. 307 p. http://books.google.com/books?id=Rbu8w7Pz8ggC&dq Date of access: 04 Feb. 2012.

Lewis, G. 1971. Van Til and Carnell—Part I. (*In* Geehan, E.R., ed. *Jerusalem and Athens: Critical Discussions on the Theology and Apologetics of Cornelius Van Til*. Phillipsburg, NJ: P&R Publishing. p. 349-368.)

Lewis, G. 1976. *Testing Christianity's Truth Claims*. Chicago: Moody Press. 363 p.

Lewis, G. 1986. Schaeffer's Apologetic Method. (*In* Reugsegger, R., ed. *Reflections on Francis Schaeffer*. Grand Rapids, MI: Zondervan Publishing House. p. 69-104.)

Lewis, G. 1993. Edward John Carnell. (*In* Elwell, W.A., ed. *Handbook of Evangelical Theologians*. Grand Rapids, MI: Baker Book House. p. 321-337.)

Lewis, G. 1999. Letter to Max Sotak about Francis Schaeffer, 8 February. Arvada, CO. (Original copy in possession of the recipient.)

Little, B.A., ed. 2010. *Francis Schaeffer: A Mind and Heart for God*. Phillipsburg, NJ: P&R Publishing. 108p.

Lundin, R. 1995. The Pragmatics of Postmodernity. (*In* Phillips, T.R. & Okholm, D.L., eds. *Christian Apologetics in the Postmodern World*. Downers Grove, IL: InterVarsity Press. p. 24-38.)

Marsden, G.M. 1987. *Reforming Fundamentalism: Fuller Seminary and the New Evangelicalism*. Grand Rapids, MI: Eerdmans. 319 p.

Mavrodes, G.I. 1970. *Belief in God*. New York: Random House. 117 p.

McCormack, B.L. & Anderson, C.B., eds. 2011. *Karl Barth and American Evangelicalism*. Grand Rapids, MI: Eerdmans. 387p.

Meek, E.L. 2009. Servant Thinking: The Polanyian Workings of the Framean Triad (*In* Hughes, J.J., ed. *Speaking the Truth in Love: The Theology of John M. Frame*. Phillipsburg, NJ: P&R Publishing. p. 611-627.)

Middleton, J.R. & Walsh, B.J. 1995a. Facing the Postmodern Scalpel: Can the Christian Faith Withstand Deconstruction? (*In* Phillips, T.R. & Okholm, D.L., eds. *Christian Apologetics in the Postmodern World*. Downers Grove, IL: InterVarsity Press. p. 131-154.)

Middleton, J.R. & Walsh, B.J. 1995b. *Truth is Stranger Than It Used to Be: Biblical Faith in a Postmodern Age*. Downers Grove, IL: InterVarsity Press. 250 p.

Montgomery, J.W. 1998 [1970]. *The Suicide of Christian Theology*. Newburgh, IN: Trinity Press. 528 p.

Morris, T.V. 1976. *Francis Schaeffer's Apologetics: A Critique*. Grand Rapids, MI: Baker Book House. 133 p.

Nash, R.A. 1986. The Life of the Mind and the Way of Life. (*In* Dennis, L.T., ed. *Francis Schaeffer: Portraits of the Man and His Work*. Westchester, IL: Crossway Books. p. 51-69.)

Niebuhr, H.R. 2001 [1951]. *Christ and Culture*. San Francisco, CA: HarperCollins Publishers. 320 p.

Nietzsche, F.W. 1968 [1901]. *The Will to Power*. Translated from the German by W.A. Kaufmann and R.J. Hollingdale. New York: Vintage Books. 576 p. http://books.google.com/books?id=Magi-iz7kIQC Date of access: 04 Feb. 2012.

Nietzsche, F.W. 2005. *The Antichrist, Ecce Homo, Twilight of the Idols: And Other Writings*. Translated from the German by J. Norman. Cambridge: Cambridge University Press. 340 p.

Noll, M.A. 1994. *The Scandal of the Evangelical Mind*. Grand Rapids, MI: Eerdmans. 274 p.

Notaro, Thom. 1980. *Van Til and the Use of Evidence*. Phillipsburg, PA: P&R Publishing. 136 p.

Orr, J. 2000 [1897]. *The Progress of Dogma*. Vancouver, BC: Regent College Publishing. 365 p.

Packer, J.I. 1986. Foreward: No Little Person. (*In* Reugsegger, R.W., *ed. Reflections on Francis Schaeffer*. Grand Rapids, MI: Zondervan. p. 7-17.)

Parkhurst, L.G. 1985. *Francis Schaeffer: The Man and His Message*. Wheaton, IL: Tyndale. 250 p.

Pascal, B. 1995 [1670]. *Pensees*. Translated from the French by A.J. Krailsheimer. London: Penguin Books. 333 p.

Patrick, D.G. 1947a. *Pascal and Kierkegaard: A Study in the Strategy of Evangelism I*. Cambridge: James Clarke & Co. 252 p.

Patrick D.G. 1947b. *Pascal and Kierkegaard: A Study in the Strategy of Evangelism II*. Cambridge: James Clarke & Co. 424 p.

Pearcy, N.R. 2004. *Total Truth: Liberating Christianity from its Cultural Captivity*. Wheaton, IL: Crossway Books. 479 p.

Perez, J. 2009. Frame's Apologetics and the Challenges of Our Time. (*In* Hughes, J.J., *ed. Speaking the Truth in Love: The Theology of John M. Frame*. Phillipsburg, NJ: P&R Publishing. p. 559-574.)

Pinnock, C. 1977. Schaefferism as a World View. *Sojourners*, 6:32-35, Jul.

Pinnock, C. 1986. Schaeffer on Modern Theology. (*In* Reugsegger, R.W., *ed. Reflections on Francis Schaeffer*. Grand Rapids, MI: Zondervan. p. 173-193.)

Plantinga, A.C. 1979. Is Belief in God Rational? (*In* Delaney, C.F., *ed. Rationality and Religious Belief*. Notre Dame, IN: University of Notre Dame Press. p. 7-27.)

Poythress, V.S. 2001. *Symphonic Theology: The Validity of Multiple Perspectives in Theology*. Phillipsburg, NJ: P&R Publishing. 128 p.

Ramm, B.L. 1972. *The God Who Makes a Difference: A Christian Appeal to Reason*. Waco, TX: Word, Incorporated. 160 p.

Ramm, B.L. 2000 [1973]. *The Evangelical Heritage: A Study in Historical Theology.* Grand Rapids, MI: Baker Book House. 180 P.

Reugsegger, R.W. 1981. Francis Schaeffer and Philosophy. *Christian Scholar's Review,* 10:238-254.

Reugsegger, R.W. 1982. A Reply to Gordon Clark. *Christian Scholar's Review,* 11:150-152.

Reugsegger, R.W., ed. 1986a. *Reflections on Francis Schaeffer.* Grand Rapids, MI: Zondervan. 320 p.

Reugsegger, R.W. 1986b. Francis Schaeffer on Philosophy. (*In* Reugsegger, R.W., ed. *Reflections on Francis Schaeffer.* Grand Rapids, MI: Zondervan. p. 107-130.)

Reugsegger, R.W. 1986c. Schaeffer's System of Thought. (*In* Reugsegger, R.W., ed. *Reflections on Francis Schaeffer.* Grand Rapids, MI: Zondervan. p. 25-41.)

Reymond, R. 1976. *The Justification of Knowledge.* Phillipsburg, NJ: P&R Publishing. 168 p.

Rogers, J. 1977. Francis Schaeffer: The Promise and the Problem. *The Reformed Journal,* 27(5):12-15.

Rorty, R. 1981 [1979]. Philosophy and the Mirror of Nature. Princeton, NJ: Princeton University Press. 424 p. http://books.google.com/books?id=go5mzgAACAAJ&dq Date of access: 04 Feb. 2012.

Rorty, R. 1989. *Contingency, Irony, and Solidarity.* Cambridge: Cambridge University Press. 201 p. http://books.google.com/books?id=vpTxxYR7hPcC Date of access: 04 Feb. 2012.

Schaeffer, F.A. 1948. A Review of a Review. *The Bible Today,* 42(1): 7-9, Oct.

Schaeffer, F.A. 1973. How and Why I Write My Books. *Eternity,* 24:64-76, Mar.

Schaeffer, F.A. 1982a. *The Complete Works of Francis A. Schaeffer: A Christian Worldview, Volume One, A Christian View of Philosophy and Culture.* Westchester, IL: Crossway Books. 395 p.

Schaeffer, F.A. 1982b. *The Complete Works of Francis A. Schaeffer: A Christian Worldview, Volume Four, A Christian View of the Church.* Westchester, IL: Crossway Books. 309 p.

Schaeffer, F.A. 1982c. *The Complete Works of Francis A. Schaeffer: A Christian Worldview, Volume Five, A Christian View of the West.* Westchester, IL: Crossway Books. 566 p.

Schaeffer, F.A. 1985. *Letters of Francis Schaeffer: Spiritual Reality in the Personal Christian Life.* Dennis, L., ed. Wheaton, IL: Crossway Books. 264 p.

Scrivener, S.R. 2009. Frame's and Van Til's Apologetic. (*In* Hughes, J.J., ed. *Speaking the Truth in Love: The Theology of John M. Frame.* Phillipsburg, NJ: P&R Publishing. p. 525-558.)

Shinn, R.L. 1958. Christian Commitment, by Edward John Carnell. (Reviewed in *Theology Today*, 15(2):278-279, Jul. Available: ATLA Religion Database. Date of access: 8-Mar. 2011.)

Singer, C.G. 1979. *From Rationalism to Irrationality: The Decline of the Western Mind from the Renaissance to the Present.* Phillipsburg, NJ: P&R Publishing. 479 p.

Smith, J.K. 2004. *Introducing Radical Orthodoxy: Mapping a Post-Secular Theology.* Grand Rapids, MI: Baker Academic. 296 p.

Sotak, M.H. 2008. Bernard Ramm: An Instrumental Case Study in Biblical Apologetics. Denver, CO: Regis University. (Capstone Project – M.A.) 47 p.

Sotak, M.H. 2016. *The Apologetics of the Evangelical Renaissance: The Quest for a General Theory of Christian Defense.* Denver, CO: Sotakoff Publishing. 222 p.

Sotak, M.H. 2017. *Evangelical Belief: A Course Guide to Christian Thought.* Denver, CO: Sotakoff Publishing. 474 p.

Spitz, L.W. 1957. Christian Commitment, by Edward John Carnell. (Reviewed in *Concordia Monthly*, 28(12):955, Dec. Available: ATLA Religion Database. Date of access: 8-Mar. 2011.)

Stackhouse, J.G. 1995. From Architecture to Argument: Historic Resources for Christian Apologetics. (*In* Phillips, T.R. & Okholm, D.L., eds. *Christian Apologetics in the Postmodern World.* Downers Grove, IL: InterVarsity Press. p. 39-55.)

Stadler, G.T. 1989. Renaissance Humanism: Francis Schaeffer Versus Some Contemporary Scholars. *Fides Et Historia*, 21(2):4-20, Jun.

Tinker, C. & Tinker, M. 2005. Fifty Years on: The Legacy of Francis Schaeffer—An Apologetic for Post-moderns. *Churchman*, 119(3):201-216, Aut. Available: ATLA Religion Database. Date of access: 15-Nov. 2011.

Torres, J.E. 2009. Perspectives on Multiperspectivalism. (*In* Hughes, J.J., *ed. Speaking the Truth in Love: The Theology of John M. Frame*. Phillipsburg, NJ: P&R Publishing. p. 116-136.)

Van Til, C. 1951. Christian Theistic Evidences. Philadephia:PA. 137 p. (Unpublished).

Van Til. C. 1955. *The Defense of the Faith*. Philadelphia, PA: P&R Publishing. 436 p.

Van Til. C. 1967. *The Protestant Doctrine of Scripture*. Phillipsburg, NJ: P&R Publishing. 156 p.

Van Til, C. 1969a. *A Survey of Christian Epistemology*. Phillipsburg, NJ: P&R Publishing. 228 p.

Van Til, C. 1969b. *A Christian Theory of Knowledge*. Phillipsburg, NJ: P&R Publishing. 390 p.

Van Til, C. 1971. *Christian Theistic Ethics*. Phillipsburg, NJ: P&R Publishing. 251 p.

Van Til, C. 1972. *Common Grace and the Gospel*. Phillipsburg, NJ: P&R Publishing. 233 p.

Van Til, C. 1997a [1969]. A Letter to Francis Schaeffer. (*In* The Works of Cornelius Van Til. Logos Research Systems.) [CD]

Van Til, C. 1997b [1977]. The Apologetic Methodology of Francis A. Schaeffer. (*In* The Works of Cornelius Van Til. Logos Research Systems.) [CD]

Veith, G.E. 1986. The Fragmentation and Integration of Truth. (*In* Dennis, L.T., *ed. Francis Schaeffer: Portraits of the Man and His Work*. Westchester, IL: Crossway Books. p. 27-49.)

Voss, E.J. 1984. The Apologetics of Francis Schaeffer. Dallas, TX: Dallas Theological Seminary. (Dissertation – Th.D.) 364 p.

Walton, J.H. 2006. *Ancient Near Eastern Thought and the Old Testament: Introducing the Conceptual World of the Hebrew Bible.* Grand Rapids, MI: Baker Book House. 368 p.

Walton, J.H. 2009. *The Lost World of Genesis One: Ancient Cosmology and the Origins Debate.* Downers Grove, IL: InterVarsity Press. 192 p.

Wells, R.A. 1983. Whatever Happened to Francis Schaeffer? *Reformed Journal*, 33:10-13, May.

White, J.E. 1994. *What is Truth? A Comparative Study of the Positions of Cornelius Van Til, Francis Schaeffer, Carl F.H. Henry, Donald Bloesch, Millard Erickson.* Nashville, TN: B&H Publishers. 240 p.

Williams, C. 2011. *Existential Reasons for Belief in God: A Defense of Desires & Emotions for Faith.* Downers Grove, IL: IVP Academic. 188 p.

Yancy, P. 1979a. Francis Schaeffer: A Prophet for Our Time? *Christianity Today*, 23:14-18, Mar.

Yancy, P. 1979b. Schaeffer on Schaeffer, Part I. *Christianity Today*, 23:19-21, Mar.

Yancy, P. 1979c. Schaeffer on Schaeffer, Part II. *Christianity Today*, 23:21-26, Apr.

Young, W.C. 1954. *A Christian Approach to Philosophy.* Grand Rapids, MI: Baker Book House. 252 p.

Zetterholm, E.E. 1958. Christian Commitment, by Edward John Carnell. (Reviewed in *Westminster Theological Journal*, 20(2):240-246, May. Available: ATLA Religion Database. Date of access: 8-Mar. 2011.)

Proof

Made in the USA
Columbia, SC
24 June 2017